Getting StartED with Dojo

Kyle D. Hayes

an Apress® company

GETTING STARTED WITH DOJO

Copyright © 2009 by Kyle D. Hayes

ISBN-13 (pbk): 978-1-4302-2521-8

ISBN-13 (electronic): 978-1-4302-2522-5

Distributed to the book trade worldwide by Springer-Verlag New York, Inc., 233 Spring Street, 6th Floor, New York, NY 10013. Phone 1-800-SPRINGER, fax 201-348-4505, e-mail orders-ny@springer-sbm.com, or visit www.springeronline.com.

For information on translations, please e-mail info@apress.com, or visit www.apress.com.

Apress and friends of ED books may be purchased in bulk for academic, corporate, or promotional use. eBook versions and licenses are also available for most titles. For more information, reference our Special Bulk Sales–eBook Licensing web page at http://www.apress.com/info/bulksales.

The source code for this book is available to readers at http://www.apress.com.

Credits

President and Publisher: Paul Manning	**Coordinating Editor:** Kelly Moritz
Lead Editor: Matthew Moodie	**Copy Editor:** Kim Wimpsett
Technical Reviewer: Peter Higgins	**Compositors:** MacPS, LLC
Editorial Board: Clay Andres, Steve Anglin, Mark Beckner, Ewan Buckingham, Gary Cornell, Jonathan Gennick, Jonathan Hassell, Michelle Lowman, Matthew Moodie, Duncan Parkes, Jeffrey Pepper, Frank Pohlmann, Douglas Pundick, Ben Renow-Clarke, Dominic Shakeshaft, Matt Wade, Tom Welsh	**Indexers:** BIM Indexing & Proofreading Services **Artist:** April Milne **Cover Designer:** Kurt Krames

To my beautiful wife, Jenn—for without
her boundless love and inspiration,
I would cease to follow my dreams.

Contents at a Glance

Contents

About the Author

 **Kyle D. Hayes** has been programming since he was ten years old. His curious and innovative mind has led him to owning many bookshelves of computer programming and technical books for which he attributes much of his knowledge. He further expanded and strengthened his skill set when he completed his bachelor's of science degree in computer information systems at California State Polytechnic University, Pomona. Today, Kyle publishes a technical blog, kylehayes.info, and is a senior web developer for a large media and entertainment company in North Hollywood, California. His passion for innovation and his drive to inspire have led him to achieve his lifelong dreams and aspirations. When he is not sitting in front of a computer, Kyle enjoys doing amateur and stock photography, listening to a wide variety of music, going out with his wife, and attending his local church. *Getting StartED with Dojo* is Kyle's first (and we hope not his last) published book.

About the Technical Reviewer

Peter E. Higgins, Dojo Toolkit project lead.

Acknowledgments

I am honored to have had the opportunity to write this book for friends of ED with its ever-patient staff. I extend my deepest gratitude to Kelly Moritz for being persistent and understanding of my hectic work schedule, to my development editor Matthew Moodie for providing unparalleled advice for my first book, to Kim Wimpsett for boldly carrying out the daunting task of correcting a programmer's publication, and to Steve Anglin for reaching out to me to author this book. I would like to also offer a big thank you to my technical reviewer, Peter Higgins, not only for being such a great Dojo resource but also for contributing the "Plug-ins" appendix. In addition, I'm grateful for the support the Dojo community has provided me through this process, especially the helpful folks on the IRC channel #dojo at irc.freenode.net.

This book would not have been possible without the large support I had from my family, friends, and co-workers—thank you for your constant interest and inspiration. Finally, I want to specifically thank my parents for always being there to hear my latest technical idioms and hobbies; without them, I would not be the passionate individual I am today.

Introduction

JavaScript can seem like an unwieldy mass feeding off today's modern websites. However, despite its apparent complexity, nestled snug against the Document Object Model (DOM), JavaScript can be a tremendous tool in your everyday web development toolkit for adding rich interactivity, animations, and advanced functionality to your websites, compelling your users to come back for more. But how do you master the skills necessary to achieve these results? *Getting StartED with Dojo* is your first step in that direction.

Dojo contains a very large set of tools that will allow you to do relatively simple tasks with ease—simple effects, Ajax functionality, powerful CSS-based document querying, JSON, and event handling—and it also contains enterprise-grade components. Some of these include a reusable, accessible, localized set of user interface widgets that are skinnable to fit any application, an entire widget framework, and a powerful event topic publish and subscribe system, as well as many more advanced components and systems.

The Dojo Toolkit is an open source project developed by a talented and enthusiastic team of programming professionals who strive to make JavaScript programming the most efficient it can be. They aim to ensure the code maintains the highest standards of quality, stability, and cross-browser compatibility. Actively developed, the toolkit's code base is updated routinely to fix bugs and provide new functionality.

Since JavaScript programming (or any programming for that matter) can be daunting if you've never done it, this book is easy to understand and very approachable to the nonprogrammer. You'll start with the basics of JavaScript programming by learning about variables, functions, loops, and conditional statements. After that, you'll be eased into learning the simple constructs of Dojo and how to integrate it with your websites.

I sincerely hope you will find the code and examples in this book inspiring and use them to advance your web development career. JavaScript, when used to its full potential, is truly a powerful language that complements today's modern web pages. My desire is for you to learn and understand it in a way that will maximize your development potential. Enjoy!

Chapter 1

JavaScript Fundamentals

"We are what we repeatedly do. Excellence, then, is not an act but a habit."

—Aristotle

If you already have a strong understanding of the basics of JavaScript such as variables, functions, and arrays, feel free to skip the next couple of chapters. I'll meet you in Chapter 3!

HTML has come a long way since its incarnation after the invention of the Internet. With its current specification in its fourth revision and the fifth nearly completed, much has been accomplished by way of more useful tags and other markup to accommodate our ever-changing hyper-universe. However, despite its many uses (and many issues!), it remains a static language at the end of the day.

Users of the Web expect to get the information they seek quickly and efficiently. In addition, as web designers and developers get more creative with their websites, a desire for a richer user experience is stronger now than ever. Much of that creativity is demonstrated through the usage of client-side technologies, which run in the user's browser, not on the web server.

Today, developers can enhance their websites' content by utilizing a variety of client-side technologies together and independently such as Adobe's Flash platform, Microsoft Silverlight, Apple QuickTime, or JavaScript. However, only JavaScript is included with all major web browsers and therefore remains the primary choice for developers to provide a richer experience to their users.

ExplainED

Despite what its name implies, JavaScript is not related to the Java programming language. It used to be called LiveScript, but Netscape later changed the name for marketing purposes. It is a dialect of the ECMAScript standard ECMA-262. You can read more about it on Wikipedia at http://en.wikipedia.org/wiki/ECMAScript, *or if you want some exciting bedtime reading, you can read the full ECMAScript 3 specification, on which JavaScript is based, at* http://www.ecma-international.org/publications/standards/Ecma-262.htm.

Even though JavaScript is a type of programming language (actually, it's known as a **scripting language**), it is fairly easy to pick up even for nonprogrammers. In the coming sections, you'll learn how to add basic JavaScript functionality to your web pages.

How does JavaScript fit in with HTML?

You can enhance your HTML a little or a lot using JavaScript. Open the introductions.html file in the folder for Chapter 1 from the code download. You'll see just some basic things that JavaScript can do. The main thing to keep in mind with these examples is where and how you can run JavaScript in your page.

LinkED

If you don't already have a local web server or development server set up to run the examples in this book, you should follow the instructions in Appendix A to set up a local web server.

Once you play with the examples, return here, and I'll go over everything.

Did you have fun? If the demo did not work, refer to Appendix A to make sure you have everything set up correctly. As mentioned, the part to focus on is that JavaScript can be run from various parts of the page.

The DOM

The **Document Object Model** (DOM) is a hierarchical tree of every element on an HTML page. What? I know, I know, it sounds daunting and complicated, but no foundational JavaScript lesson is complete without at least briefly mentioning the DOM. You don't need to fully understand it at this point in time; that will come as you learn JavaScript. For now, just think of it as the tree of life for any given HTML web page. Every branch represents the relationship of a DOM element (the leaf) to other elements.

Take a look at the HTML document in Figure 1-1. Now compare it to the diagram in Figure 1-2. Each tag block is an object and is related to other objects in the DOM.

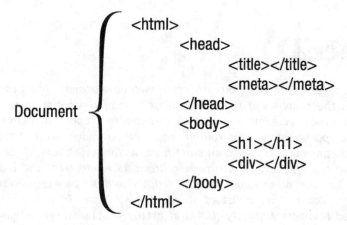

Figure 1-1. A basic HTML document

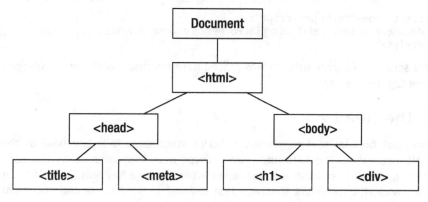

Figure 1-2. The HTML document from Figure 1-1 represented as an object model

The script tag

When the browser renders a web page, it assumes that any text between HTML tags is to be rendered as some type of text. If you attempted to simply write a JavaScript statement in the middle of the page, the browser would display that text to the user, rather than executing it.

To tell the browser to treat a block of text as JavaScript code, you always have to wrap the code in a script block, with two exceptions that I will cover in another section. The script tag is used to tell the browser that *some* type of script is going to be executed here. To distinguish the scripting language, the tag requires a single attribute, type, which defines the MIME type of the script. For JavaScript, this will always be text/javascript, as shown in the following script block.

NotED

A MIME type is used in various aspects of web development. In all cases, it notifies the members of the system what type of content is about to be sent or processed. This allows each member to prepare to deliver the content appropriately. This content could be an image, an MP3 file, an HTML document, or a JavaScript statement. As for script *tags, if you were to leave the type empty, all modern browsers would treat the block as JavaScript. Any other value, and the script would not be executed by the browser. You can see a list of standard MIME types from the Internet Assigned Numbers Authority (IANA) at* http://www.iana.org/assignments/media-types/.

```
<script type="text/javascript">
  document.write("<em>I was placed here because JavaScript...</em>");
</script>
```

This script will simply write "I was placed here because JavaScript…" wrapped in em tags to the page.

In the head

The most popular spot to place JavaScript statements is in the head of the HTML document. The following code excerpt from the demo shows the code that causes an alert window to pop open after the page has finished loading. It is a JavaScript statement that was first defined in the head of the document and then was instructed to execute only once the page was loaded. Don't be concerned with the details of the code; I'm just giving some simple examples of where code can be defined.

NotED

The code snippet that contains the code for the alert box was defined in a JavaScript function. Functions provide a few uses for developers. The first is reusability; once you write the code inside a function, the name of the function can be called anywhere on the page as many times as you like. Another useful benefit of a function is it allows you to write code that you want to call later and not as the page is loading.

```
<!DOCTYPE html PUBLIC "-//W3C//DTD HTML 4.01//EN"
    "http://www.w3.org/TR/html4/strict.dtd">

<html>
<head>
  <title>Chapter 1 - Introductions</title>
  <script type="text/javascript">
  var pageLoadedAlert = function()
  {
    alert('The page has finished loading!');
  }
  </script>
</head>
<body onload="pageLoadedAlert()">

...
```

NotED

Did you notice the double forward slashes in the code block near the alert statement? This is a single-line comment. JavaScript comments do not get executed as JavaScript statements; they are completely ignored. Their sole purpose is to communicate to the developer what any given line is doing. If you have a little bit more to say than what would fit on one line, wrap your comment inside a multiline block, like this: /* This is my multi-line comment */.

This is a great place to set variables and define functions—both of which we will cover later in this chapter. It's for this reason that this ends up being such a popular spot to find JavaScript. The developer is preparing the page with functionality that will be used when the user interacts with the page. Additionally, JavaScript that is defined in the head vs. the body will begin to load first, allowing it to be ready to execute sooner.

In the body

JavaScript can be placed in the body as well. You'll still wrap it in a script tag as before. The document.write statement in the demo, and shown next, immediately writes out the text in the spot the statement was placed. Once the browser processes that part of the page, it knows to immediately execute that JavaScript. The user will see the output as if it were normal HTML written in the page. However, if you were to view the source of the page, you would actually see the JavaScript statement, not the outputted HTML.

```
<h2>JavaScript can execute as the page is rendered</h2>
<script type="text/javascript">
  document.write("<em>I was placed here because JavaScript wrote me here
when the page loaded.</em>");
</script>
```

Keep in mind that not all the JavaScript on the page is immediately available as soon as the page starts loading in the browser. The browser loads and executes JavaScript in a procedural manner, processing each piece as the page loads from top to bottom. This is why document.write works as the page is loading and not after. When the browser encounters that method, it has processed all the page content up until that point, nothing afterward. After document.write executes and outputs its result to the page, the HTML then continues to get processed by the browser.

NotED

Although using View Source in your browser will show you only the JavaScript code that you wrote and not what its result was, there is a way around this. The option is called View Generated Source. It is not available by default in browsers. If you are using Firefox, you can install the Web Developer Toolbar add-on (https://addons.mozilla.org/en-US/firefox/addon/60). Once installed, you can select View Source ➤ View Generated Source. If you are using Internet Explorer (IE), you can install the IE Developer Toolbar or Developer Tools; you can find links to these tools on Wikipedia: http://en.wikipedia.org/wiki/Internet_Explorer_Developer_Toolbar. Once you have installed one of these IE tools, you can select View ➤ Source ➤ DOM (Page).

It is less often that you will see developers defining JavaScript statements in the body of the HTML. The main reason is that the page becomes harder to maintain since the code cannot be found in one common area.

The only time that it makes sense to find JavaScript in the body of the page is if the site is broken up into many different files that comprise a single page, known as **modules** or **includes**. This is a common practice for large sites that use a back-end technology to merge these files into a single web page. It is in those individual files that you will likely see JavaScript blocks at the top of the file to define functionality for that part of the page.

Inline in an element

There were two exceptions to using the script block to denote JavaScript code. A good portion of HTML tags have a special set of attributes that are known as **event handlers**. It is this type of attribute in which you can execute JavaScript statements without first needing to wrap them in the script block. The most popular and probably easiest to understand of these is the onclick event handler.

```
<h2>JavaScript can be inline, listening for the click of a button</h2>
<input type="button" value="Click me!" onclick="alert('POW!!!')" />
```

The value of the onclick attribute must contain a JavaScript statement. Event handlers are extremely useful tools when working with user interaction. The code inside the attribute runs when that event occurs. For instance, when the button shown previously is clicked, an alert message is displayed to the user.

Although event handler attributes in elements such as the input one shown earlier are easy to use, they are not favored in modern web development. They're obtrusive to the HTML and should be separated and placed in a common JavaScript block with other code for the page.

LinkED

You'll learn more about event handlers and how to properly create them in Chapter 2.

Altering elements

JavaScript can help you alter the look of elements. For example, you can change CSS attributes via JavaScript. As you can see, they are named in a slightly different manner to correspond with JavaScript naming conventions (for example, backgroundColor as opposed to the CSS attribute background-color). The following is the source code for the functions I used in the demo to alter a few of the elements and text in the page:

```
<h2>JavaScript can change the look of just about anything on the
page</h2>
<script type="text/javascript">
    var makeBold = function(element)
    {
        // CSS equivalent: font-weight: bold;
        element.style.fontWeight = "bold";
    }

    var makeHuge = function(element)
    {
        // CSS equivalent: font-size: 44px;
        element.style.fontSize = "44px";
    }
    var makePink = function(element)
    {
        // CSS equivalent: background-color: pink;
        element.style.backgroundColor = "pink";
    }
    var hide = function(element)
    {
        // CSS equivalent: display: none;
        element.style.display = 'none';
    }
    var show = function(element)
    {
        // CSS equivalent: display: block;
        element.style.display = 'block';
    }
</script>
```

Notice how I separated the functionality of each style change into a separate function. This allows me to reuse that code easily and alter any element I tell it to alter.

LinkED

In Chapter 4, I will be talking about how to use Dojo to animate elements on a page. At the core of this functionality, the code is changing the styles of elements in a programmatic manner such as their position on the page, color, font styling, size, and so on.

How do you create variables and strings?

Think of **variables** as cups—there are many different sizes, and they all have the capacity to hold something that is similar in size. Cups, in turn, allow you to remove that item that is being stored at will. Variables in the same manner store all different types of data. Some variables hold large amounts of data and some small. In JavaScript, after you store something in a variable, you can always retrieve it again, that is, as long as you haven't replaced the contents of the variable with something else. Some types of data in variables get treated a little bit differently, which I will explain in a bit, but first, let's run a small demo. You can run the example called Variables and Strings for Chapter 1 to see the demo.

LinkED

Certain types of data in variables get treated a little bit differently. I'll discuss this in more detail in the section "Declaring variables" later in this chapter.

If you think this stuff is a bit dry, I promise we will have much more fun later when we start working with Dojo. These fundamentals, however, are absolutely necessary if you have never programmed before. For now, you're doing great, so I'll delay no more!

JavaScript can store different types of data in variables: strings (which are just a collection of characters) and numbers. Actually, JavaScript really stores only one thing in variables, and that is an object. An object is as general as it sounds. An **object** is a blueprint of how JavaScript will store this data in the computer's memory. JavaScript works with this data differently depending on its type. Strings, numbers, and booleans (`true` or `false`) when assigned to a JavaScript variable are actually transferred into their associated types of objects automatically: a string into a String object, a number into a Number object, a boolean into a Boolean object, and so forth.

NotED

Booleans are special variables found in every programming language. Believe it or not, they are the most basic of all datatypes. Even though they appear to be strings, since you assign the words true *or* false *to them, they in fact are not. The words* true *and* false *are simply representations of 1 and 0, respectively, or on and off. A Boolean is not only used when setting variables, but as you'll see later in this chapter in the section "How do you control the flow?" they are also used to communicate whether expressions are true or false.*

JavaScript's ability to create objects like this is where its true flexibility lies. Once you have assigned a value to a variable, that variable automatically assumes other functionality associated with its datatype. For instance, if you wanted to make the characters in a String variable all uppercase, you could do the following:

```
var myStr = "I want this whole string to be all uppercase!";
myStr.toUpperCase();
document.write(myStr);
```

The toUpperCase function was possible only because the variable was a String. If it were some other datatype like a Number, it would not have been able to do that. JavaScript saw that I wanted to create a String object (by using the double quotes around my sentence), so it created that special datatype. By doing this, my String variable received a bunch of functions that can be called from it.

Variables are used to make it easier for developers to use and move around the data in their application.

Declaring variables

You declare a variable in JavaScript with the var keyword followed by a name for your variable. Naming a variable allows you to refer to its contents later by simply using its name. The name will always stay constant, but its value may change. There are a few rules you must abide by when naming variables in JavaScript, as shown in Table 1-1.

Table 1-1. Rules for naming variables

Rule	Examples
Must not start with a number.	5goldenRings, 7primeNumbers
Must not contain punctuation with exception to the underscore.	foo:bar, !fooBar
Must not contain spaces. Use an underscore (_) in place of a space if you so desire. Note, hyphens (-) may not be used unless it is in quoted notation such as foo["bar-baz"] = "Dojo rocks my world!".	telling_the_truth
Must not contain mathematical operators.	ying/yang, multipleSt*rs
Must not be the exact name of any JavaScript keyword. A full list of reserved keywords follows this table.	var, function, else
Should not be the same as a name you've provided in an ID of an element on the same page. It will work in Firefox but will break in Internet Explorer.	var fooBar = false;, <div id="fooBar"></div>

Reserved JavaScript keywords

The following is a list of JavaScript keywords. They are words that are used within JavaScript for other functions and cannot be used as variable or function names.

- abstract
- as
- boolean
- break
- byte
- case
- catch

- char
- class
- continue
- const
- debugger
- default
- delete

- do
- double
- else
- enum
- export
- extends
- false
- final
- finally
- float
- for
- function
- goto
- if
- implements
- import
- in
- instanceof
- int
- interface
- is
- long
- namespace
- native
- new

- null
- package
- private
- protected
- public
- return
- short
- static
- super
- switch
- synchronized
- this
- throw
- throws
- transient
- true
- try
- typeof
- use
- var
- void
- volatile
- while
- with

Another very important thing to keep in mind is that JavaScript variable names are case-sensitive! This is a wonderful thing because it allows for many more combinations of variable names; however, it can also be a curse when you are attempting to execute a statement and it isn't working. Be sure to check the case on all your variable names.

In addition, it is generally good practice to follow a naming method known as **camel case**. This means that the first letter of the variable is lowercase, and each first letter of a word in the variable afterward is capitalized. Some examples are firstName, emailAddress, and mobileComputerName.

Assignment operator

To assign a value to a variable, you must use the assignment operator. In the case of JavaScript—and most programming languages, for that matter—the operator is the equals (=) sign. As you can see in Figure 1-3, the left side of the equals sign is the variable name you are declaring; the right side is the value that you are assigning to the variable.

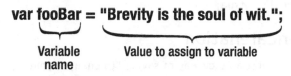

Figure 1-3. A dissected look at variable assignment

Strings

To declare a string, you must enclose it in a set of single or double quotes:

```
var myStr = "There are three faithful friends, an old wife, an old dog,
and ready money."
```

Beware, however, if the string you are creating contains either a single or double quote. To maintain the string, you have to **escape** the quotations you want to be part of the string, not part of defining the variable. To escape a quote in the string, simply precede it with a backslash (\ ):

```
var myEscapedStr = "You only killed the bride\'s father, you know."
```

As you can see, if the apostrophe was not escaped in the word *bride's*, it would actually have closed the string block for that variable, and the browser would have attempted to run the rest of the text as JavaScript code. You need to escape the quotation only if it is the same type that was used to create the string. If you used double quotes to declare the string, then single quotes do not need to be escaped. If you used single quotes to declare the string, then double quotes do not need to be escaped.

Numbers

Assigning numbers to variables is very straightforward. Unlike strings, you must not enclose the number in quotes.

```
var answerToLife = 42;
var oneEighth = 0.125;
```

Booleans

Despite the English keywords true and false being used to represent Booleans, they are actually seen as numbers to the computer, 1 and 0, respectively. In the same manner, when defining a Boolean variable, you must not enclose it in quotes:

```
var visitedBefore = false;
var glassHalfFull = true;
```

String concatenation

Concatenation is just a fancy way of saying "to chain or join together." In the case of strings, it is very easy to concatenate multiple String variables to form a single String variable. The concatenation operator in JavaScript is the plus sign (+). Simply use it in the same manner you would add a series of numbers together.

```
<script type="text/javascript">
  var rndNum = Math.floor(Math.random() * 21);

  var displayName = function()
  {
    var firstName = document.getElementById('txtInp').value;
    alert('Hello, ' + firstName + '!');
  }

  var combineStrings = function(str1, str2)
  {
    return str1 + str2;
  }

  var showCombinedString = function()
  {
    var inputA = document.getElementById('inputA').value;
    var inputB = document.getElementById('inputB').value;
    document.getElementById('pString').innerHTML =
combineStrings(inputA, inputB);
  }
</script>
```

You've got this stuff down pat, right? I think you deserve a little break. Step away from the book, and stretch for a few seconds. I'll just wait here until you are ready to proceed.

How do you perform arithmetic?

Performing arithmetic is very straightforward in JavaScript. The standard mathematical operators are used in sequence in the same way you would write an equation. This means that the order of operations used in mathematics is followed as well. The following is a list of the operations that are executed first in an equation:

- Parentheses
- Exponents and roots
- Multiplication and division
- Addition and subtraction

This means that if you had the equation 5 + 3 * 3, the result would be 14, not 24. In fact, one easy way to remember this rule is by changing the equation around so that your operators are in the order by which they'll be evaluated. Instead of 5 + 3 * 3, it would read 3 * 3 + 5. If you want to force precedence on part of the equation, you can use a pair of parentheses. In our example, if you wanted 5 + 3 to evaluate first, you would write the equation as (5 + 3) * 3. This format would result in 24.

Table 1-2 lists the operators that you can use in JavaScript.

Table 1-2. JavaScript operators

Operator	Function
+	Addition
-	Subtraction
/	Division
*	Multiplication
%	Modulus

ExplainED

You use numbers without quotations so that JavaScript knows to treat them as a number and not as strings of characters.

JavaScript also provides the Math library with a variety of functions to make more advanced calculations such as sine, cosine, tangent, powers, and square roots. It's also home to the function that produced a random number in the demo from the previous section. Table 1-3 lists the additional mathematical functions available to you to use from the Math library.

Table 1-3. Math functions

Function	Description
Math.abs(x)	Absolute value of x
Math.acos(x)	Arc cosine of x
Math.asin(x)	Arc sine of x
Math.atan(x)	Arc tangent of x
Math.atan2(x,y)	Arc tangent of x,y
Math.ceil(x)	Integer closest to x and not less than x
Math.cos(x)	Cosine of x
Math.exp(x)	Exponent of x
Math.floor(x)	Integer closest to and not greater than x
Math.log(x)	Log of x base E
Math.max(x,y)	Maximum of x and y
Math.min(x,y)	Minimum of x and y
Math.pow(x,y)	x to the power y
Math.random()	Random number in the range 0 to 1
Math.round(x)	Integer closest to x
Math.sin(x)	Sine of x
Math.sqrt(x)	Square root of x
Math.tan(x)	Tangent of x

How do you read a method signature?

Now that I'm discussing functions in more detail, I'll touch on a few pieces of information. Functions are also sometimes called **methods** and have a way of defining how to interact with themselves (in other words, the interface they offer to your code). This special description of a method is called a **method signature**. In the documentation for a programming language, method signatures are illustrated all the time. They inform the programmer specifically what to pass into the method, whether it be a String, a Boolean, or other datatype, and they also tell you exactly what to expect the method to return. Figure 1-4 illustrates the method signature for dojo.byId.

NotED

Technically speaking, in programming, a function is different from a method. A function is simply a subroutine or section of code that performs a specific task. A method, on the other hand, is a term in object-oriented programming that describes a subroutine specifically associated with a class or an object.[1]

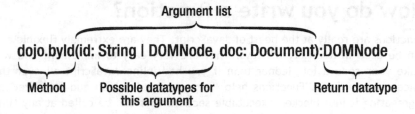

Figure 1-4. A method signature broken down

The signature in Figure 1-4 looks strange at first, but once you learn what each of the pieces mean, it makes more sense. First notice the :DOMNode at the end of the method. This tells you that the method is going to return a DOMNode when it is finished processing. You can assign this return value to another variable in the code that calls the method, or you could nest this method call

---

[1] Wikipedia contributors, "Method (computer science)," *Wikipedia, The Free Encyclopedia,* http://en.wikipedia.org/wiki/Method_(computer_science) (accessed August 30, 2009)

inside another method call and have the return value passed directly to the next method.

As you can see in the argument list, the variables have the same notation as the return type. These specify what datatypes the method expects to receive. The order of the arguments is also very important and should be taken literally. Looking at id, you can see it shows two datatypes separated by a pipe (|)—this means that this method argument can accept either one of the datatypes, in this case, either a String or another DOMNode can be passed to the method.

Finally, if an argument is optional, it will have a question mark (?) following it.

ExplainED

The words foo and bar are often used in place of actual variable names in programming examples. When used, there isn't a difference between one or the other; they are just placeholders for real variable names. You can read more about the origin of these funny words on Wikipedia (http://en.wikipedia.org/wiki/Foobar).

How do you write a function?

Functions are really at the heart of JavaScript. They are extremely flexible and can be used in a variety of ways. They are very easy to implement and will make your code a lot cleaner than if you had inline JavaScript all over the place on your page. Functions help keep your code clean and organized by segregating it into blocked executable sections that can be called at any time by the name of the function. This is much better than writing inline JavaScript code everywhere on the page that you want to use it. For instance, if you were writing an event handler for a button, you wouldn't want to write all the code within the declaration; you would simply want to refer to a function name where you've already written the code in a legible format.

LinkED

I briefly described functions earlier in this chapter in the "In the Head" section.

Keep in mind that, unlike the statements that you have written directly inline with the page, statements inside functions *do not* get executed when the page loads. This is because when the browser loads the JavaScript in a page, it knows that function blocks are meant to be called at another time, not at the time that the browser reads it. In fact, JavaScript functions are actually stored in variables just like a String, Boolean, or any other datatype. A function is another datatype of JavaScript. This is why you use the assignment operator in the examples to declare a new function:

```
var fooBar = function(args)
{
  alert("I'm a function named fooBar!");
}
```

Play with the examples for this section. I think you'll like what you see and begin to consider the ways that functions will make your life easier. Come back here when you are done, and I'll discuss in more detail what functions are. Run the Functions example for this chapter to see the demo.

You've seen those things before, right? Yep, you saw them in the previous examples. Even though you hadn't learned about functions yet, it was more efficient for me to use functions to help demonstrate previous examples.

Declaring functions

Functions are very simple and straightforward in JavaScript, as shown in Figure 1-5.

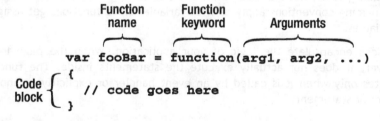

Figure 1-5. A dissection of a JavaScript function declaration

To declare a function, you start out in much the same way that you do when you declare a variable. In fact, the whole left side from the beginning to the equals sign is identical to declaring a variable. The right side is where things change.

The right side of the declaration starts with word *function* followed by a set of parentheses. Inside the parentheses is where you provide a list of arguments

19

that you want the function to be able to access. Finally, the declaration ends with a block of code, surrounded by a pair of curly braces. These tell the browser that this code is not to be executed right now, and it should be run only when the function is called.

LinkED

You'll learn more about arguments in the next section, "Passing data to functions."

ExplainED

When a function is called, it means that you are explicitly telling the browser to run the block of code that you defined in a function declaration. You can call a function anywhere you can write JavaScript. Simply write the name followed by a pair of parentheses. That's all you need to execute the function. If your function requires attributes to be passed along as well, then you provide those between the parentheses.

The keyword function is one of the reserved JavaScript keywords that you can't use as a variable name, and quite frankly, you can't name your function "function" either, not that you should want to do so. In fact, pretty much the same naming conventions apply as with variables since functions get assigned to variables.

Functions encapsulate the logic of your application. When the page loads, however, it does not actually execute the statements inside. The function executes only when it is called by an event handler or explicitly in another JavaScript statement.

LinkED

You can see an event handler calling a function earlier in this chapter when I discussed executing code after the page was finished loading.

You can also define variables inside a function just like you would anywhere else in the page. The difference is that when you define a variable from within a function, it will not be available to another function or from an inline statement on the page. This is known as a **local variable**, because it is local to the function it was declared in. Variables declared outside functions are called **global variables** and can be accessed and modified from within any function on the page.

Passing data to functions

Functions may also be written to receive data input that they can then process. These inputs are commonly known as **arguments**. Many times, if you are passing data into a function, you also want to receive something from it. Return statements in a function will send a variable back to where the function was called. A caveat about return statements is that they can return only a single variable, which can be a String, Boolean, Array, Object, or any other datatype. Figure 1-6 gives you a better idea of how this works.

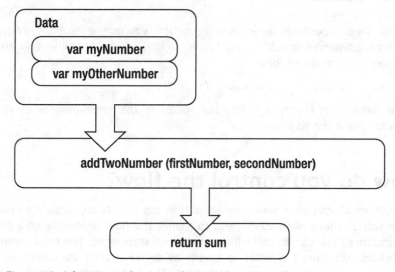

Figure 1-6. A function with two attributes and a return value

You define the inputs that you want to receive in the function and what is going to leave the function via an output. Remember, you can pass only one variable in a return statement. The following is a simple example of what a function looks like with some arguments being passed in and some code inside the block:

```
function addTwoNumbers(firstNum, secondNum)

{
```

```
var sum = firstNum + secondNum;
return sum;
}
```

This is a basic function that wants to receive two numbers as arguments to simply add them together and return the sum. Most of the time when you are executing a function that contains a return statement, you are going to want to prepare a variable to receive the return value:

```
var numA = 10;
var numB = 13;
var sumTwoNumbers = addTwoNumbers(numA, numB);
```

The result of calling the function addTwoNumbers with numbers numA and numB is 23. This value is stored in the variable sumTwoNumbers.

NotED

If you need to pass data to execute a function, you do not necessarily have to create separate variables first to pass to it. You could have written the previous statement as follows:

```
var sumTwoNumbers = addTwoNumbers(10, 13);
```

Just make sure that you define the values in the same manner as you would create the variables.

How do you control the flow?

You will not always want your program to flow top to bottom, straight through. There will be times when you'll need to change the flow depending on a given circumstance. You can do this with a conditional statement. The most common conditional statement is what is known as an if...then statement or an if...then...else or simply an if statement. The logic pretty much works the way it reads: "If *this* condition is *true*, then do this; *else* do this." Look at the following example, and then I will break it down to talk about each piece.

```
var accountBalance = 65;
if(accountBalance < 100)
{
  alert('Your account is running low! Learn Dojo so ' +
  'you can make more money!');
}
```

The magic of an if statement lies in its *expression* statement. In the previous example, (accountBalance < 100) is the expression. This expression must result in true for the block of code between the curly brackets to execute. In our example, I'm storing a dollar amount of the user's account balance; then in the expression I'm testing if it is less than $100. If it is, the expression is true, the block of code executes, and I alert them that their balance is running low.

In the previous example, if the user's balance was greater than $100, then the program would simply skip over the alert and continue as usual, because the expression would be false. However, if you had another set of statements that you wanted to execute, you might put them in an else statement. This basically says that if the first expression was not equal to true like you wanted, then execute the code in the else block. Here's an example of this type of statement:

```
var userLoggedIn = false;
if(userLoggedIn == true)
{
  document.write('Welcome, you are logged in.');
}
else
{
  document.write('Please login, so you can access all the great
features.');
}
```

In this case, the user would be prompted to log in since userLoggedIn is not equal to true. You'll also notice that to determine equality, you must use two equal signs (==). In our example, if we had used a single equal sign between userLoggedIn and true, it would have assigned true to userLoggedIn, causing the expression to evaluate to true and making it look like the user is logged in when they're not. Knowing the difference between inequalities is very important in ensuring accurate if statement execution. Use Table 1-4 to see what inequalities you can try.

Table 1-4. Sample inequalities

Sign	Definition
a == b	Is a exactly equal to b
a != b	Is a not equal to b
a < b	Is a less than b
a <= b	Is a less than or equal to b
a > b	Is a greater than b
a >= b	Is a greater than or equal to b

if...then statements can contain multiple if blocks to test multiple conditions. Think of the else block as a default action in case none of the other if expressions is equal to true. The first if statement in a conditional block is the only one that is required; you do not have to have an else if or an else statement follow.

What is an array, and why is it so important?

Arrays are extremely valuable tools in programming. At their core, they allow you to store a set of data in a single variable. Most often these sets will contain similar categories of data (Figure 1-7). You may have an array of names, a grocery list of items, or perhaps DOM elements with the same class name. You can retrieve any one item out of this data set via an index, or you can loop through the entire set.

ExplainED

Need a quick refresh on the different datatypes you can use for variables? Strings are sets of characters enclosed in a set of quotes. Booleans store either true or false, without quotes. Numbers are any integer or decimal. Keep in mind that technically functions are a datatype as well and are assigned to variables as well.

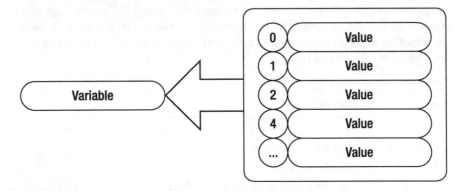

Figure 1-7. An array with multiple elements

LinkED

Arrays are especially useful in JavaScript when working with the DOM. You'll discover this later when you learn how to query the DOM to return sets of DOM nodes in Chapter 4.

How do you create an array?

Creating an array variable is simple and straightforward:

```
var namesArr = [];
```

The expression on the right of the equals sign is called an **array literal**, and it will create an empty array and assign it to the variable namesArr. The previous code creates an empty array, which means there are no elements for you to retrieve.

ExplainED

In previous examples where you created a new variable and assigned a string to it, you were using a String literal. The same goes for Booleans; you used a Boolean literal. With numbers, when it was an integer, it was creating a new variable using an Integer literal, and when it was a decimal, it used a floating-point literal.

Adding elements to an array

To add new items in an array, you can call the push function from the array and pass in a value to add:

```
var namesArr = new [];
namesArr.push("Jenny");
namesArr.push("Peter");
namesArr.push("Walt");
```

If you wanted to print the values of this array, you could write the following:

```
document.write(namesArr[0]);
document.write(namesArr[1]);
document.write(namesArr[2]);
```

When you add elements to an array using the push function, an index is used to keep track of the position of elements in the array. The first element in an array is not stored with the index 1 as you might expect, but actually index 0. This is because arrays in JavaScript are **zero-index** arrays. That means that any time you loop through an array to retrieve the data, you need to start with zero and then work your way up from there. This is very common in most programming languages. It is something you have to get used to. Keep in mind that if you are trying to retrieve an element, you take its numerical position and subtract one; that will give you the index. For instance, for the fifth element, you use index number 4.

How do you loop through array elements?

More often than not, you won't be interested in processing only one element of an array and leaving the rest behind. You'll usually want to do something to the entire set. Typically you won't know how long the array is going to be either. You need to use an automated method of processing every single item, without having to write a lot of code. The perfect type of loop for this kind of task is the for loop.

For loops

There are different types of loops in programming; the most common one is the for loop because of its usefulness when working with arrays. Just like an array, a for loop uses an index—an index that keeps track of the number of times it has run the loop. The index that is used is an actual JavaScript variable. You basically tell the loop to count to a specified number. It will base its starting count on the index you provide it. You also control how many steps the loop increments the index.

Given the namesArr array from the previous example, here is a basic for loop to display those names:

```
document.write('<ul>');
for (var i = 0; i < namesArr.length; i++)
{
   document.write('<li>' + namesArr[i] + '</li>');
}
document.write('</ul>');
```

There is a lot going on here, so we will break it down into smaller chunks. The first document.write() function displays whatever string you give it at the point in the page where you call the function. In this case, it will simply start an unordered-list block.

The next line is where it gets tricky and will require some extra explaining. A for loop requires three things to work: a variable that will hold the current index count (var i), followed by an expression to determine whether the loop should execute (i < namesArr.length), ending with how many steps you want to increment the index (i++). By calling .length on the namesArr function, you can get the length of the array. For the index, you provide var i = 0 since you are actually creating a new variable and setting it to 0. This is your starting point for the index. If you had set it to 8, the count would start at 8.

The expression to test against is usually an inequality when it comes to looping through arrays. The expression that the for loop is testing is just like the expressions within if statements. And in the same manner, this must be equal to true in order to proceed with executing the code in the for block. In this case, we are checking whether the current index (i) is less than the number of elements in the array. Each time the loop repeats, the index increases by one because of the i++ statement.

NotED

The double plus (++) operator in most programming languages when appended to a variable that contains a number will increase that number by one. Note that when you use it as described before, one is added to the number and then returned; if you prefix the variable with the double plus (as in ++i), the value is returned first and then incremented. By the same token, a double minus (--) can be used in the same manner, but it will decrement the value.

Summary

You may be feeling a little lightheaded right now, but I hope you can see the value of JavaScript in web development. It can be very powerful but also very confusing at times. Bear with me in the chapters ahead, and I can guarantee you'll love what you can do with the language. Let's recap what you've learned in this chapter:

- A few examples that show you the basics of JavaScript
- How to name variable and functions

- How to create arrays, which are special variables that allow you to store groups of related data and also how to loop through that data to work with it

- How to control the flow of your scripts with conditional statements

- How to write functions that help to encapsulate functionality

You should feel good about what you accomplished. When you are first learning to program, it can be intense and overwhelming at times. The best part about this being a book is that you can always go back and read it again.

Chapter 2

Digging Deeper

"The obstacle is the path."

—Zen proverb

In this chapter, you'll take a look at what sets JavaScript apart from other languages. The DOM is a mysterious entity to many, but learn to tame it, and it will become your best friend. JavaScript is your whip, and with it you will harness the DOM's power to build engaging and rich websites.

If you don't feel quite comfortable with some of the programming concepts from Chapter 1, don't worry about it too much unless you really feel the urge to revisit it. If you are new to programming, it will take some time to get used to and really understand the concepts. Much of what you do when you first learn to program is copy and paste from examples. The more you do, the more you'll see the common patterns and be able to start doing stuff from scratch.

Start getting excited for what lays ahead in this chapter. We'll be looking at how to find specific elements in the DOM, style elements, fill them with content, and listen for interaction from the user and the page. Understanding these concepts is vital to understanding the benefits of what Dojo brings to the table.

Manipulating the DOM

The DOM can be a scary beast at first glance. OK, it can be really scary, but fear not, because by the end of this book, you will be fully comfortable treading the depths. The next few sections lay the groundwork to ensure your understanding of the magic that JavaScript provides to HTML.

How do you get a reference to a node on the DOM?

One of the main reasons a developer chooses to develop parts of their web page using JavaScript vs. a server-side language (Java, PHP, Python, and so on) is because you can interact with the page after it loads to respond to user events and interaction, create animations, or submit data while allowing the user to stay on the same page. JavaScript allows the developer to do this because the technology is intermingled with HTML and the browser. You can reference any of the pieces on a page and manipulate them, change their state of appearance, and so on; JavaScript makes this all possible.

Users tend to have a more positive experience when these types of things happen vs. if the page were to simply reload with something new. It engages them and encourages them to stay on the site because it is enjoyable to use.

Let's go over some terminology. You already know what the DOM is, so let's talk about **nodes**. Everything in an HTML document is represented in the DOM as a node. For example, consider a contact form on a page with a few input fields for name, email, and comments. Each one of those items, the form, and the input fields are all separate nodes. Since the input fields actually reside between the form tags, you can access the input nodes just by getting a reference to the form container itself. See Figure 2-1 for a visual example of this.

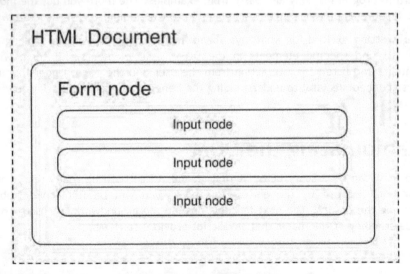

Figure 2-1. A form node that contains three input nodes

30

By ID

As you may already be aware, you can assign any element in an HTML document an id attribute. In CSS you can style an element by referring to its given id. JavaScript can also use this special property. Look at the following code example:

```
<div id="sidebar">
  <p>Sidebar content</p>
  <p>More sidebar content</p>
</div>

<script type="text/javascript">
  var sidebarDiv = document.getElementById('sidebar');
</script>
```

ExplainED

Variables allow you to store data for later use. You can store Strings, Numbers, Booleans, and functions. You can also store references to HTML elements on the page such as divs.

As you can see, I assigned an id to the div, which contains two basic paragraphs. In the JavaScript block in the next few lines, I create a new variable called sidebarDiv and store a reference to the div. This is a good time to introduce the global document object. The document object is globally accessible, which means that you can access it like I did earlier in the JavaScript block or from inside a function or from any place that you write JavaScript statements. It is just like any other variable that you declare, except that you don't have to explicitly declare it. It is created automatically by the browser and placed in a variable called document.

ExplainED

Keep in mind that a DOM is actually a convention used to represent various types of documents whether they be HTML, XML, or similar. There is no variable in JavaScript called DOM. However, in the case of JavaScript and HTML, there is a variable called document that refers to a container that holds everything on an HTML page.

The document object is a container for all the elements on the HTML page and thereby represents the DOM of the page. You could traverse the entire DOM through the document object. I won't go over that in detail; it would be too painful because of the size of any given HTML document. However, the document object provides some useful methods that allow you to get around the DOM in a quicker, more efficient manner. In the previous example, you call the method getElementById and pass in the id of the div element as a String. This expression returns to you a JavaScript reference to that node in the DOM.

NotED

In the world of programming web pages, all the data on a page is stored in the computer's memory. When you create variables, you are creating "references" to a specific location in memory where the data you want to store exists. Sometimes you are creating that data and then getting a reference to it (for example, declaring a new String or Number or even a function). Other times you are getting a reference to something that already exists in memory. In the case of the JavaScript example, the div *was placed in memory when the page loaded. When you used* document.getElementById(), *you were actually only getting a reference or pointer to that object in memory. If that object changes on the page, the variable will reflect those same changes.*

By children nodes

When you obtain a reference to an element, it contains not only the properties of the element but also the child elements inside it as well. To enable you to get references to these child elements, this node reference also has a special property called childNodes. When this property is accessed, it returns a reference to an array. Each element in the array is a reference to each individual node that is contained within the parent element. Let's look at an example:

```
<div id="sidebar">
  <p>Sidebar content</p>
  <p>More sidebar content</p>
</div>
<script type="text/javascript">
  var sidebarDiv = document.getElementById('sidebar');
  var sidebarArr = sidebarDiv.childNodes;
  alert(sidebarArr.length);
</script>
```

The bold code is what you're interested in. You create a variable called sidebarArr that will reference the array that sidebarDiv.childNodes represents. You create a simple alert statement to tell you how many nodes are contained in that div. The alert will display "2" since there are two paragraphs inside the div.

ExplainED

It is sometimes beneficial to name your JavaScript variables with an abbreviation of the type of data they contain. For instance, if it is a String, you may want to call it strFirstName, or a Boolean boolVisitedBefore. Another one you'll see me use from time to time is arr for an array such as sidebarArr. There are no set rules amongst developers for what to use exactly or to use them at all. Sometimes it helps, but it can also make variables unnecessarily long.

By tag name

What if you wanted to apply the same style or get information from elements with the same tag name on the page? You certainly would not want to access each one individually by their assigned id; sometimes they may not have a known id. There is a handy method that the document object provides called getElementsBy TagName(). When it's called and a name of an HTML tag is passed in, it will return an array of all the elements on the page with the specified tag name.

NotED

*JavaScript supports a concept known as **scoping** where you can create variables that hold references to other JavaScript statements or methods. For instance, since document.getElementById() is rather long to type, you could say var byId = document.getElementById;. By that same token, if you wanted to work with a specific section of your document, you could first get a reference to a high-level element of the section like var f = document.getElementById('foo'). Then any time you wanted to call the methods that would be available to the document variable, you would call them directly from the variable f, such as var paras = f.getElementsByTagName('p'). This would only return paragraph elements that are within the element "foo".*

Observe the following code:

```
<div>
  <dl>
    <dt>42</dt>
    <dd>The answer to life, the universe, and everything</dd>

    <dt>boanthropy</dt>
    <dd>A type of insanity in which a man thinks he is an ox</dd>

    <dt>peristerophobia</dt>
    <dd>Fear of pigeons</dd>
  </dl>
</div>

<script type="text/javascript">
  var terms = document.getElementsByTagName('dt');
  for(var i=0; i<terms.length; i++)
  {
    document.write(terms[i].innerHTML + "<br/>");
  }
</script>
```

Given a div with a definition list (dl) of terms (dt) and definitions (dd), you can get a reference to only the terms and display their values. First, you have to get a reference to an array of all the dt tags. I created a variable called terms that I then assigned the array that document.getElementsByTagName returned to me. Notice that for the getElementsByTagName method, I only needed to give it the alphabetical characters of a tag name and not the angled brackets (<>) of the tag.

LinkED

You learned about for loops in Chapter 1 in the section "How do you loop through array elements?" Recall that they need a variable that tracks the current loop count (which you can use to reference an index in the array), an expression that has to evaluate to true *to allow the loop to proceed, and an increment statement that will tell the loop how much to increase the counter each time the loop is executed. Using ++ will increment the Number by one after the loop executes.*

Now that I have an array of dt elements stored in terms, I can use a for loop to write out the value of each element. Variables that are references to tags on the page will have a property called innerHTML. This property will return the data that sits between the opening tag and the closing tag. In the document.write statement, for example, you can first refer to an array element by using the counter variable (i) as the index and then get the innerHTML property. Since document.write will physically push output directly to the page as it is loading, you can use it to write data out to the page when it loads. You do this simply by concatenating a String (with the plus sign) with a br tag. When you run the example, the output will look similar to the following.

LinkED

You learned that you can concatenate Strings using the plus (+) operator in Chapter 1 in the section "How do you create variables and strings?"

42
boanthropy
peristerophobia

How do you change the style of a DOM element?

Ideally you are already familiar with using CSS and HTML together. If not, you may want to check out *Beginning HTML with CSS and XHTML* (Apress, 2007). You can also change the look and style of elements using JavaScript to manipulate special properties on elements that reflect their look and feel. These properties are similar to the ones that you find in CSS. Keep in mind, however, that you don't want to do all your styling through JavaScript. That would not make sense when you have the option of the much more powerful CSS rendering engines in browsers that are meant to handle full-page styling efficiently. Instead, you should use this approach to change the look of an element after a user interacts with it or to get the user's attention.

Using the style property

ExplainED

Don't forget that you can easily get a reference to a node or element on the DOM by using document.getElementById *or* document.getElementsBy TagName.

Before you can the change the style of an element, you'll need a reference to a node on the DOM. You already know how to do that! Once you have that, you can modify the style via the style property. The style property is an object that is stored in the style property of the node and has properties that you can modify such as fontFamily or color. Many of the CSS properties are available, but not all. Table 2-1 lists the CSS properties that are available and their JavaScript equivalent name.

Table 2-1. CSS properties

CSS Property	JavaScript Style Property
background	background
background-attachment	backgroundAttachment
background-color	backgroundColor
background-image	backgroundImage
background-position	backgroundPosition
background-repeat	backgroundRepeat
border	border
border-bottom	borderBottom
border-bottom-color	borderBottomColor
border-bottom-style	borderBottomStyle
border-bottom-width	borderBottomWidth
border-color	borderColor
border-left	borderLeft
border-left-color	borderLeftColor
border-left-style	borderLeftStyle
border-left-width	borderLeftWidth
border-right	borderRight
border-right-color	borderRightColor
border-right-style	borderRightStyle
border-right-width	borderRightWidth
border-style	borderStyle
border-top	borderTop
border-top-color	borderTopColor
border-top-style	borderTopStyle
border-top-width	borderTopWidth
border-width	borderWidth
clear	clear

CSS Property	JavaScript Style Property
clip	clip
color	color
cursor	cursor
display	display
filter	filter
font	font
font-family	fontFamily
font-size	fontSize
font-variant	fontVariant
font-weight	fontWeight
height	height
left	left
letter-spacing	letterSpacing
line-height	lineHeight
list-style	listStyle
list-style-image	listStyleImage
list-style-position	listStylePosition
list-style-type	listStyleType
margin	margin
margin-bottom	marginBottom
margin-left	marginLeft
margin-right	marginRight
margin-top	marginTop
overflow	overflow
padding	padding
padding-bottom	paddingBottom
padding-left	paddingLeft
padding-right	paddingRight
padding-top	paddingTop
page-break-after	pageBreakAfter
page-break-before	pageBreakBefore
position	position
float	styleFloat
text-align	textAlign

CSS Property	JavaScript Style Property
text-decoration	textDecoration
text-decoration: blink	textDecorationBlink
text-decoration: line-through	textDecorationLineThrough
text-decoration: none	textDecorationNone
text-decoration: overline	textDecorationOverline
text-decoration: underline	textDecorationUnderline
text-indent	textIndent
text-transform	textTransform
top	top
vertical-align	verticalAlign
visibility	visibility
width	width
z-index	zIndex

NotED

Camel case refers to a variable naming convention in programming. When the variable name is only one word, all letters are lowercase: var name. *If the variable name is composed of more than one word, the first word is lowercase, and each subsequent word begins with an uppercase letter, as in* var firstName *or* var userStreetAddress.

The difference is that CSS properties that contain a hyphen (-) get stripped of that hyphen and converted to camel case in JavaScript. For instance, if you wanted to apply a certain font family in CSS to an element, you would specify it using the font-family property; in JavaScript, this is expressed as *node*.style.fontFamily. Let's try it.

```
var paraText = document.getElementById('pText');
paraText.style.fontFamily = "Arial";
```

The syntax is very similar to CSS. The advantage of doing it with JavaScript is that you can alter it after the page has loaded, as opposed to CSS, which renders as the page is loading.

LinkED

Actually, it is possible to change an element's style on the page using only CSS for the style and a little JavaScript for the updating. You'll see this in the next section, "Using the className property."

Using the className property

Using styles can be tedious if there are multiple properties of an element you want to change. Let's say you wanted to change not only the font family but also the text color and the background color. If you used the style property for that, you would have to write four long lines to accomplish that task:

```
var petuniaP = document.getElementById('petunia');
myPara.style.fontFamily = "Arial";
myPara.style.color = "#336699";
myPara.style.backgroundColor = "#cccccc";
```

In addition, it is usually best to keep presentation code (CSS and styles) separate from the logic of the application. JavaScript provides a way to make it easier to apply a set of styles to an element and integrate both CSS and JavaScript together.

By first defining a CSS class with the proposed styles you want to apply, you can then assign that class name to your node's property, className. Since this would then cause the element to instantly have that class name as if it had it when the page loaded, the styles instantly transform it by modifying all the properties of the node in correlation with how they are defined in the CSS class.

```
<style type="text/css">
  .vibrant {
    font-family: "Arial";
    font-weight: bold;
    background-color: #A9FF00;
    color: #00E87E;
  }
</style>
```

```
<p id="petunia">Curiously the only thing that went through the mind of
the bowl of petunias, as it fell, was, 'Oh no, not again.' Many people
have speculated that if we knew exactly *why* the bowl of petunias had
thought that we would know a lot more about the nature of the universe
than we do now.</p>
```

```
<script type="text/javascript">
  var flowerQuote = document.getElementById('petunia');
  flowerQuote.className = 'vibrant';
</script>
```

Notice that in the JavaScript you don't need to include the period that precedes the class name in the CSS declaration. One thing to keep track of in this case is that you are setting the className property equal to vibrant. If the paragraph already had another class name, it would get replaced with vibrant. If you didn't want this to happen and you wanted to *append* the new class, you could write the code as follows:

```
flowerQuote.className += ' vibrant';
```

There is a space after the first single quote on purpose. This is because the browser uses spaces between class names to distinguish between them. If you did not provide a space, the two class names would be merged together, making it appear to the browser as a single class name.

ExplainED

When you make changes that change the properties of an element, such as giving it a new class name, if you were to view the source of the page in your browser, you would not see the class name applied to the element. This is because the source only shows what the page initially rendered as, not anything that is changed after it is done loading. Firebug, a common development tool for the Firefox browser, can show you the "current" rendered state of the page in its DOM tab.

How do you change the HTML content of an element?

Besides sending Ajax calls, which I'll cover later in the book, something that makes your websites seem more responsive is dynamically adding content into the page while the user is using it. Be careful, though, because this method can become difficult to keep track of at times. As long as you do a little planning, you can minimize the risk of making your code messy and unreadable.

All DOM nodes have an innerHTML property that allows you to provide a String of HTML content. Essentially this is the same as putting a block of HTML between the opening and closing tags of the element you are referring to innerHTML on. Take a look at the innerHTML demo for this chapter to see how this can be used.

Pretty great, right? I hope you see how this can truly make your visitors feel like the page is more responsive to their interactions. In addition, the demos have a very low usage of colors and other graphics. You could certainly make it look even nicer with the appropriate stylizations.

Let's break these down a little bit to go over all that is happening. Here's the JavaScript code from the Form Submission example:

```
var sendSubmission = function()

{
  var alertBox = document.getElementById('greenAlert');
  var name = document.getElementById('txtFirstName').value + " " +
    document.getElementById('txtLastName').value;
  var email = document.getElementById('txtEmail').value;
  alertBox.innerHTML = 'Thank you, ' + name + ', your submission has
been sent. '+
    'You will be notified at ' + email + ' if you are a chosen winner.';
  alertBox.style.display = 'block';
}
```

In the first line, I'm defining a new function, but you already know how to do this. Let's move on. Skipping the curly bracket line, you can see that I am getting a reference to the div that has an id of greenAlert. Of course, I didn't have to call the variable that I am storing it in alertBox; I could have used any descriptive variable name.

ExplainED

When you get a reference to a text input element, you can reference its value *property to return the value that the user typed into the textbox.*

Next, I get the name of the submitter using an efficient approach that uses less code than if I wrote separate statements that received and stored the value of the txtFirstName field as well as the txtLastName field in separate variables. Instead, I chose to get them all at once and concatenate them together into one variable. Notice also that I put a space in between the two values to ensure it displays correctly later. On the next line, I grab the value from the txtEmail field.

ExplainED

Concatenation is the process of combining more than one String together to form a single String that can be assigned to a variable or sent to another process. You can concatenate anything that is a String or that returns a String. Since the value property of a text input element returns a String, you can use the plus operator (+) to concatenate it to a regular String defined in quotes.

Finally, once you have all the values, you construct the statement that you want to set the HTML content of alertBox to. As soon as the browser executes that statement, the innerHTML is instantly set and reflects on that page instantly. Lastly, you change the style of the alertBox to be display = 'block' to make the box be visible to the user—since in the CSS you made it hidden by setting display:none for the element:

```
<style type="text/css">
  #greenAlert {
    background-color: lightgreen;
    font-weight: bold;
    font-family: "Arial";
    padding: 5px;
    display: none;
  }
</style>
```

The JavaScript code for the second example, Preview Before Submission, is as follows:

```
var updatePreview = function()

{
  var prvwTxt = document.getElementById('txtComment').value;
  var prvwArea = document.getElementById('prvwComm');
  prvwArea.innerHTML = prvwTxt;
}
```

On the first line in the function, I get a reference to the text input form field the user is typing into, and I get its current value (which is the text the user typed). Then on the next line, I get a reference to the comment preview element where I will show the user what their comment will look like. Finally, in the last line of the function, I set the preview area's innerHTML property to the value I pulled from the input element. It instantly sets the preview area to this text and displays it to the user. Users love this kind of interaction. It keeps them engaged and interested in your site because it contains immediate feedback and confirmation of an action they took.

I hope you had some fun with this example by experimenting with some HTML inside the comment area. It's really a great way to see how powerful the innerHTML property can be, despite its simplicity. It also goes to show that such power can be extremely simple to implement. There was a special magic that was presented to the user thanks to the innerHTML property. However, what really made this a *rich* experience was that while the user types their comment, they instantly see the preview update itself. This was made possible by simply adding the onkeyup property to the textarea and pointing it to the updatePreview() function.

LinkED

The property onkeyup *is an event listener. When the user types on their keyboard and any individual key comes back up after they press it, the browser will execute the* updatePreview() *function. You'll learn more about this in the "Events" section next.*

```
<script type="text/javascript">
  function updatePreview()
  {
    var prvwTxt = document.getElementById('txtComment').value;
    var prvwArea = document.getElementById('prvwComm');
    prvwArea.innerHTML = prvwTxt;
  }
</script>
<fieldset>
  <legend>Leave a Comment</legend>
  <textarea id="txtComment" cols="45" rows="5"
    onkeyup="updatePreview()"></textarea><br/>
  <input id="btnSubmit" type="button" value="Submit Comment" />
</fieldset>
<fieldset>
  <legend>Preview your comment</legend>
  <p id="prvwComm"><em>Your comment will be previewed here when you
    start typing.</em></p>
</fieldset>
```

Events

Did you know that pretty much every interaction your users make within your website causes events in the background to be fired off? Events are one of my personal favorite topics of discussion when it comes to programming. They are incredibly powerful and can help control the flow of your application in an organized, reusable way.

What is a JavaScript event?

An **eventevent** is a packet of information about something that has occurred on the page. It can be passed to different parts of your application by way of an **event variable**. An event can be fired because of user interaction such as moving their mouse on the page, clicking a button, typing in a text field (sound familiar?), or submitting a form. JavaScript may also fire off events from internal sequences, such as receiving a response from the server after an Ajax request, after a timer finishes, after the page finishes loading, or when an error occurs.

View the demo Events for this chapter to get a better idea of the kind of information you can find out from events.

Without listening and acting upon events, a user's experience on a website will be dull and, quite frankly, uneventful! By responding to events that occur on the page, you can make your web page much more interactive and provide more reasons for the user to stay on the page. As an example, it is a much better user experience when a user is filling out a form and to have a form field show an error immediately after the user leaves the field if it is invalid. This allows the user to fix it, rather than filling out the entire form, submitting it to the server, and then having to go back through the form to fix all of the issues. Users get a warm and fuzzy feeling when they know that the developer had their best interests in mind when designing the user interaction. You wouldn't be able to provide this special treatment without the concept of events and event handling.

Events are so much fun, right? At the surface they are simple, but they also have a very powerful set of features that could be more fully covered over a couple of chapters. We will be concerned only with their surface functionality for now.

How do you attach an event listener?

Let's go over some of what you just saw in the demo. First, you'll take a look at the code from the Click event:

```
var clickEvent = function(event)

{
  var timestamp = "Timestamp: " + event.timeStamp + "\n";
  var type = "Event type: " + event.type + "\n";
  var shift = "Shift key: " + event.shiftKey + "\n";
  var screenCoords = "Coordinates: " + event.screenX + "," +
    event.screenY + "\n";
  var txtClickEvents = document.getElementById('clickEvents');
  txtClickEvents.value = timestamp +
    type + shift + screenCoords + "-----------------------\n" +
  txtClickEvents.value;
}
```

Notice on the first line where I am declaring my function that I specify I would like to have a variable passed to it. In this case, the variable will hold an event object. Let's look at the HTML where this function is called:

LinkED

Setting up event listeners inline with HTML tags is not considered best practice. It's more conventional to create them in JavaScript to separate the presentation from the logic of the web application. You can see how Dojo makes this a breeze in Chapter 5 in the section "How do you listen for an event with Dojo?"

```
<input id="btnClick" type="button" value="Click me!!!"
  onclick="clickEvent(event)"/>
```

I specify the property onclick since I want the clickEvent function to execute when the user clicks my button. Look at the next part of that property; not only do I specify to execute the clickEvent function, but I also tell it to pass in the event object. This special object captures all kinds of information about the event that occurred. When passing it to your function like this, it must be called event. This is because it is a local variable that is created when the event occurs. Once the event is completed, the event object can be inspected to retrieve the information it captured. By specifying the function in the onclick property, the function becomes an event listener. This term really is as simple as it sounds; the function at this point begins to listen for the onclick event and executes when it hears it being fired. The process of associating the function with the onclick property is known as **attaching** an event listener.

Going back to the JavaScript code after the function declaration, you can see our first piece of data that we got back, the timestamp. Normally you won't use this particular property, but I used it in the example to distinguish each event's separate data sets.

NotED

Timestamps are used in programming for a variety of different reasons. Most of the time it is to give a context as to when something occurred. In the case of an event, a timestamp is created at the point the event is fired, which is immediately after the event occurs.

The next line captures the type of event that was sent. Although the example is only ever going to send a type of click, if you were using the same function for multiple events, you could check to see what type was fired and do the appropriate action for that event.

LinkED

You can use what you learned in Chapter 1 to implement an if statement and choose the appropriate programmatic path for that event.

Both click events and key events provide Boolean properties on whether the user was holding the Ctrl, Option (Mac), Command (Mac), Alt, or Shift key when they performed their action. In the example, I was looking for the Shift key, so I output the value of event.shiftKey. You can see that I captured this information on the next line of the JavaScript code. This really helps you create pages that seem to act more like applications that your users use on their computer.

I also capture the screen coordinates in which the button was clicked on the next line, even though you can click the button only in its own area. I hope you noticed that as you clicked the button from different areas of its surface that the coordinates changed. This isn't quite as useful on this particular button, but you could use this same type of statement on a more interactive page where you need to perform certain functions for certain parts of the page.

The rest of the code in the function you are already familiar with.

As for the other examples, they touch on the same topics as covered here, only they are listening for different events. Study that code, and play with it on your own to get a better feel for what is happening.

Summary

Whew! That was intense, right? You did it, though; you made it through that chapter! You should feel good with yourself right now because the content I covered includes topics that are so important to understand when developing projects with JavaScript and Dojo. In this chapter, I covered the following:

- Manipulating the DOM by getting references to different nodes
- Styling DOM elements to dynamically change the way they look
- Modifying DOM elements' innerHTML property to provide dynamic and rich content
- Working with the event architecture so that you can properly listen and execute statements when events occur

Chapter 3

Enhancing with Dojo

If you worked through Chapters 1 and 2 because you are new to JavaScript, you should feel so proud of yourself right now, because you have accomplished a lot. I hope you have learned a lot as well. I've covered much of the foundational terminology and concepts that you need to understand in order to proceed. Of course, you can always return to the earlier chapters and review that material; I suggest, however, that you move ahead and give the new lessons a try. It's now time to get into the fun stuff, which is the main reason you bought this book, right?

Dojo indeed is fun to develop with. However, just like JavaScript, there are some fundamentals that I need to go over so that you can see how you can use it to accomplish the same tasks in plain JavaScript as well as see how you can more easily do advanced functionality that would otherwise be very difficult and time-consuming to create yourself in plain JavaScript.

What makes a good JavaScript toolkit?

Before getting into Dojo, I'll go over some core concepts that JavaScript toolkits tend to have in common. This is important so you can see the greater picture of what each JavaScript toolkit is trying to accomplish.

What is a JavaScript toolkit?

It's likely that you already know a little bit about what a **JavaScript toolkit** is, since you picked up this book. Even so, let's clear some things up, just in case. A JavaScript toolkit is *not* a framework. What's the difference? Imagine that a toolkit is analogous to a toolbox you might have in your garage. Each tool inside the toolbox has a specific function to accomplish a specific task. These tools can be used independently of each other or together. Now imagine that a framework is analogous to a set of standards when using certain tools together.

A **framework** is the foundation to build higher-level systems and usually will not contain any specific functionality. With this, you could certainly build a framework using a toolkit. By that same token, you can build a framework without a toolkit.

What are some popular JavaScript toolkits?

In the past couple of years, many JavaScript toolkits have popped up around the Internet, each one strong in its own way at accomplishing certain tasks. Many of them also tend to have many of the same features implemented in different ways, claiming to be better than the next. Who are some of the big players in the JavaScript toolkit realm? At the time of this writing, the following list represents the JavaScript toolkit community fairly well:

- Dojo Toolkit (http://dojotoolkit.org)
- jQuery (http://jquery.com)
- Prototype (http://prototypejs.org)
- Yahoo! User Interface (http://developer.yahoo.com/yui)
- MooTools (http://mootools.net)
- ExtJS (http://extjs.com)
- QooxDoo (http://qooxdoo.org)

*Much of the time in the JavaScript world, the term **toolkit** and the term **library** are used interchangeably. There is no substantial difference between the two; it's a matter of naming preference.*

I recommend visiting each of those sites to poke around and see what the toolkits have to offer. Some of the toolkits, such as jQuery, aim to be very small and lightweight. Others such as Dojo have a lightweight part (Dojo Base), but the project as a whole offers so much more, such as widgets, dynamic drawing capabilities, advanced data access, and internationalization support.

What comprises a JavaScript toolkit?

Many things can comprise a JavaScript toolkit. The following sections are just what I see as common threads and what developers expect the toolkits to provide. If I don't mention a feature that you know a toolkit to have, that doesn't mean it's not a toolkit. By the same token, if a toolkit doesn't have one of the following features, that doesn't mean it's not a toolkit.

LinkED

Wikipedia offers a high-level comparison of features available in many of the JavaScript toolkits. Despite the name of the article being "Comparison of JavaScript frameworks," it is indeed a comparison of both frameworks and toolkits; see http://en.wikipedia.org/wiki/Comparison_of_JavaScript_frameworks.

CSS selector engine

CSS selectors are what allow you to define specific styles for elements in an HTML page. You can use custom class names, tag names, IDs, or even special positioning and pseudo-selectors. The point is, CSS has a very powerful method of filtering the elements in a document and picking out the ones that match a certain criterion.

JavaScript, on the other hand, does not have this same power out of the box. Instead, you are left with more basic functions such as getElementById or getElementsByTagName. Let's say, for instance, that you want to choose all the button elements in a page that have the class navigation associated with them. You'd first have to use getElementsByTagName to choose all the buttons on the page and then loop through that array and figure out which ones contain the navigation class. This would be extremely tedious.

LinkED

You can see an example of Dojo's selector engine in the dojo.query() *section of Chapter 4.*

As a solution, most of the JavaScript toolkits provide a CSS selector engine that allows you to pass a query to a function in CSS syntax, and the function will return an array of all the elements that match that query. In addition, the selector engines usually support a large subset of CSS3 selectors. CSS3 supports many more combinations of selectors, allowing you to style more specifically. The toolkits usually do not support the full CSS3 range of selectors because it would slow down the function a lot. Instead, they provide all the popular ones and then some.

LinkED

You can find a list of the CSS selectors that Dojo supports at http://api.dojotoolkit.org/jsdoc/1.3/dojo.query.

DOM manipulation

In addition to querying the DOM and being able to grab any element or set of elements you want easily, you'll also want to be able to manipulate the DOM easily. This could be taking existing elements and moving them somewhere else or inserting brand new elements that you created based on data you received from an Ajax call. It's not real easy to manipulate the DOM in plain JavaScript. Most people who try use the innerHTML approach I discussed in Chapter 1.

Good JavaScript toolkits will provide you with functions that allow you to get an element and pretty much place it anywhere on the DOM with a single line of code. All you need is the element you want to move and a reference point in the DOM that you want to move it to. For example, if you had two lists side-by-side on a page, you could take an element out of one list and use the second list as a reference element to place the item into. It's really that simple and straightforward. This is a great way to engage the user.

Cross-browser compatibility

As web developers, we should jump at the opportunity to use any tool that helps eliminate the hassles of making websites act and look the same in Internet Explorer 6 (God forbid), Firefox 3, Safari, or the browser of the day. If you were to ask a sample of web developers what they hate most about their jobs, I bet they would say cross-browser compatibility. With this being such a major issue, it's a relief to know that JavaScript toolkits can help.

All the major JavaScript toolkits implement their functionality in a cross-browser way. The code base for the JavaScript engines that are included in today's popular browsers are a little different from each other, both in the functionality they provide as well as the actual names of functions in many cases. One of the most popular examples is making Ajax calls. In Firefox, you can make this call using the XMLHttpRequest object; in Internet Explorer 6, you have to use the XMLHTTP object instead. What toolkits do for you is they create their own name for an Ajax function and wrap the support for all the browsers in it. That way, you only have to worry about one function. This brings me to the next feature of JavaScript toolkits, Ajax support.

LinkED

You can learn more about how Dojo handles making Ajax calls in Chapter 7 when I discuss dojo.xhrGet().

Ajax

Ajax is a very popular technology to use in modern websites. It allows the developer to load data from the server or another external source, after the user has loaded a page, without doing a page refresh. As I mentioned earlier in the "Cross-browser compatibility" section, the classes to use to make Ajax calls can be different from one set of browsers to another. In addition, actually working with Ajax techniques can be a nuisance as well and generally has been disliked. Each of the toolkits has its own way of making all this easier and more straightforward. They do this by providing separate functions that do different types of Ajax calls. They also usually provide a nice way of allowing the developer to pass a reference to functions that they want to fire when the request was a success or when it failed. These are known as **callbacks**.

LinkED

You'll learn more about callbacks in Chapter 7 when I discuss making Ajax calls.

Unfortunately, when working with Ajax, making the request to the server and getting the data back is only half the battle. When working with Ajax in plain JavaScript, that request would come back in plain text. That may not sound too bad, but imagine that you are requesting that the server send you an XML file that lists all the items in a user's online shopping cart. That could get large! In addition, imagine that the request came to you as plain text with all the XML in it. You would have to parse the file to get the data you wanted. What if it came back to you in another format such as JSON; would you know what to do with it? Would you care? Probably not. You don't want to have to concern yourself how to parse the data—what you care about is that you get the data in a format that you can use on your page easily.

All that is to say that the toolkit will probably provide a way for it to parse the data coming back for you so that you get a nice clean JavaScript object to work with.

Animations and effects

Modern websites like to catch the user's attention and keep them engaged in their content. Besides pulling in dynamic data through Ajax, one of the ways sites can focus the user on a certain part of the page and draw them in is by using animations and effects on the page. This can be anything from a photo gallery that fades images in and out as the user navigates from one to the next, or it might also be a content area expanding smoothly to a larger size, revealing more content. Whatever the case may be, users love it, so developers need to implement it.

Programmatically creating animations has always been a more challenging task because it can require complex mathematic algorithms. You don't want to have to concern yourself with this kind of thing when you need to get a job for a client done in a little amount of time. What you would likely rather do is simply say that you want this image to fade out and that the animation should span for one second. Perhaps you don't even care about the time, just so it's at a reasonable speed; you want to simply say, "Fade this image out." You can do this in most of the popular JavaScript toolkits.

Many of them implement a few popular animations out of the box but also allow you to build more complex ones if you are interested in doing so. They all pretty much allow you to animate many of the CSS properties an element may have, such as opacity, width and height, position on the screen, and so on. From there, you can specify start and end values for these properties, and the toolkit figures out the rest.

If you study how you can make Ajax calls with the different toolkits, you'll notice that some, like Dojo, provide a much wider selection of functions that allow you to get remote data in numerous ways.

Attaching and listening to events

Event handling in JavaScript goes back to the issue of cross-browser compatibility. As I mentioned in Chapter 1, it is generally not good practice to create event listeners with tag properties but to use JavaScript instead. However, the method for doing that is different in Firefox than in IE, for example. What does a web developer do? Well, you could write a function that handles this difference for you, or if you were using a toolkit, you could use a standard set of methods provided by the toolkit that handle all the browser differences for you.

The nice thing about this is that you get a set of functions that are consistent in the way they are called and how they handle the events.

Which one?

The million-dollar question you might be asking is, which toolkit should you choose in your projects? Frankly, I would take a look at each one and see how each one handles the types of tasks that you need. You could also look at the syntax and see whether it is something you are comfortable writing on a daily basis. The point is, use the right tool for the job. The nice thing about the Dojo Toolkit is that you can use it as stripped down as you want to match some of the other lightweight frameworks, or you can maximize its use and bring in some very advanced logic and operations—it's up to you. Considering what you've read this far in the book, I'm going to assume that you've already chosen Dojo, and might I say, what an excellent choice you've made.

What is Dojo?

The more you program JavaScript, the more you will develop a style in which you develop it. For instance, your functions will begin to take on a similar style and will start to follow your own unique pattern. In addition, as you get more advanced and your start implementing features that are more powerful and complex, you will notice some of the annoyances and difficulties JavaScript has. These annoyances are not necessarily bad because it was built to be an extremely flexible and mutable language. However, at the time that JavaScript was conceived, the expectations for the Web were not nearly what they are today. Users want rich experiences, and they want certain parts of websites to act like the applications on their desktops.

At this point, you may be thinking, "Well, isn't that what Adobe Flash and Microsoft Silverlight provide?" Although the answer is yes, those solutions have different goals. Since those types of technologies live in the context of what are essentially movie files, they have a certain restriction to how they integrate with websites. JavaScript, on the other hand, is meant to be interwoven with HTML. The good news here is that JavaScript has the physical capabilities to provide an extremely rich and interactive experience; the bad news is that it is very difficult and complex to code by hand. In addition, the

JavaScript versions included in each browser are all different. This means that when you program and test that something works one way in one browser, it may not work the same way in a different brand or even a different version of another browser. I know you what you are thinking, but don't jump ship yet! I have some more good news!

NotED

Although the World Wide Web Consortium (W3C) goals are to modernize the Internet by defining a set of standards by which to develop by, not all browser manufacturers implement features in the same manner; in a sense, they define their own standards. This is an issue for us as developers since we have to make our pages work in any browser our users might have installed. This not only affects HTML development but also affects CSS and JavaScript development. Fortunately, Dojo holds extremely high standards for ensuring its code is compatible with all the popular modern browsers.

Developing to a pattern

A little bit ago I mentioned that you will begin to develop patterns as you become a more advanced developer. You may even create special shortcuts to accomplish certain tasks. Well, many others have done the same thing; in fact, some have even standardized practices so that other developers can follow the same patterns. These are known as **design patterns**. Patterns are common solutions for common problems when programming. Design patterns are a globally accepted phrase in programming, and there are many books that cover various types of design patterns, most of which are theoretical. They also contain practical examples, but there are times when a pattern won't fit exactly into your problem.

JavaScript developers have devised their own set of patterns and ways of accomplishing tasks. Instead of them providing a theoretical pattern to follow, they have provided JavaScript code that you can use in your websites or applications that utilizes these patterns and ways of doing things. These are often called **JavaScript frameworks**, **toolkits**, **Ajax toolkits**, or simply **libraries**. There are many available to use, and most of them are open source and free. Each one has its own strengths and weaknesses, but the one we will be focusing on in this book is Dojo.

LinkED

Many well-written books are available on the topic of programming design patterns. One of my personal favorites is Martin Fowler's Patterns of Enterprise Application Architecture (ISBN: 0321127420). A good introduction design patterns is Eric Freeman's Head First Design Patterns (ISBN: 0596007124). Finally, an excellent book for JavaScript design patterns is Ross Harmes and Dustin Diaz's Pro JavaScript Design Patterns (ISBN: 159059908X).

Many of the toolkits build their code base in what the programming world knows as a **class**. A class is an encapsulation of properties and methods that are grouped together and can act as a single unit to achieve a particular goal. For instance, if you had a set of functions that you created on your page that controlled the animation of a graphic, those functions might be play(), pause(), and stop(). Instead of having those in the page or even in just an external JavaScript file, those functions could actually be part of an animation class called AnimateGraphic. This class would actually be part of a separate file, which would allow you to move it around or reuse it easily since the functions are encapsulated inside that class.

LinkED

You'll learn more about classes and how to create them in Chapter 9.

Keeping it simple

Dojo is about making your life easier by providing a JavaScript toolkit that will help you write code that is simpler, more maintainable, and more robust, which is less likely to cause cross-browser issues. At the same time, it provides a lot of built-in features and shortcuts to make it easy and fun to implement richness and responsiveness in your websites. Loaded with useful functions and utilities, Dojo saves you time by making it easier to get references to elements on the DOM, and it provides useful DOM manipulation capabilities, animation, effects, prebuilt widgets, and extensions. It also has an awesome community to support it all.

Collectively, the Dojo Toolkit refers to the full suite of libraries: Dojo Base, Dojo Core, Dijit, and DojoX. I'll go over their differences next and when to use each one.

LinkED

The Dojo Toolkit home page is at http://www.dojotoolkit.org. *You can download the toolkit at* http://www.dojotoolkit.org/downloads. *I'll discuss how to install it in "Installing and configuring Dojo."*

Base

Dojo Base contains the basic functionality that other JavaScript toolkits contain, such as in jQuery, Mootools, or Prototype. This includes well-designed Ajax functions, animation support, object-oriented programming support, and a lot of other stuff.

Core

Core is the core of the whole toolkit. The Dijit and DojoX libraries cannot function without a reference to Core on your page. Core provides a lot of functionality in a little package. It provides you with basic DOM manipulation, Ajax support, a consistent cross-browser approach to adding event listeners, CSS3 selector engine, CSS style and position utilities, and much more that won't make sense at this point and time but that you will certainly dive into later. Believe it or not, everything I just mentioned can actually be extracted even further from Core into the aforementioned Base. Base provides all the previous functionality in a tiny footprint. The additional functionality of Core is actually optional when you load Dojo on your page.

Dijit

Of course, you want to provide a richer experience to your users, but you don't want to spend a lot of time making nice calendar widgets, photo slide shows, charts, light boxes, or drag-and-drop functionality, right? Thanks to Dijit, you don't have to. Dijit provides a full library of premade skinnable, themeable widgets that you can easily drop into any of your Dojo-powered websites. These special widgets are not only easy to use for your user and easy to program for you, but they also cater to your international audience by being fully localizable to support more than a dozen languages out of the box. In addition, you can provide the accessible functionality your disabled users need to read and navigate your website via Dijit out of the box.

DojoX

DojoX is a library that contains many special and experimental projects that push Dojo to its limits, provides an incredible array of tools that allow you to create 2D and 3D drawings right onto your web page, makes your web pages work even if they are offline, and offers incredible dynamic charting. These are just a few of the features that are available in the ever-growing DojoX. It is a very large library of projects that truly give you the power of the future, today.

Why should I use Dojo over other libraries?

A common struggle that many developers have when they first hear about Ajax libraries and toolkits is knowing which one to choose. I always say choose the right tool for the right job. Luckily, thanks to Dojo's smart package system and distinctly separate libraries, in addition to its custom build tool, I don't see why Dojo wouldn't be the choice for every project.

Many of the other libraries available, while also free and open source, offer only a subset of everything that Dojo offers.

Installing and configuring Dojo

Dojo is unique in how easy it is to install and get up and running. In addition, once you do, you don't need to include any other files on the page to have access to all of its features. One `script` definition at the top of the page, and you will instantly have all the Dojo goodness available to you. Normally with Ajax and JavaScript libraries, for any additional packages you want to use, you have to specifically include them at the top of your pages for each module you want to use. With Dojo, any time you want to use a feature that is not available in the base of the library, you simply call the function `dojo.require([package name])` and pass in the package name (without the brackets, of course). You'll see the benefit of that function and how easy it is to use later.

How do you install Dojo?

You can load Dojo in your page in two ways. The most straightforward and easy way is to load the library from an external server such as from Google or AOL. Simply drop one of the following `script` tags in the head of your HTML page.

Here's the code for Google:

```
<script type="text/javascript"
  src="http://ajax.googleapis.com/ajax/libs/dojo/1.3/dojo/dojo.xd.js">
</script>
```

Here's the code for AOL:

```
<script type="text/javascript"
  src="http://o.aolcdn.com/dojo/1.3/dojo/dojo.xd.js"></script>
```

That's it! You don't need to download any files and upload them to your site or anything. These types of servers are known as **content delivery networks (CDNs)**. These special sites represent a distributed network of servers all over the world that attempt to find one that is closest to your users when they access your site. This allows the files to be delivered to your site much quicker than if the files were hosted in a single location.

The alternative is hosting the files yourself. To do this, follow these steps:

1. Open your browser, and navigate to http://download.dojotoolkit.org/.

2. Click the link at the top that says, "Download latest stable release...."

3. From the list of files, choose the latest version of the toolkit in the correct format that will work best for your computer (that is, for Windows/Mac you can download dojo-release-1.3.0.zip).

4. Once the download has completed, unarchive the files to a directory of your choice where you may store your JavaScript files. Oftentimes, this may be under /js from the root of your website. See Figure 3-1 for an example of this.

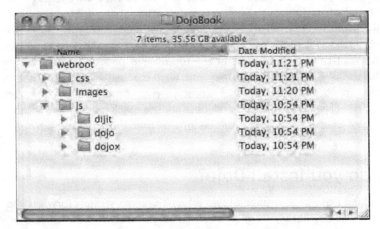

Figure 3-1. Put the Dojo Toolkit files in your common JavaScript folder.

At this point, you will want to point to that folder using the `script` tag similar to the previous method:

```
<script type="text/javascript"
  src="/js/dojo/dojo.js"></script>
```

Technically you could start writing Dojo code with this setup, but it is best to configure how you want Dojo to run on your page.

How do you configure Dojo for your website?

A unique feature of Dojo is that it gives you the ability to configure it to work the way you want it to work. Some of these options are available to make it easier to develop and debug your scripts. Other options are for more advanced usages of Dojo and will not be covered at this time.

LinkED

You can learn more about configuring Dojo and the `djConfig` *variable at DojoCampus; see* http://docs.dojocampus.org/djConfig.

The mechanism that supports this special type of configuration is an attribute in the `script` tag called `djConfig`. The two most common parameters for this attribute are `parseOnLoad` and `isDebug`. You write these into the `djConfig` attribute like so:

```
<script type="text/javascript" src="/js/dojo/dojo.js"
  djConfig="isDebug:true, parseOnLoad:true"></script>
```

You can also configure Dojo with a global JavaScript variable. You could rewrite the previous statement like so:

```
<script type="text/javascript">
  var djConfig = {isDebug:true, parseOnLoad:true};
</script>
<script type="text/javascript" src="/js/dojo/dojo.js"></script>
```

As you can see, you set it up in way that is known as **name-value pairs**. You have a name and its value, which is separated by a colon. Each name-value pair in the `djConfig` attribute should be comma-separated from one another.

LinkED

Learn how to see debugging information in your browser in the "How do you debug Dojo and JavaScript?" section.

The isDebug parameter tells Dojo whether it should provide debugging information to your debugger console (which I'll cover in the next section). The parseOnLoad parameter tells Dojo whether it should specifically look for special Dojo syntax on the page that it may need to parse, such as dojoType properties in tags. For example, you can add the property dojoType to some HTML elements to load Dojo widgets in the page. The parseOnLoad property tells Dojo to look for those attributes once the page loads. If you set this to false, then you need to explicitly tell Dojo when to parse the page.

NotED

After including the Dojo parser on your page using dojo.require ("dojo.parser"), *you'll need to call* dojo.parser.parse() *to start the parsing manually.*

LinkED

You can learn more about Dojo widgets and the Dojo parser in Chapter 8.

How do I write my first bit of Dojo?

I'll now show how write a quick bit of Dojo to help you get started and test your installation of Dojo. In the next chapter, you will actually start digging into it; there I'll explain what everything does and how it works. For now, create a new HTML document in the root of your website, and write the following code.

LinkED

In Chapter 4, you'll learn the basics of Dojo and how it differs from plain JavaScript. You'll see how Dojo will help you program JavaScript more efficiently.

```html
<!DOCTYPE html PUBLIC "-//W3C//DTD XHTML 1.1//EN"
"http://www.w3.org/TR/xhtml11/DTD/xhtml11.dtd">
<html xmlns="http://www.w3.org/1999/xhtml">

<head>

  <title>Hello World!</title>
  <link rel="stylesheet" href="js/dijit/themes/tundra/tundra.css" />

  <script type="text/javascript" src="js/dojo/dojo.js"
    djConfig="parseOnLoad:true, debug:true"></script>

  <script type="text/javascript">
    dojo.require("dojo.parser");
    dojo.require("dijit.form.Button");
    dojo.require("dijit.form.TextBox");

     var init = function()
    {
      dojo.connect(
        dojo.byId('btnSayHello'),
        "onclick",
        this,
        helloButton_onClick
      );
    }
// button onClick listener
     var helloButton_onClick = function(event)
    {
      alert('Hello World and hello ' +
        dojo.byId('txtName').value + '!');
    }
    // start initializing
    dojo.addOnLoad(init);
  </script>
</head>

<body class="tundra">
<h1>Hello World Example</h1>
<hr/>
  <label for="txtName">Your Name:</label>
  <input id="txtName" type="text" dojoType="dijit.form.TextBox"/><br/>
```

```
<button id="btnSayHello" dojoType="dijit.form.Button">
    Say Hello</button>
</body>
</html>
```

Don't be too concerned with anything that doesn't look familiar in the previous block. It is easier to understand than it appears. I'll now break it down a little bit so you aren't completely in the dark with what's happening. After all, it can be a slow process learning something new like this.

Just after the title tag, you'll notice that I bring in a new CSS style sheet. This particular one loads a theme provided by Dojo to make the form elements look nicer and not so boring. Next, you'll see that I'm using the script tag from earlier to bring Dojo into the page. Notice that I'm using the djConfig property in the tag, but as mentioned before, you could set a global variable beforehand.

In the next script block, via dojo.require(), I load some Dojo classes that I am going to be using the page. This special function allows you to load classes in a very simple manner. Other toolkits require you to write separate script statements for each new class you want to load. When the require() function executes, it fetches the file for me through Ajax and puts it in the scope of the page to use. In this case, I load the code for the Dojo parser, a button widget, and a textbox widget.

After the require() statements, I create a new function called init(). I like to create these special functions on pages that are to be executed once the page has finished loading. I make this happen by calling dojo.addOnLoad() in the last line of that script block. It's a single place to put statements that you want to run after the page is done loading; you can also set up some default variables or even make some Ajax calls. In the case of my example, I'm using it simply to attach an event listener that will listen for the click of the button.

LinkED

Remember event listeners? I discussed the less popular way of creating them, which is adding a property to the input tag, in Chapter 2's "How do you attach an event listener?" section.

Next, helloButton_onClick is the actual function that gets executed when the user clicks the button. The function contains the basic logic of showing the user an alert box with a sentence and their name.

Skipping down to the `body` tag of the page, you'll see that I added a `class` attribute with the value of `tundra`. This corresponds with the CSS file that I brought in at the top of the page. This class is what will activate all the styles in the CSS file to be applied to the page.

Moving on to the textbox and the button, notice that both of these elements have a `dojoType` property. Each of them also references a class. These class names are the same as I told `dojo.require` to load. It's at this point that I'm actually using them. When the Dojo parser runs through the page, it will pick up these two elements and swap them out with the Dojo widgets of those class names. You can still set regular attributes that you would normally use on those tags, and they'll get carried over to the widgets.

NotED

*Classes in JavaScript can be referenced using **dot notation**. This conforms to a similar style that is seen in many modern programming languages such as Java and C#. Technically speaking, each word between the dots is known as a **package**, with exception of the last word, which is the name of the class. Packages are pretty much just folders in the filesystem where your JavaScript is stored. In the realm of JavaScript, there is no such thing as packages. The dot notation at this point simply represents a namespace, which basically makes this class unique in what's called so that it doesn't conflict with other JavaScript classes that may have the same name. It does still, however, relate pretty much to a folder structure within Dojo. If you were to look in the Dojo directory, you can find the source of the classes by following the dot notation. For instance, if you wanted to see the source for* `dijit.form.Button`, *you would go to your Dojo source and then go into* `dijit/form/Button.js`.

That pretty much covers it, and after running the previous code in your browser, you should have something that looks similar to Figure 3-2.

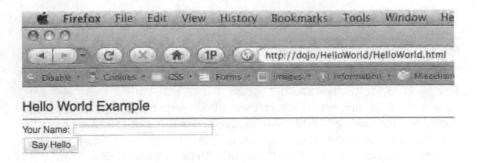

Hello World Example

Your Name:

Say Hello

Figure 3-2. Browser screen after running the demo code

Typing your name in the textbox and clicking the Say Hello button will yield an alert box, as shown in Figure 3-3.

Figure 3-3. Alert box after clicking the Say Hello button

Getting help

If you are new to JavaScript programming, especially if you are new to Dojo, you'll most likely need some help along the way as you go through this book and when you are on your own. Developers who know where and how to find help are the most successful and the most proficient when programming.

How do you debug Dojo and JavaScript?

As a web developer, you should already be testing your pages in all the major browsers. When it comes to developing your pages with JavaScript, though, Mozilla's Firefox browser is your best choice thanks to its add-on architecture. You'll still need to test your JavaScript code as well in other browsers, but an invaluable add-on called Firebug helps you along the way of building your page with JavaScript.

LinkED

Thousands of add-ons are available for you to install into Firefox, but you should probably know a little bit more about what an add-on is. Mozilla has an excellent article on how you can customize Firefox with add-ons; see http://support.mozilla.com/en-US/kb/Customizing+Firefox+with+add-ons.

LinkED

You can download and install the popular Firefox browser at www.getfirefox.com. *A couple of good add-ons to install after you've installed Firefox are Firebug (*www.getfirebug.com*) and Web Developer (*https://addons.mozilla.org/en-US/firefox/addon/60*), which is great for manipulating web pages on the fly in a high-level manner.*

Firebug

Firebug is the industry-standard tool for helping you find errors and work with JavaScript and HTML code in a real-time manner. It is an add-on that installs right into your installation of Firefox. The process of testing and fixing your code is known as **debugging**. Firebug's basic features are very easy to get started with, but it also offers a wealth of powerful tools as you get more advanced. In addition, it's perfect for looking under the hood of other websites that may impress you to see how they tick or how they are constructed.

Starting Firebug

Once you've installed Firebug and restarted Firefox, you'll notice that you have a new icon on the bottom right of the Firefox window, as shown in Figure 3-4.

Figure 3-4. The new bug icon on the bottom right of Firefox is what you click to open the Firebug panel.

Inspecting HTML code

One of my favorite features of Firebug is the ability to inspect the HTML of a web page easily. Note that this is not the same as viewing the source HTML of a web page, which every major browser can do and which shows you the source that was served to you by the web server. What that does not show is any HTML that was generated or manipulated by JavaScript. Firebug does show you the generated source as well as a very easy way of navigating it.

After you've opened Firebug from the icon at the bottom right of Firefox, you'll be focused on the HTML tab of Firebug, as shown in Figure 3-5. This is the generated source of the web page, meaning that it is the current state of the page after any modifications by JavaScript and CSS have been applied.

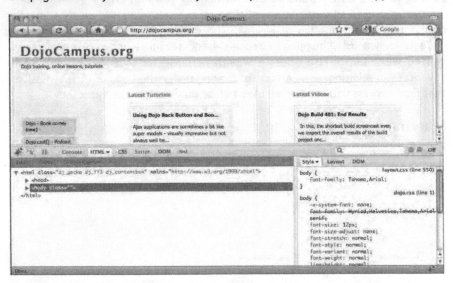

Figure 3-5. HTML tab of Firebug showing the generated source of the web page

Once in this mode, you can click any of the disclosure triangles to the left of the lines of code to dig deeper into the document. However, this could take a lot of time and is really better for fine-tuning your selections. The best way to find the code of what you want is by clicking the Inspect button on the top left of the Firebug toolbar, as shown in Figure 3-6. This tool allows you to hover your mouse pointer over any of the visible elements of the web page and click them to instantly be taken to their generated source in the source code viewer. You can see this action in Figure 3-7.

Figure 3-6. The square icon with an arrow in it is the Inspect button for Firebug.

Figure 3-7. Hover over any visible element on the web page after clicking the Inspect button to instantly see its related source.

After you chosen an element to inspect, you can use the disclosure arrows to drill down further in the source. This method of inspecting can be incredibly powerful on websites that you are exploring to see how they are architected.

Altering the page in real time

One of the most powerful features of Firebug is the ability to alter the page's HTML and CSS in real time. Doing so is incredibly simple and intuitive. If you want to change the value of any of the attributes of one of the elements, you are free to do that simply by clicking the value in the source; it will instantly become editable, as you can see in Figure 3-8. Type the new value, press Enter/Return, and the change instantly commits itself to the page. You can apply the same action to text between HTML tags such as headers, paragraphs, lists, and so forth. The beauty of this is that these changes don't get saved to the actual web page, so you can't do any harm. Once you refresh the page, it will go back to its default settings.

Figure 3-8. Real-time editing of the class property of an HTML element

The HTML is not the only thing you can edit live; you can also alter and append to the CSS styles for the page as well. With the HTML tab still selected, you have a pane on the right that shows you the current CSS styles, as shown in Figure 3-9, that are applied to the selected element on the page. It will group them automatically by style sheet and order of precedence based on standard CSS rules. All parts of the CSS in this pane are editable. You can change any of the existing property names or their values simply by clicking them. You can also add a new CSS property to a selector by right-clicking or Ctrl+clicking (on the Mac) the selector and choosing New Property, as you can see in Figure 3-10. You can type any valid CSS property name followed by the value, and it will instantly be applied to the selected element. This is helpful when you are building a new website and want to see how different CSS styles affect an element on the page or when you are fixing bugs of an existing website.

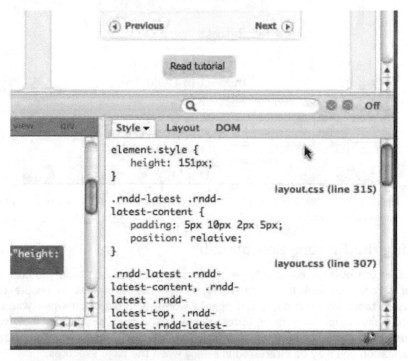

Figure 3-9. Current applied CSS styles to the selected element

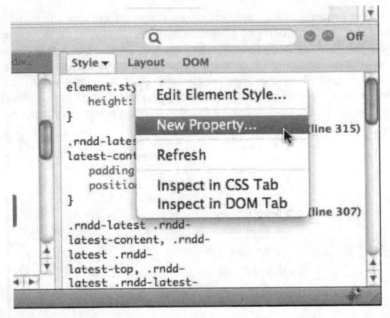

Figure 3-10. Context menu on a CSS selector allowing you to add a new property to the selected element

Using the Firebug Console tab

Another useful feature of Firebug is its Console tab. The first time you click it, your screen will look like Figure 3-11. Follow the directions to enable the Console tab. Once you do, you'll open a world of information when you are writing JavaScript for your websites. Not only will the Console tab show you errors that have occurred on the page, but it also allows you to send it information you may be interested in seeing when the page executes.

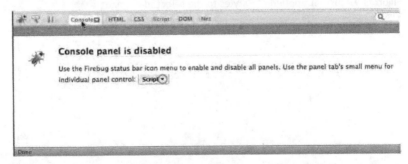

Figure 3-11. You need to enable the Console tab in Firebug the first time you run it.

You'll frequently see the following JavaScript code both in this book and online when viewing JavaScript code samples:

```
console.log('debugging info goes here');
```

The console object is a special object to aid in debugging your JavaScript code. It has a function called log, which allows you to write out information to Firebug's console for you to see when the page is executed. You can provide strings or native JavaScript objects, and it will display them in the console, allowing you to further inspect them if you want. Take a look at the following code to see how this can benefit you when programming JavaScript:

```
<script type="text/javascript"
  src="http://o.aolcdn.com/dojo/1.3/dojo/dojo.xd.js"></script>
<script type="text/javascript">
  dojo.addOnLoad(function(event)
  {
    dojo.connect(dojo.byId('btnFoo'), "onmouseover", button_over);
  });

  var button_over = function(event)
  {
    console.log('Oh you touched me!', event);
  }
</script>
<button id="btnFoo">No Touchy!</button>
```

This code is pretty basic, and at a high level it is loading the Dojo Toolkit from the AOL CDN, adding a page onLoad event where I create an event listener for my button when the user moves their mouse over it. Finally, it creates the event handler function called button_over where I use the important console.log() function. This is the line you want to focus on right now. In my event handler, I receive an object called event that contains information about the button event that just occurred. In my console.log() statement, I have provided a string that says something descriptive of what just happened (this can be anything you want); after the string, I have a comma followed by the event object. Figure 3-12 shows what this does when I move my mouse pointer over the button.

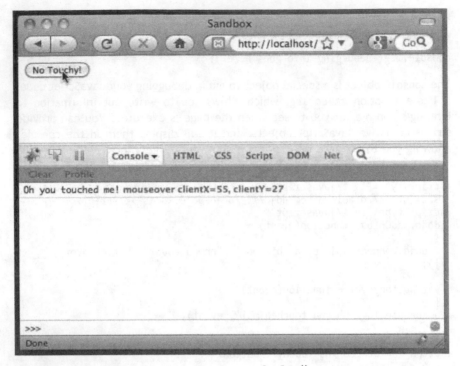

Figure 3-12. A message provided by the `console.log()` statement in the sample code

You can see that when I moved my mouse pointer over the button, the event was fired, and I was able to see some information about it. Not only did my message display, but Firebug also gave me a small snapshot of the event, showing me the `clientX` and `clientY` variables and their associated values.

NotED

You can chain as many JavaScript variables separated by commas as you want in the `console.log()` statement. It will automatically display snapshot views of these when it executes the statement on the Console tab.

From here you can click the variable snapshot that it provided to see a detailed look at this variable, as shown in Figure 3-13 and Figure 3-14.

LinkED

Read more about Firebug logging on Firebug's website at http://getfirebug.com/logging.html.

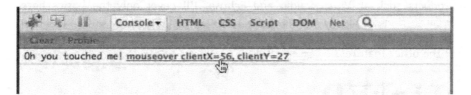

Figure 3-13. You can click any of the variables that you passed to the console.log() statement to see more information.

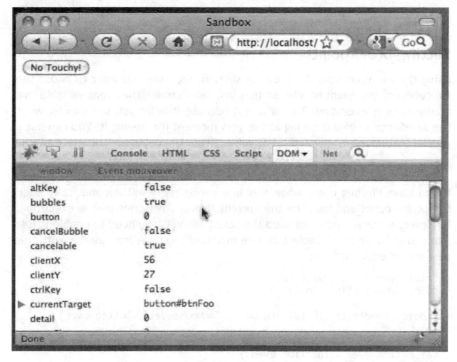

Figure 3-14. A detailed look at the event variable that was passed when the button was hovered over

JavaScript debugging with Firebug

Logging is great to provide general information about what is going on in your JavaScript code. However, there are times when you have bugs that you are trying to solve them and need to look at the code on a much more granular basis. Enter the Script tab of Firebug. The Script tab provides you with debugging tools that are very similar to modern IDE tools that are found in products such as Visual Studio and Eclipse. I'll cover only the basics here because there is simply too much for the scope of this book. Once you know the basics, though, you'll be able to browse around and learn how to use some of the other features.

LinkED

You can learn more advanced tips and how-tos on the Firebug website for JavaScript debugging and profiling at http://getfirebug.com/js.html.

Setting breakpoints

Using the example from the previous section, let's say you want to pause the execution of the event handler so that you can examine the event variable live as the page is executing. This is useful because it helps you see exactly what the JavaScript engine is seeing at the very moment it is seeing it. You can put a special statement in your code that will activate the debugger automatically:

debugger;

If you have Firebug open, when this line executes, it will automatically open the Script panel and focus on the current line of JavaScript that is executing. However, since you have not used the Script tab yet, you need to enable it just like you did with the Console tab. I've modified the code from earlier with this new statement as follows:

```
<script type="text/javascript">
  dojo.addOnLoad(function(event)
  {
    dojo.connect(dojo.byId('btnFoo'), "onmouseover", button_over);
  });

  var button_over = function(event)
  {
    debugger;
    console.log('Oh you touched me!', event);
  }
```

```
</script>
```

Figure 3-15 shows what happens when the debugger statement is encountered. The JavaScript has paused execution on the very line that the debugger statement is on. The line is highlighted in Firebug so you can clearly see what it's currently executing. At this point, you have a lot of information, which is displayed in the right pane in the Watch tab. The bold words in this pane are the variables that are available at this time on this line of code. In this case, it is the this object and the event object. The latter is available because it was passed in to this function. Since you currently reside in the event handler, you have access to that event object.

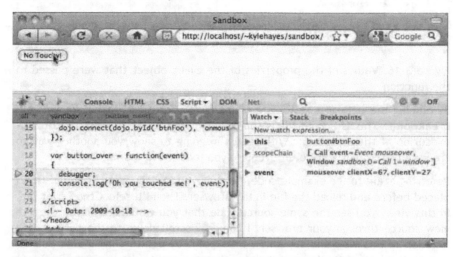

Figure 3-15. The execution of JavaScript pauses when a debugger statement is encountered.

If you want to see more information about the variables on the Watch tab, you can click their disclosure arrows to see their properties and values, as shown in Figure 3-16.

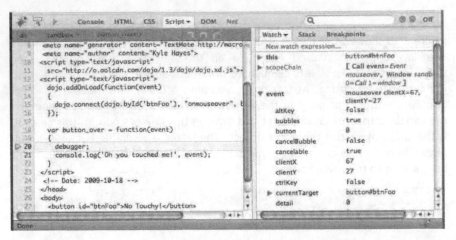

Figure 3-16. Values of the properties of the event object that were passed to the function

By placing the debugger statement in my code, I created what is known as a **breakpoint**. This is because it is the point in which you "break" the flow of execution of the JavaScript. With that, I'm going to show you another way to create a breakpoint that doesn't require you to edit the source file.

Referring again to the example code, I'll remove the debugger statement that I placed before and reload the file in the browser. Then I'll select the Script tab. In this view, you see the same source code that you would see if you were to view source through your browser. I can now scroll down to the button_over function in this view and set a new breakpoint by pointing my mouse pointer just to the left of the line number for the statement with my console.log() function in it, as shown in Figure 3-17. A small red circle will now appear in this spot. This is a breakpoint and will act just like the debugger statement did before, except now it will break on the console.log() function immediately before this line is executed. In other words, a breakpoint will occur before the code on that line runs. For a breakpoint to be triggered after it has been set, the code just simply needs to be reexecuted. In this case, you can just hover the mouse pointer over the button again. However, if you were trying to trigger a breakpoint that occurred as the page was loading, you would have to refresh the page.

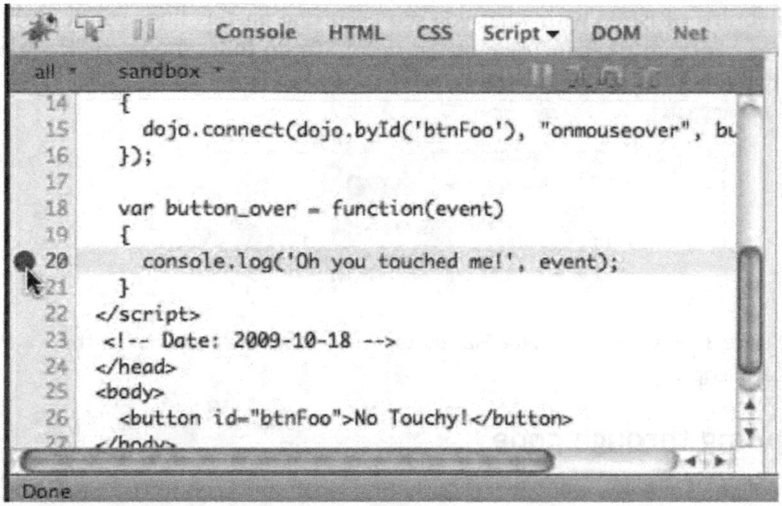

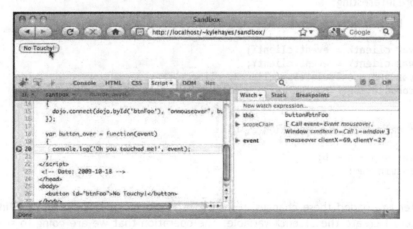

Figure 3-17. Use your mouse to set a breakpoint by clicking to the left of the line number on the line you want to "break."

You can see the effects of hovering over the button in Figure 3-18. You'll notice that since you are in the same function again at the same point, the variables that are on the Watch tab are the same as well. Any time you don't want the breakpoint to be triggered again, you can simply click the red circle, which will remove the breakpoint.

Figure 3-18. The execution of the function stopped where a manual breakpoint was set.

After you're satisfied with what you see occurring on this line, you'll probably want to continue the execution of the script. To do that, simply click the blue Play button in the bar below the tabs, as shown in Figure 3-19.

Figure 3-19. Clicking the blue Play button will resume the execution of the JavaScript.

Stepping through code

Much of the time you won't necessarily find what you need in the first line of a breakpoint. For instance, if you discover the logic of your code is not executing properly and you want to go through it with a fine-toothed comb, you'll want to set a starting breakpoint and perform the action that is known as **stepping** through the code. This is the ability to step through, line by line, the JavaScript code. It can be handy to inspect complicated pieces of a function or blocks of code. You may have noticed some extra arrow buttons to the right of the Play button. Each one is utilized when you step through your code. Before we proceed, let's add some lines to the function to make the stepping process more interesting:

```
var button_over = function(event)
{
  var clientX = event.clientX;
  var clientY = event.clientY;
  var sum = calculateSum(clientX, clientY);
  console.log('The sum is: ', sum);
}

var calculateSum = function(a, b)
{
  var sum = a + b;
  return sum;
}
```

After I reloaded these changes in the browser, I put a breakpoint on the line where I create the clientX variable. The operation that we are going to step through is rudimentary but will serve in demonstrating the different stepping tools. I am simply going to calculate the sum of the clientX and clientY values

80

and then display that sum in the console. These two values represent the coordinates of my mouse pointer at the time it triggered the mouseover event.

As Figure 3-20 shows, I have a breakpoint on line 20, just inside the button_over function. You'll notice that I have a few more variables I can watch in the Watch tab: clientX, clientY, and sum. At this point, the assignment of the clientX variable is just about to happen, which is why clientX still shows as *undefined* in the Watch tab. To proceed with this execution, you don't want to hit Play because that would cause all the JavaScript to continue to execute. You want to run only this one line and stop on the next. For this, you'll use the Step Over button, which looks like a U-turn symbol with the arrowhead on the right side, as shown in Figure 3-21. This allows you to step over the current line and stop on the next breakable line. When I do this, the code will execute and will stop on the line where the clientY variable is assigned. You can see the result of this action in Figure 3-22.

ExplainED

Lines that don't contain any executable code such as a trailing bracket or parenthesis, are not breakable lines since they don't contain any code of interest.

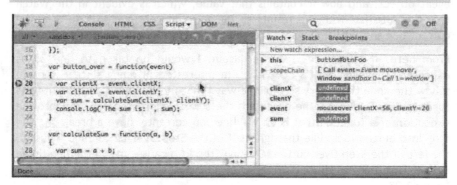

Figure 3-20. Breakpoint set and triggered on line 20

Figure 3-21. Step Over button on Firebug's Script tab

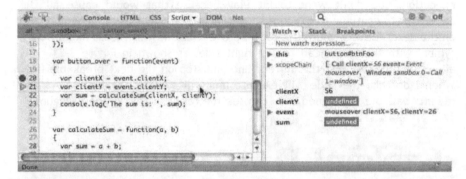

Figure 3-22. The result of stepping over line 20: the debugger executes line 20 and stops again on line 21.

After I stepped over line 20, the variable clientX received its value from the event object, and now it contains that value, which is evident in the Watch tab. I'm satisfied with the results so far and will continue to step over the current line so that I land where the calculateSum() function is being called.

From here, if I were to step over again, I would be taken to line 23 as expected. However, that's not what I'm interested in doing since I want to follow the code trail every step of the way. That means I want to step into the function that is about to be executed: the sum function. You can step into the execution of a function that is on the line you currently have a break on. The Step Into button looks like the right half of the Step Over button and is just to the left of the Step Over button. Clicking Step Into causes me to then be taken to the first line of the calculateSum() function that I added, as shown in Figure 3-23.

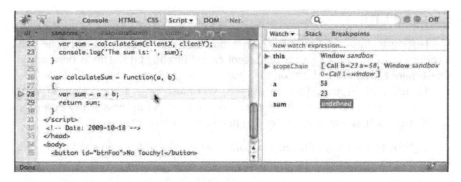

Figure 3-23. The first line of the function that I stepped into

I can now step over this code in the same manner that I would have previously. Once I got to the end of the function and clicked Step Over again, I would be taken back to the line where I called that function. But instead, let's say I'm satisfied with the results of where I'm at now (the first line of the calculateSum() function) and I simply want to return to the line I was on before; in that case, I simply click the other step button known as the Step Out button. By doing this, I am immediately taken back to line 22 where I initially called the function. While using any of these buttons, each time you stop on a line, you can inspect the variables and how they change by looking at the Watch tab. You'll be surprised by all the information you can find out about what's going on when your code executes. It's especially useful to look into system objects such as event objects to see all the data they make available to your code.

That is everything I wanted to cover in this introduction to Firebug, but please review the LinkED sidebars to learn how to maximize your use of the tool when writing JavaScript; you won't regret it. The Dojo Toolkit works very well with Firebug by providing special error messages, warnings, and other pieces of information while you are debugging your code.

LinkED

Introduction tutorials and help are available for Firebug at the very bottom of the following page: http://getfirebug.com/docs.html.

Firebug Lite

For testing in Internet Explorer or on a browser that doesn't support the full Firebug, Dojo includes a handy little tool called Firebug Lite. This is basically a small panel that will show up on your page that resembles some of the functionality of Firebug. To turn this on, you must have `debug: true` in your `djConfig` settings. Once you have this, Firebug Lite will automatically open for you if it doesn't see an instance of Firebug or if Firebug is turned off.

Throughout the book, you'll see a couple of areas where you can send messages to Firebug to give you information.

LinkED

You can see an example where I use `console.log()` *in Chapter 4 in the* `dojo.query()` *section. Additionally, you can see it in Chapter 7 in the fail callback example in the* `dojo.xhrGet()` *section. The latter shows a very common use of Firebug.*

If I get stuck, where can you find help?

Among the features of Dojo itself and the functionality it provides to you as a developer, it also comes with a strong and passionate community. If you run into issues with your code or have a question about how a particular function, class, or feature works, you can always reach out to the community for help. Various channels are available to you to seek guidance:

- **Frequently asked questions**: http://dojotoolkit.org/support/faq
- **Forums**: http://dojotoolkit.org/forum
- **IRC**: irc.freenode.net, #dojo channel
- **Mailing list**: http://dojotoolkit.org/mailman/listinfo/dojo-interest
- **Commercial support provided by SitePen**: http://sitepen.com/services/support.php

All these options are great. My personal favorite is joining the folks on IRC; you'll frequently see me there during the weekdays. Also, the developers of the toolkit hang around there as well as do many of the active users of the toolkit. All these people are very good at JavaScript and Dojo development, and you're almost sure to get your questions answered.

Summary

In this chapter, you learned what the Dojo Toolkit is all about and why it is such a great choice for your projects. You learned that it is important to program to patterns and that Dojo helps you stick to predevised patterns that are proven to work in web development. Not only does it help you program consistently, but it also provides many shortcuts to keep your JavaScript more readable and maintainable. You should feel proud that you learned about the following:

- What the Dojo toolkit is
- What design patterns are
- Where to find help when you need it
- How to write your first few lines of Dojo code
- How Firebug can be an invaluable tool when debugging your code

Chapter 4

Dojo DOM Basics

Now that you know how to include the Dojo Toolkit in any of your projects, it's finally time to start looking at its application programming interface (API). Luckily, the core functions that you need to know about Dojo are very easy and straightforward, yet they will give you a lot of power that you didn't have before in plain JavaScript. Some of the functions that are provided are not only brief alternatives, but they also contain more features than their JavaScript counterparts (such as dojo.byId vs. document.getElementById); others are new functions that were created to extend JavaScript's functionality and solve common problems that developers came across when programming with JavaScript (such as dojo.query). Without further ado, let's get started!

How do you get an element by its ID?

LinkED

You learned about getElementById *in Chapter 2.*

It's common to get a reference to an element by its ID using document.getElementById. However, what you may have noticed while working with this function is that it has a long name. For a function that is used so frequently in JavaScript programming, it would have been nice if the original developers of the language created something a bit more eloquent. Well, you are not alone in feeling this way. In fact, most JavaScript libraries come packaged with a shorter function for getting an element by its ID. With Dojo, you use dojo.byId. That's a 40 percent reduction in characters that you have to type! Not to mention that there is only a single capitalization as opposed to the three in getElementById. You may laugh that I'm pointing these statistics out, but as a programmer, you always want to find ways to develop faster. The quicker that you can put the logic you have in your head into code, the more efficient you can be—and the more money you can make and the more time you have on your hands to program more JavaScript!

Let's say you have a product-listing page for a particular category of products. All the products are in an unordered list, and you want to get a reference to that list. All you need to do is provide an id to the ul, such as productList, and call dojo.byId('productList'). As you can see in Figure 4-1, that will provide you not only with the ul container but also with all of its list items.

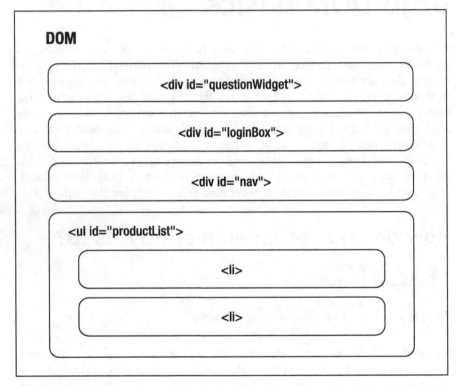

DOM

<div id="questionWidget">

<div id="loginBox">

<div id="nav">

<ul id="productList">

<li>

<li>

Figure 4-1. Calling dojo.byId('productList') gives a reference to the entire ul and all of its children.

This function appears to be identical in functionality to document.getElementById, but in fact, it is slightly different. The following is the function signature for dojo.byId again:

```
dojo.byId(id:String|DOMNode, doc:Document):DOMNode
```

ExplainED

Much of the time when a Dojo function requires a element's id to be passed, you may pass a reference to a DOMNode *instead of the* id. *A* DOMNode *reference is what you worked with before when you used* document.getElementById. *It's an object representing part of the DOM. When a Dojo function asks for an* id *and you pass one, in the background it will convert that* id *to a* DOMNode. *It's a convenience to be able to use one or the other. Any time you use* dojo.byId, *you'll get a reference to a* DOMNode *returned.*

As you can see, id will accept either a string *or* a DOM node. Dojo is usually very consistent in that DOM-related functions have similar ways of accepting arguments. If a function needs an id, it will always allow you to pass a String with an id or to pass an actual DOM reference. In the case of dojo.byId, however, the fact that you are trying to get a reference to an element with a specific id means there is no point for you to pass in a reference to the element you want (in other words, you already have the reference). So, if you are going to pass a DOM node to this function, then it is what is called a **no-op**, meaning that no operation will actually occur, and you will just simply get the reference sent back to you.

NotED

You might be wondering why you would even program the functionality of a no-op function. If dojo.byId *will always want an id, what's the point of allowing it to accept a* DOMNode? *The answer is that you may not always know what you are working with when using the* dojo.byId *function. For instance, if you were creating your own special function where you wanted to do something to an element that was passed in, you could allow an id or a* DOMNode *to be passed in as well and simply call* dojo.byId *to get a reference to the* DOMNode. *If a* DOMNode *was passed in, there would be no reason to change the internal logic of your function; you would still pass that* DOMNode *to* dojo.byId *to be consistent and write less code. Since* dojo.byId *conveniently allows you to pass in* DOMNodes *and have it not do any additional operations on it, this becomes useful when writing utility functions for your projects.*

The second argument allows you to look for an id in a separate document than the one you are currently executing from. An example of that would be a new window that you opened, a frameset page, or an iframe page.

I'll now show some simple examples of how to use the dojo.byId function.

Getting reference to a node

This is a very simple and straightforward use of this function. It is also the most common use, and you will be seeing and using it a lot:

```
var fooBarNode = dojo.byId("foobar');
```

Calling dojo.byId and passing in the id of an element will return a reference to a DOMNode object to the variable fooBarNode.

Checking whether a node exists

In JavaScript, you can write conditional statements without equality statements if you want to see whether the object exists. If JavaScript sees an object in the if statement, as opposed to null, it will return true. In the case of dojo.byId, if the id is found, a DOM node is returned, and therefore the statement will evaluate to true and would continue executing. However, dojo.byId will return null if the id was not found, and the internal statements of the if statement block will execute.

```
var n = dojo.byId('foobar');
if(n)
{
   console.log('The node exists');
}
```

When the previous statement is executed, the variable n will hold the value that dojo.byId returns. If the element on the page does indeed exist, then n will contain a reference to a DOMNode; if it doesn't exist, then n will contain the value null. For the former, the if statement will execute its block of code; for the case of the latter, it will not execute the block of code within the if statement.

How do you get an element using a CSS selector?

dojo.byId is a great function to get only a single element, but oftentimes you'll need a reference to a group of elements. You'll likely want to perform a similar action to all those elements as well. dojo.query is the Swiss Army knife of the Dojo Toolkit. With it, you can use CSS3-style selectors to return an array of elements to work with. View the first demo, dojoQuery.html, for this chapter to see a few examples. When you return, I'll go over why those examples were so special.

The fun part about that demo isn't so much about what happened but *how* it happened. Thanks to Dojo, each one of those actions was actually very simple to do. Before I break down the pieces of the demo, I need to go over a few things first.

CSS3 Selectors

As you already know, CSS is an extremely powerful styling language (it would be even better if you didn't have to worry about cross-browser issues). You can style elements on an HTML pages in many different ways all depending on how you construct your CSS selectors. This selector syntax is how you tell dojo.query what elements you want to select. Obviously, instead of styling these elements, you'll get an array of DOMNodes (more specifically a dojo.NodeList) that you can manipulate, style, add events to, or do whatever you like. If you wanted to select all the items in a list on the page, but not from another one, you could do that by giving a class or an id to each of the lists and specifying only the list that you want to use in the query:

```
<ul class="shoppingList">
  <li>Milk</li>
  <li>Bread</li>
  <li>Soup</li>
  <li>Cornbread</li>
</ul>
<ul class="todoList">
  <li>Mow the lawn</li>
  <li>Learn Dojo</li>
  <li>Fix door hinge</li>
</ul>
```

To select the items in the shopping list, you could use the following dojo.query statement:

```
var shopListItems = dojo.query('ul.shoppingList li');
```

With the previous statement, I'm asking dojo.query to pass back a NodeList of all the li elements from a ul with the class shoppingList.

If the CSS query that you run does not match any elements on the page, then you will get back an empty NodeList. If it matches only a single element, you will still get back a NodeList with a single element in it. No matter what, you'll always get a NodeList back.

If you were to look at the shopListItems in Firebug, it would look like what is shown in Figure 4-2. You can see in the screenshot that the variable contains four list items and that the shopListItems length is four.

LinkED

You learned how to use the Firefox extension Firebug in the previous chapter in the "Getting help" section.

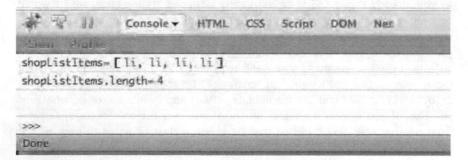

Figure 4-2. The console view of Firebug when outputting the value of shopListItems

NotED

If you want to determine whether you got any elements back in your NodeList, you could always find out how many elements are in the NodeList by getting the value of its property length. In the shopping list example, you could have called shopListItems.length, which would have returned a value of 4.

Dojo's query function is known for its speed in selecting the elements you specified. One of the reasons it is so fast is that it does not support 100 percent of the CSS3 selector language. Instead, it supports the most commonly used selectors and then some. Table 4-1 and Table 4-2 list the supported and unsupported selectors.

Table 4-1. Supported selectors

Selector	Example
Class	".foo" or ".bar"
ID selectors	"#foo"
Node type (such as tag names)	"span"
Descendant combinatory	"ul li"
Child combinator	"div > span"
Universal selector	*
Adjacent sibling combinator	+
General sibling combinatory	~
Attribute presence	[foo]
Attribute with exact value	[foo='bar']
Attribute with a value in a whitespace separated list of words	[foo~='bar']
Attribute begins with value	[foo^='bar']
Attribute ends with value	[foo$='bar']
Attribute with at least one substring instance value	[foo*='bar']
Structural pseudo-classes	:first-child, :last-child, :only-child, :empty, :checked, :nth-child(n), :nth-child(2n+1), :nth-child(even), nth-child(odd), :not(...)

Table 4-2. Unsupported selectors

Selector	Example
Namespace-differentiated selectors	@namespace fooBar url(http://startDojo.com); fooBar|h1 { color: blue }
Any :: pseudo-element selector	::first-line ::first-letter
Visual and state selectors	:root :active :hover :visited :link :enabled :disabled
Uncommon pseudo-selectors	:root :lang() :target :focus
of-type pseudo-classes	:nth-of-type() :nth-last-of-type()

Don't worry if you are not familiar with many of the aforementioned selectors. You will most likely not need all of them immediately. Over time you will likely want to expand your queries and get more specific; when that time comes, they are here ready for you. In the meantime, I'll discuss the demo you viewed a moment ago.

NodeList

When you first look at what the dojo.query function does, you likely assume that it will return to you an array of elements that match the criteria of the query you specified. You are absolutely correct for thinking this! Only, it's not the normal JavaScript array datatype that you are getting back—in fact, it's an extended version called a dojo.NodeList. Dojo has this special NodeList class because it packs in a lot more functionality than you would get from a normal array. It actually reflects a lot of Dojo's core APIs for array iteration and manipulation, functions for manipulating the DOM, and event handling. Some of these functions include addClass(),, style(),, and connect(),, to name a few.

LinkED

You can see many of the functions that NodeList *has and notice that they are just like the ones within Dojo Base in these examples on DojoCampus:* `http://docs.dojocampus.org/dojo/NodeList`. *However, a* NodeList *already knows about each of the elements when it calls those functions, so you don't need to pass in an* id *or a* DOMNode *when the functions are called like you do with the normal Dojo Base functions.*

dojo.query()

The function signature for dojo.query is as follows:

```
dojo.query(query: String, root: String|DOMNode?, listCtor: Function?):NodeList
```

ExplainED

Remember, a question mark following an argument means that the argument is optional when the function is being called.

The only argument required is query, which is a String. The second argument, root, is optional and is either the id of an element or a DOMNode that you want the query to apply to. Finally, listCtor stands for "list constructor." This is an Noted argument that you don't need to concern yourself with, but it basically allows you to send the result of dojo.query to another function in case you don't want to receive a NodeList in return.

On the demo page, you played with various different buttons that each call a special function. What makes this demo different from other demos in previous chapters is that this one is powered by Dojo and, more specifically, dojo.query. First I'll talk about the buttons in the Highlight section. Clicking any of these buttons causes a function to be called to find all elements with that particular CSS selector. When clicking the .foo button, all the elements with foo in their class attribute are highlighted. In normal JavaScript (without Dojo), the code to perform this type of action may have looked like the following:

```
var highlight = function(class, color)
{
  var divs = document.getElementById('elements').childNodes;
  var fooDivs = new Array();
  for(var i=0; i<divs.length; i++)
  {
    if(divs[i].className.match(class)==true)
    {
      fooDivs.push(divs[i]);
    }
  }
  for(var i=0; i<fooDivs.length; i++)
  {
    fooDivs[i].style.backgroundColor = color;
  }
}
```

Thanks to Dojo, the complexity is greatly simplified and results in the following:

```
var highlight = function(query, color)
{
  dojo.query(query).style("backgroundColor",color);
}
```

Each of the other buttons also calls the same highlight function but just passes in query strings and color hex codes:

```
<button onclick="highlight('.foo', '#71B095')">
  .foo
</button>
<button onclick="highlight('.bar', '#D13F32')">
```

```
.bar
</button>
```

ExplainED

When you call dojo.query(),, *you'll always get a* dojo.NodeList *returned to you. Even if it has no elements, you'll get an empty* NodeList *with a length of 0 back. Read the documentation on* NodeList *at* http://api.dojotoolkit.org/jsdoc/1.3/dojo.NodeList.

One minor thing that I don't show in the previous code block is that there is also a clearHighlight function that I call right before calling the style function. I put it there to more clearly illustrate which divs are being affected when highlighting. The dojo.style function is a normalized way of setting the style properties of elements. This would be instead of using the style property on an element such as dojo.byId('fooBar').style.backgroundColor.

```
var highlight = function(query, color)
{
  clearHighlight();
  dojo.query(query).style("backgroundColor",color);
}
var clearHighlight = function()
{
  dojo.query('.col div').style("backgroundColor", "#fff");
}
```

In the demo, when I wanted to style every element that I got from dojo.query, I didn't have to put it through a loop. I was simply able to call the style function right after I called dojo.query. This is because the style function exists in the NodeList class, just like onmouseover, orphan, and place. Those functions perform all the necessary loops that would be needed, which helps keep the code readable and easier to maintain.

In the Events section, when you clicked the "Add mouseover listeners to all divs" button, this performed a similar search as you did before with a query statement, but instead of chaining a style call after, you executed an onmouseover function to add a listener to all the divs. Open Firebug's console to inspect these events; you should see something similar to the result in Figure 4-3.

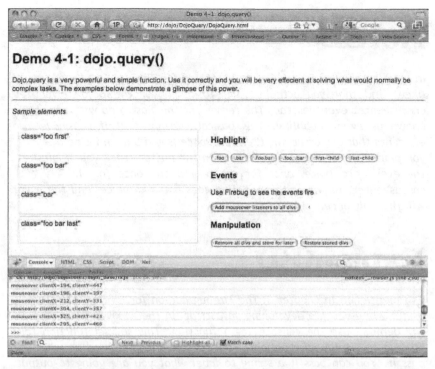

Figure 4-3. Mouseover events firing off in the Firebug console while rolling over the divs with the mouse

The code I used to make this happen so painlessly is as follows:

```
var addOver = function(query)
{
  dojo.query(query).onmouseover(function(e){
        console.log(e);
  })
}
```

NotED

In most cases where you want to listen for the onmouseover *event, you'll likely find that you actually want to listen for the Dojo normalized* onmouseenter *event instead. The reason for this has to do with something known as* **event bubbling**. *This basically means that if you have two elements that are occupying the same space (say a button inside a* li*) and you placed the* onmouseover *listeners on the button, then you would hear the event fire twice, once for the button and once for the* li. *With* onmouseenter, *however, this bubbling does not take place, and the event will fire only once.*

ExplainED

As I mentioned in Chapter 3, the Firebug add-on for Firefox is extremely useful while you are developing JavaScript. In the addOver *function from the demo, I use the* console.log() *function. This special function tells Firebug to display information in the console window based on what you pass it. You can pass it a string to label what you are going to output, followed by an object or two. This might look like this:* console.log('Tracing the mouseover event', e);.

The final examples in the dojo.query demo are the Manipulation buttons. When you click the first button, it removes all the divs from the document, and clicking the second button restores them all. The functions to provide this functionality are as follows:

```
var storedDivs;
var orphanDivs = function()
{
  storedDivs=dojo.query('.col div').orphan();
}
var restoreDivs  = function()
{
  storedDivs.place(dojo.byId('elements'));
}
```

As you can see, I used a special function called orphan. This basically takes all the DOMNodes that were matched by the query statement, removes them from the document, and returns them to my variable, storedDivs. Then I simply called the place function from storedDivs and told the function where to place these elements. In this case, it was right back where I originally got them. But they could certainly have been placed elsewhere.

Chaining

Every time you call a function from NodeList, such as style or orphan, you will get another NodeList object returned to you, meaning that you can call more functions on that NodeList and so forth. This is called **chaining** and can help create eloquent JavaScript statements. Be careful, though, because this type of development can get difficult to maintain if you attempt to chain just for the sake of chaining. The goal is not to make your code all fit into a single statement. You also want it to be clear what is going on so that if a problem arises or you want to add a new feature, you can easily make your changes. The following is a simple example of what chaining could look like:

```
var foo = dojo.query('.foo')
            .onclick(function(e){console.log(e)}
            .style('backgroundColor','#ccc')
            .addClass('foobar');
```

This will select all elements with a class of foo and attach an event listener to the onclick event, change the background color to gray, and finally fade out the elements.

How do you loop through a NodeList or an array?

When using dojo.query and seeing the NodeList functions execute, it's easy to forget that there is any kind of looping involved because everything seems to just work. That's because it is all done in the background using one of Dojo's core functions, the forEach function. You can use it too both via dojo.forEach and from a NodeList. This special type of loop allows you to specify an array you want to loop through and to specify a function you want each element to pass through separately for processing. Play with second demo for this chapter called DojoForEach, and then return here for an explanation of what is happening.

LinkED

In Chapter 1, I discussed the native JavaScript datatype Array in the section "What is an array, and why is it so important?" You learned about how to create them, add data into them, and how to loop through them.

dojo.forEach

You may have thought that the demo was perhaps the wrong one at first when you started playing with it. I wanted to make it interactive to allow you to create the array, element by element. Each time you do this, the application actually clears the element list and re-creates it with the new set of elements.

First was the function that handled the "Add element" button:

```
var arrElements = [];
var addNew = function(str)
{
  arrElements.push(str);
  displayElements();
}
```

I first initialized a global array variable to store all the elements. Then each time you clicked the button, your text got sent to the addNew function. This simply added the element to the array and called the function to display the list. No Dojo here, so let's move on to this:

```
var displayElements = function()
{
  var dojo.empty("elements");
  dojo.forEach(arrElements, displayCallback);
}

var displayCallback = function(element, index, arr)
{
  dojo.place("<li>" + element + "</li>", "elements");
}
```

The displayElements function first uses the dojo.empty() function to remove the children elements from the element with the id of elements. The function dojo.empty() needs an element id or DOMNode of an element with children, such as a list, a form element, and so on. It then deletes all the children from that element. When this function is run for the first time on the page, this particular query won't return any nodes since there isn't anything in the list yet. But, we don't have to worry, because when that's the case, the function won't attempt to loop when you reach the forEach function.

The next line is where I actually call the forEach function. As you can see, I'm simply passing the global array to the function and specifying the name of the callback function, which is displayCallback. The forEach function then loops through all the elements in the array passing each one as an argument to the callback function. One by one, the callback function processes its logic for that one element it gets passed.

Callback functions

Callbacks are special functions that get called by another function during a process. Most of the time callback functions need to have a specific function signature so that when the internal process tries to call it, it can pass the appropriate variables. The function signature for the forEach callback function is as follows, and all forEach callback functions must match this signature:

callback(element:Object, index:int, array:Array)

LinkED

*Callbacks are also heavily used when making Ajax calls. When a request is sent off to the server, you usually don't want to have JavaScript physically pause and wait for a response. The server may not respond at all or may take a long time. Instead, you use what is known as an **asynchronous request**, which allows you to continue along with the JavaScript processing after the Ajax request is sent. The issue is, what happens when the server finally does respond with a response? Initially, when you send the request, you will also give it a callback function to execute when it responds. You can learn more about this when I talk about Ajax in Chapter 7.*

You can see that I followed this signature in the example for displayCallback. When the callback is executed by the forEach loop, it is passed the current element in the loop, the current index count, and the array through which I'm looping. This is very handy since it pretty much gives you everything you may need to execute an action for this element. In this case, I create a new li DOMNode and set its innerHTML to be the text that you entered from the form. Then I simply add that li to the ul in the document. All of this processing happens in the blink of an eye.

How do you filter an array of elements?

Filtering is a feature that users expect these days when presented with some sort of data set. In the past, it was time-consuming to create a function to allow the user to filter. With Dojo, of course, it's easy. Take a look at the little demo called DojoFilter to see the filtering function at work (Figure 4-4).

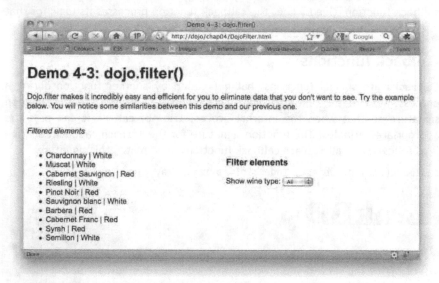

Figure 4-4. When launching the DojoFilter demo, you shoud should see this screen.

I hope that, besides me pointing it out, you immediately noticed a similarity in functionality of this demo compared to the previous one. The key similarity is that I reused some code to remove and display elements in the central list. I bet you were surprised how quickly the data refreshed after it was filtered, not to mention how easy it was to implement the filter. Let's go over it.

The importance of a data model

Since this is a demo, any data I want to have, I need to create inline or have you create it in the demo. You'll see that instead of creating an empty array for arrElements, I am initializing it with all the data it is going to need in the beginning. I also create a global variable called currentWineType that will keep track of which wines I should be showing in the list (a full explanation of the code is shown in a bit, so don't worry).

I'll take this moment to briefly discuss a concept here that many developers may not know about or use in their code. This concept is a data model and is a good practice to follow to help make your code flexible among many other benefits. A **data model** is a representation of data in your application. It could be multiple variables that are holding the data, or you could even build classes that just hold data and their job is just to return the data to the application when it is requested. This only really applies for data that you are using in the JavaScript, not to static content on the page. By having one array that contains all the wines you have, you can always revert to that full list if you want to restore the default data set. Otherwise, if you were to filter on top of the same array, you would have nothing to go back to without refreshing the page.

LinkED

If this example were a real application where you were really pulling in information about wines, you wouldn't have it embedded in the page as you do here. Instead, you would have a database that holds all the data with its various properties. Then, you could build a server-side application using Java, PHP, Python, or something similar, that would read the data from the database and return it via an Ajax call to the page. You could develop the back-end application to return it in a format that works best with JavaScript such as JSON. I discuss how to do this in Chapter 7.

A data model also implies a sense of state in your application or web page. By having a variable called currentWineType and having it store the current wine type that the filtered list is showing, you have put the page in a state that is showing that particular wine type. For argument's sake, let's say you wanted to remember what the user had chosen for that filter so if they came back to your site, they would see where they left off. You could store the currentWineType value in a cookie on their system and set the same variable to the value of the cookie when they returned. At that point, you would know to automatically filter that data with whatever they had before. In the displayElements function, I actually create a new array, which is temporary, called filteredArray that contains the result of the filtering. If I had kept the code the way I had it in the previous demo and set the filter result to the arrElements array, I would have lost the original data. I was able to do this filtering thanks to the magical function dojo.filter().

This concept of a data model will become clearer the more you see me use it throughout the book. Here's an example of the wine data model:

'Chardonnay | White'

The model here is that I have a set of attributes separated by a pipe. The first attribute is the type of wine, and the second attribute is the color of the wine. You can duplicate this numerous times for each wine you have and create an array. A combination of the array and the elements in it is the data model for the page. You can parse the different attributes out of the strings since the pipe is a delimiter.

LinkED

Representing data models in this linear format is not ideal and is not easy to work with when more data and attributes are provided. JSON is much better at this, and I will discuss it in detail in Chapter 7.

Let's move on by breaking up the code that I used in the demo.

dojo.filter()

I'll break this up into the order of execution starting with the moment the page is done loading. I use the following line to check when the DOM has fully loaded and therefore when I can start working with it:

```
dojo.addOnLoad(displayElements);
```

ExplainED

The function dojo.addOnLoad is a quick and easy way to add an event listener for the onload event. Listening for this event is such a frequent need that this special function will add the function you pass to it to the list of functions to be called once the page is loaded. They will be called in the order they were added through this function.

I'm simply telling the addOnLoad function to call the displayElements function once the page is done loading. Unlike the previous demo, I actually have data to display right off the bat. The displayElements function is therefore called to draw the data out on the page:

```
function displayElements()
{
```

```
dojo.empty("elements");

    var filteredArray = dojo.filter(arrElements, wineTypeCallback)
    dojo.forEach(filteredArray, displayCallback);
}
```

The empty function removes all of the children from the element with the *id* of elements. The next line creates a temporary local variable to store the result of the dojo.filter function. I pass dojo.filter our arrElements since it contains the original data that I'm filtering, and I reference a callback function to call for each element. The callback function needs to have the same function signature as dojo.forEach.

All you need to do in your callback is figure out whether the element should be displayed in the final result. The NodeList that gets returned contains the elements that were not filtered out. That's it! It's looking for you to return a basic Boolean, true or false. It's true if you want the element to show in the final result, and it's false if not. In my case, I wrote the callback function like so:

```
var wineTypeCallback = function(element, index, array)
{
  var show=true;
  if(currentWineType != 'all')
  {
    if(element.split(' | ')[1] != currentWineType)
    {
      show=false;
    }
  }
  return show;
}
```

Most of this you should be able to understand, but I brought in a few new concepts here. First, whenever I have a function that has to return a value, I always like to call return only once at the end of the function. You can call return at any point, and when you do, the function stops further processing and returns the value to the calling statement. However, I prefer to have only a single return statement. That makes it easier since I can always expect that my returns are going to be at the end of my functions.

With that, I create a local variable at the top of the function that keeps track of my return value. In this callback, I call it simply show (as in should I *show* this element?). I set it to true at the beginning so that all I need to do in my statements is check if it ever needs to be set to false; otherwise, it will default to true. It's a basic concept but helps keep the code readable and maintainable.

ExplainED

Variables that are declared inside functions are only accessible internally to the function that they were created in. Variables declared outside a function are available to the global scope and can be accessed outside the functions as well as inside any of the functions in that global scope.

Next, I check whether the global variable, currentWineType, is not set to all. In the flow I'm following, it would be set to all since I just loaded the page and that is the default value. The callback function in this instance will therefore return true for all the items, and you'll see all the items on the page.

To make this demo more interesting, let's take a small detour and see how to change the value of currentWineType. This will in turn affect the execution of the if block. The wine type select box has an onchange handler set up to listen for the user changing the value. When it does, it calls the appropriate function, which is shown next:

```
var selWineType_change = function(event)
{
  currentWineType = event.target.value;
  displayElements();
}
```

All you do here is change the global currentWineType variable to be the value of the option the user selected. This will change the state of the application. Then you go in and call the displayElements() function just like you did when you loaded the page. Let's get back to the callback statement that I was discussing a moment ago and go over what happens if the value is not set to *all* but perhaps red.

If the selection was red, that would mean that currentWineType would be equal to red at this point and therefore would continue to execute the inside of the if statement block. If you were to look at the element value at this time, it would display something similar to this:

wine type | color

JavaScript has a great function called split. You can pass it a string and a delimiter. It will search the string and will split the string up each time it encounters the delimiter value. The end result is an array of all the elements that were before and after the delimiters. In our case, this split function results in an array with only two elements: wine type and color. Since element.split() returns an array, I can reference an index in that array. I like to keep my code eloquent, so I've referenced the index (1) after the split function, eliminating the need to take an extra step and create an extra variable. By referencing the 1 index, you'll have a value of Red or White at this point. From there, it's a simple matter of comparing that value to the selected value in currentWineType. If they are equal, then you don't modify the return value (since it is already set to true). However, if the element you received is not equal to currentWineType, then you return false.

Once the filter function is complete, I have a new array stored in filteredArray:

```
...
var filteredArray = dojo.filter(arrElements, wineTypeCallback);
dojo.forEach(filteredArray, displayCallback);
...
```

This is where you use the trusty forEach function to display the newly filtered data on the page. Unlike the previous demo, I don't want to pass arrElements this time; I want to pass the new array that has the filtered data in it, filteredArray . This all instantly updates the document to reflect the newly filtered data. Changing the select box again will refilter the raw data and display that.

How do you create an element?

Oftentimes in the world of dynamic web pages, you'll need to create a new DOM element and place it in the document. Imagine for a moment that you wanted to make an Ajax request to list the current users in a group. Once you get a successful request back that contains an array of users, you'll want to display that on the page. Take a look at the demo DojoCreate to see how this is done (Figure 4-5).

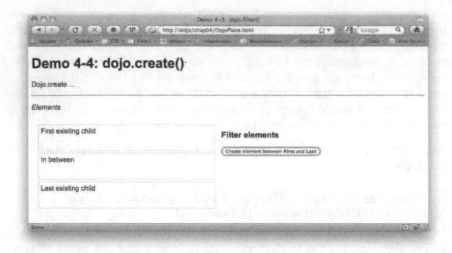

Figure 4-5. After clicking the button in the demo, this is what the screen should look like.

JavaScript provides a function called `createElement`, but it is not very powerful at all and is tedious to use. Dojo, on the other hand, provides an excellent alternative to creating elements on the fly without writing HTML. This is beneficial because when the elements are created, they are already represented as `DOMNodes`. Let's take a deeper look at what makes this demo interesting.

Positions

Before I get into exactly how you can create and place `DOMNodes` and other things in the document at will, I'll go over some special position values that both the `dojo.create` and `dojo.place` function use. In addition, both of these functions need a reference node to base the position on. Don't be concerned about the syntax and usage of the functions themselves for now because I will cover those next—just focus on the position terms listed here:

- `first`
- `after`
- `before`
- `last`
- `replace`
- `only`

These values are provided as strings when `dojo.create` and `dojo.place` ask for a `position` argument. The default for both functions is `last`. These are visualized in Figure 4-6.

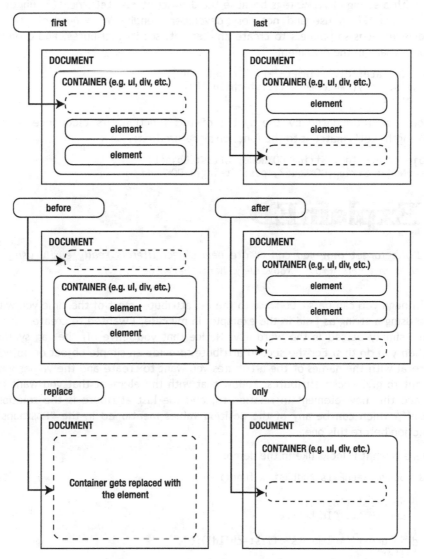

Figure 4-6. Each floating element represents the node attribute. Its name represents the value that would be used for the position. The reference node in each example is the Container element.

dojo.create()

Whenever I've had to create new elements in the past, I've always just created it with a string of HTML tags because the JavaScript createElement() function is so painful to use and not very developer-friendly. With dojo.create(), however, it is so painless to create an element, set its attributes, and drop it somewhere in the document:

```
dojo.create('div',{innerHTML: "In between"},
  dojo.query('#elements :first-child')[0],
  'after');
```

Don't be intimidated by the syntax of this function. Its eloquence is its strength. Let's match it to the function signature first:

```
dojo.create(tag: String|DOMNode, attrs: Object,
 refNode: String|DOMNode?, pos: String?):DOMNode
```

ExplainED

Don't forget that you can create new object literals really easily using curly brackets: {foo: 'fooValue', bar: 'barValue'}.

Although you can pass a DOMNode to the tag attribute, most of the time you will be using a string as I did in the example. In my case, I wanted to create a div, so I simply passed in the word div. Notice that you leave off the tag syntax when you do this. For the second attribute, provide an simple object or object literal with the names of the attributes you want to create and the values you want to give those attributes. Follow that with the element that you want to place this new element in relation to, and the last attribute is the relation itself, which can be any of the position values mentioned in the "Positions" section before this one.

Here is what it looks like in the demo:

```
var addBetweenFirstAndLast = function()
{
  dojo.create('div',{
    innerHTML: "In between"
  },
  dojo.query('#elements :first-child')[0],
  'after');
}
```

I created a div whose innerHTML is simply the text In between. Then I used dojo.query to look for the container whose id was elements and give me its first child (which is the top div inside that container). Since NodeList is an array, I grab the first item with a zero-index—this is my reference node. Finally, I tell it to insert my newly created div right after my reference div.

How do you move elements around in the DOM?

Often you'll want to place preexisting elements somewhere else in the page. Luckily, dojo.place satisfies this desire by allowing you to specify the element you want to move, an element you want to use as a reference to where to move it, and the position to move in regard to the reference element. Sound familiar? It should, because this is the same stuff you needed to place an element with dojo.create()!

The function signature for dojo.place() is as follows:

```
dojo.place(node:String|DOMNode, refNode:String|DOMNode, position:
String|Number?):Boolean
```

NotED

Following a function's parentheses in a function signature, sometimes you'll notice a colon and a datatype. This means that this function is going to return a value of that datatype. In the case of dojo.place, *it will return a Boolean for whether the placement of the node was successful. It of course doesn't have to be native JavaScript datatypes;* dojo.query *looks like* dojo.query(...):NodeList.

The position argument is optional, as denoted by the question mark following this attribute in the function signature. It is identical in functionality to the position (or pos) attribute in dojo.create. If you don't provide it, then the element that you pass in will become the last child of the reference node. An easy way to think about this is that if you wanted to place a list item (li) from one ordered list into a separate unordered list, you would provide the li as the node and the unordered list as the reference node:

```
dojo.place('myLi', 'myUl');
```

When you don't specify a position for the third argument, as I did earlier, it uses the default last as the value for position. last refers to the last child in

111

an element. In this case, it would put `myLi` as the last list item in the unordered list. The same position values can be used as in `dojo.create`.

How do you set the attributes of an element?

`dojo.create` is great for creating elements and setting their attributes at that time, but if you need to change the attributes *after* an element is created or on an existing attribute that was rendered by the HTML, then you should use `dojo.attr()`. This function allows you to have a consistent function for setting attributes on an element. In addition, it makes it easier than if you were to do it with plain JavaScript (you should expect nothing less from Dojo!).

The function signature for `dojo.attr()` looks like this:

`dojo.attr(node:DOMNode|String, name:String|Object, value:String?)`

Notice right away that this function does not return anything, which you can see by the lack of a colon and datatype following the parentheses. You are going to pass it a `DOMNode` or an element's `id` that the attribute modification will apply to. It will modify this element directly, so it has no reason to return it to you as well.

You can use this function to change one attribute at a time:

`dojo.attr('fooBar', 'selected', 'true');`

Provide a `DOMNode` or id as the first argument, the property name that you want to modify as the second argument, and the property value as the third argument.

Or you can use it to set many properties at a time:

```
dojo.attr('txtName', {
  "type": "text",
  "value": "Type your name here",
  "tabindex": "1"
});
```

Notice this differs from setting one function in that you actually pass only two things to the function: an `id` and an object literal. The object literal's properties are used as the properties in the element, with the values following suit. In the example, I want to change the attributes of the input element `txtName`. I set its type to `text`, give it a default value, and set its `tabindex`, which will allow it to focus in the right order in a form when the user tabs through the inputs.

You can even use it to add event handlers along with the properties:

```
dojo.attr('txtName', {
  "type": "text",
  "value": "Type your name here",
  "tabindex": "1",
  "onkeyup": function(event) {
    console.log('You typed ', e.keyCode);
  }
});
```

The previous is just like the earlier one except that I added an event listener as well. When you define the event listener, you simply pass it a function that you want it to run when the key on the keyboard is released. If the previous were an HTML statement, it would look like the following:

```
<input id="txtName" type="text"
    value="Type your name here" tabindex="1"
    onkeyup="console.log('You typed', event.keyCode)" />
```

The previous code will output the following in the Firebug console after typing **dojo** into the textbox:

```
You typed 68
You typed 79
You typed 74
You typed 79
```

You can also modify the style of an element with dojo.attr(). Keep in mind that if you choose to style the element via this function, you must provide another object literal for the style property.

NotED

Remember that object literals are created with a set of curly braces and a set of name/value pairs inside. Each name is separated by its value with a colon, and each pair is separated from the next pair by a comma.

```
dojo.attr("fooBar", {
    alt:"My foo bar",
    style:{
      backgroundColor:"#ccc",
      padding:"5px",
      margin:"10px",
      width:"200px",
      height: "250px",
    }
});
```

How do you get and set the style of an element?

Just like getting an element by its `id`, the Dojo way of getting and setting the style of an element is different from the plain JavaScript function. This is because of the browser incompatibilities that exist when using the regular function. Dojo normalizes the `element.style()` function you are familiar with so that it works consistently no matter which browser you are in.

Before proceeding, let's first inspect the function signature for `dojo.style()`, which you'll use to get and set styles:

```
dojo.style(node:DOMNode|String, style:String|Object, value:String)
```

Only the `node` attribute is required every time you use this function. Whether you include the `style` or `value` attributes or none or both of them will depend on what the function will do for you. Before you see it in action, however, you need to look at computed styles.

Computed style

When you view a page that has JavaScript that modifies the style of the elements on the page, the modified style isn't reflect in the source if you were to choose View Source in your browser. This is because of something called a **computed** style. The page will render its default view, which is whatever is programmed in a style sheet or inline with the page. This is what you see when you choose View Source. However, after JavaScript changes a style of an attribute, it becomes a computed style that is active for that particular load of the page.

You need to know and understand this concept so that you don't receive unexpected results when working with Dojo's style function.

Getting the style of an element

If you want to get the computed style of an element, call `dojo.style` with an `id` or a node, and it will return to you an object that contains the computed style of that element. This object is quite large because it represents most of the CSS attributes that an element can have:

```
var barStyle = dojo.style("foo");
```

NotED

When accessing CSS attributes from the computed style object, you should try to eliminate the use of shorthand properties such as font. *Instead, use their individual properties (for example,* fontFamily, fontSize, fontWeight, *and so on). This is because they are not necessarily reflected as expected since they aren't actual CSS but instead JavaScript styling that is similar to CSS. You'll also note that the attributes use camel case instead of hyphens just like the regular JavaScript* style *equivalents. I talked about this in "How do you change the style of a DOM element?" in Chapter 2.*

If you want to get the value of only a single property without returning the full object, you can pass the property you want in the style argument as a string:

```
var barStyle = dojo.style("foo", "borderWidthTop");
```

This statement will return to you a String of the value of the property. You'll also see here that I'm not using a compound property to get a style. Even if I had asked for simply borderWidth, I may not have received my expected result. You should be as specific as possible as to what you want to get back.

Setting the style of an element

You'll be using the third argument for this one, value. If you were to modify the example from before slightly to set the property instead, it would look like this:

```
dojo.style("foo", "borderWidth", "5px");
```

This is very straightforward. You provide the same value that you would to a CSS element. If you want to set multiple properties of an element, I recommend you don't set them separately by calling the previous function each time. Luckily, it is built to support multiple properties. Instead of the third value, you provide an inline object as the second argument:

```
dojo.style("foo", {
    "borderWidth": "5px",
    "borderStyle": "solid",
    "borderColor": "#ccc"
    });
```

115

Styling many elements

You can't use dojo.style for an array of elements unless you were to loop through them. However, you can style them from dojo.query:

```
dojo.query(".foobar").style("color", "#ff0000");
```

That's good for changing one style on many elements. If you wanted to change more than one style on many elements, you would use something similar to this:

```
dojo.query("#nav li").style({
    "fontSize": "16px",
    "fontFamily": "Arial"
});
```

dojo.style is straightforward to use and can be effective in situations where you want to draw the user's attention to something happening on your page, such as a set of errors or other special focus points.

Summary

You now know some great foundational skills to work with the Dojo toolkit. The functions you saw and worked with will probably be some of your most frequently used while working with Dojo. You'll continue to see these basics throughout the book and will get more comfortable in working with them. To summarize, you learned about the following in this chapter:

- Reading a function signature, which is the special documentation of a function's ins and outs
- The Dojo way of getting elements by their IDs
- An extremely efficient and powerful function selecting elements using CSS3 selectors
- Looping through arrays and NodeLists using the special forEach() function
- Callback functions that are used in many different aspects of Dojo

- Filtering arrays to only include the elements you want using the `filter()` function
- Creating elements without using HTML and using purely Dojo via the `dojo.create()` function
- Moving elements around in the document programmatically using a simple English keyword-based system (for example, `after`, `before`, `last`, `first`, `only`, `replace`)
- The efficient and compact Dojo function for styling elements using `.style()`

Congratulate yourself on a job well done. When you are finished recuperating, turn the page to learn the exciting world of using Dojo to interact with the user.

Chapter 5

Managing User Interaction with Dojo

User interaction is the most important part of Ajax/DHTML web pages. Knowing how to work with the data that is provided from the interactions is even more important. In this chapter, I will go over in detail how to listen for events and interpret their encapsulated data.

Events are one of the most powerful parts of modern programming and can really enhance how you develop web applications and widgets. With proper use, your code will be more loosely coupled and modular, making it easier to reuse while keeping it tidy; now that's a combo! Events and event handling will most likely be quite confusing at first. In fact, many web developers don't truly understand the concepts of an event model unless they have prior programming experience. This chapter aims to change that and helps you get up to speed.

How do you listen for an event with Dojo?

LinkED

Listening for events is an important part of programming JavaScript and web development. You learned about adding event listeners in Chapter 2.

Listening for events shouldn't be new to you. However, as I'm sure you can guess by now, you are going to find that doing event handling in Dojo makes a little more sense and is more innovative. In Dojo, event listeners are basically created by connecting functions to other functions. However, we don't always see it as that. These are some examples of when you need to connect an event listener:

- Connecting to a DOM event, such as the click of a button.
- Connecting to a custom function call (yes, you can execute a function after another one has finished executing).
- Connecting to another event that dispatched from an object.
- Using the subscribe and publish model. This allows a publisher to broadcast its data to interested parties who are subscribed to a specific topic. It's kind of like choosing to watch a channel on television.

Connecting to DOM events

Remember DOM events? They are the events that are announced primarily with user interaction such as the user clicking a button, hovering over an area, or even loading the page. Setting up event listeners to catch these types of events (as well as others) is different from the way you learned previously in Chapter 2, but you'll catch on quickly!

dojo.connect() is the main function that you will be working with the most when you want to create event listeners. It's the glue between the event and the functions that you want to execute when the event occurs. Its method signature is as follows:

```
dojo.connect(obj: Object|null, event: String, context: String|null,
  method: String|function, dontFix:Boolean):Object
```

ExplainED

*The terms **event listeners** and **event handlers** are related but not the same thing. An event handler is the actual method or function that will be receiving an event object and doing something when the event fires. An event listener is the connection of an event to an event handler. Much of the time you may hear these two terms used interchangeably to describe both pieces as a whole.*

The dojo.connect() function's use is more straightforward than it appears, because you don't need to provide all those properties. You can get by with just providing values for the first three:

- obj is the source object that the event will be coming from. If it is a DOMNode such as a button or a link, then the DOM event manager handles the connection just like it would be handled in plain JavaScript. With connect(), you don't have to link only to DOMNodes or native events; you can actually link just about anything such as another function so that when it is called, the event handler is fired as well.

- event is the string representation of the event you want to listen for. With a button, you may want to listen for onclick, and with a link, you may want to listen for onmouseover. This value must always be all lowercase, and it also must be enclosed in quotes since it is a string.

- method is the third attribute if you are providing only three attributes. This is the method on the page that you want to call. This has to be a global function declared on the same page or an inline anonymous function.

Figure 5-1 illustrates the dojo.connect() function. Imagine that dojo.connect() is kind of like the messenger. It knows about the sender of the message and the receiver of the message. It also knows the route to use to get the message to its intended recipient. In the diagram, this is represented by the dotted line, which is the glue of the whole process. It will take the onclick function that is executed from the button and connect it to the button_click function event handler, passing it an event object.

dojo.connect(Button, "onclick", button_click);

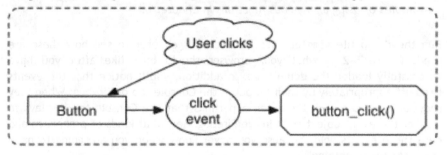

Figure 5-1. dojo.connect() is the glue that hooks up an event to an event handler.

You learned before that you could set up an event listener for, say, a button by giving it an attribute such as onclick:

```
<input id="btnFoo" value="Foo" onclick="btnFoo_click(event)" />
```

In Dojo, you would set this up when the page loads and use `dojo.connect()` like so:

```
dojo.addOnLoad(function(){
  var foo = dojo.byId('btnFoo');
  dojo.connect(btnFoo, "onclick", btnFoo_click);
});
```

Here you are simply starting off with the Dojo `addOnLoad()` function to make sure the event connection occurs after the page has fully loaded; then you get a reference to the button you want to connect to by using `dojo.byId()`. Once you have that, you call `dojo.connect()` and pass in the button reference, which is a String that represents the type of event you want to listen for (others might by `onmouseover`, `onkeydown`, and so on), which in this case is `onclick`; that's followed by a reference to the function you want to execute when the event is fired.

NotED

*An **anonymous function** is a JavaScript function that is declared inline within another statement. Anonymous functions are often used to write code faster since a separate function block is not written. Although it's an accepted practice, it is generally better to refer to a named function instead for better code readability. Using an anonymous function with an* onload *listener would look similar to this:* dojo.addOnLoad(function(e){console.debug(e)});. *You'll see many more examples of using anonymous functions in Chapter 6.*

Run the demo file `simpleEvents.html` for this chapter to see how these are used. Figure 5-2 is what your browser should look like after you have successfully loaded the demo page. In addition, you'll notice that the events fired off appropriately by their output in the Console tab of Firebug. When they show up, you can click the green hyperlinks that the Console tab displays to inspect the event object right inside Firebug. See what kinds of properties and data these events hold, because you never know when you are going to need that data for something.

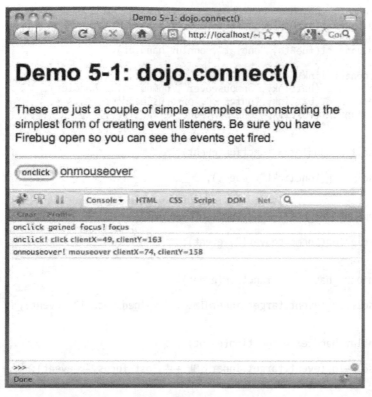

Figure 5-2. The `simpleEvents.html` demo should show the events in the Firebug console.

LinkED

If you need to brush up on Firebug a little, see the "Getting help" section in Chapter 3, where you'll find a tutorial on using Firebug in Firefox.

Easy, right? I'm glad you think so. Just in case, though, I'll go over a few things in that demo. You'll notice that I put all the connect methods inside an init() function:

```
var init = function()
{
  var fooBtn = dojo.byId('fooBtn');
  var barLink = dojo.byId('barLink');
```

```
   // connect button
   dojo.connect(fooBtn, "onclick", onclick_handler);
   dojo.connect(fooBtn, "onfocus", onfocus_handler);
   dojo.connect(fooBtn, "onblur", onblur_handler);

   // connect link
   dojo.connect(barLink, "onmouseover", onmouseover_handler);
   dojo.connect(barLink, "onfocus", onfocus_handler);
   dojo.connect(barLink, "onblur", onblur_handler);
}

var onclick_handler = function(event)
{
   console.log("onclick!", event);
}

var onmouseover_handler = function(event)
{
   console.log("onmouseover!", event);
}

var onfocus_handler = function(event)
{
   console.log(event.target.innerHTML + " gained focus!", event);
}

var onblur_handler = function(event)
{
   console.log(event.target.innerHTML + " lost focus.", event);
}
...
dojo.addOnLoad(init);
```

If it is feasible and it makes sense in your situation, it is good practice to create event listeners in one spot, which is usually after the page has loaded. That way, you can see at a glance the different connections you have and where they are going. In addition, since I'm calling the init() function after the page is loaded (via dojo.addOnLoad()), it will be guaranteed that the elements I'm connecting will be available. If you need to make any other changes to DOM elements, this function is a good place to do it in. This way, you don't have numerous calls to dojo.addOnLoad() all over the place. Keeping them one spot will help you keep your sanity.

ExplainED

You don't want to try to connect an event to the DOM without an addOnLoad *listener. This is because the* DOMNode *may not have been loaded yet when you try to connect to its events.*

Since I'm referencing the button and the link a lot in the connect() statements, it was better to get a reference to these elements first, which is what I'm doing in the first two lines using dojo.byId(). Now, look at the connect methods, and notice how I first pass in the object that is going to announce the event (the button fooBtn and the hyperlink barLink). Then I pass the event name as a string and finally a function reference that is going to be called when the event occurs. Each event handler receives an event object just like it would if it was set up inline with a button from the event attributes. This special object contains the data and information that you want to know about the event.

Let's take a look at one of the simple event handlers to understand the process a little better. Here is the connect statement followed by the event handler function:

```
<script type="text/javascript">
...
// connect button
dojo.connect(fooBtn, "onclick", onclick_handler);
var onclick_handler = function(event)
{
  console.log("onclick!", event);
}
...
</script>
<button id="fooBtn">onclick</button>
```

First, you call the dojo.connect() function and pass in the object that you got reference to earlier, followed by a string with the value of the type of event you are listening for, a click event or onclick. Finally, you pass the event handler (function) name as the third argument. By default the event object will be passed to the event handler when it is executed; that's why you have an argument named event. This is the most descriptive name, but you could have named it anything.

Inside the event handler, you simply call the console.log() function to show you when you run the page that the event was fired. This will display on Firebug's Console tab or Firebug Lite's console.

NotED

In JavaScript, you can pass a reference to a function to other objects and functions. When you do this, however, you don't add the parentheses like you do when you are executing the function. Simply provide the name of the function without the pair of parentheses. Think of it as a variable, since that is actually all it is; that's why you don't include the parentheses.

Table 5-1 shows all the events you can listen for.

Table 5-1. Available events to listen for with `dojo.connect()`

Event name	Description
onclick	A node was clicked.
onmouseover	A node was hovered over with the mouse.
onmouseout	The mouse hovered off the node.
onmouseenter	This is a normalized version of onmouseover that will dispatch only on first enter.
onmouseleave	This is a normalized version of onmouseout that will dispatch only on first leaving.
onkeypress	A key on the keyboard was pressed.
onkeydown	This is passed to onkeypress.
onkeyup	A key on the keyboard was released.
onfocus	A node received focus on the page.
onblur	A node lost focus on the page.
onchange	The value of an input was modified.
onsubmit	A form was submitted.

Let's say your method handler was actually inside another object, and you wanted to connect an event to it. This is where you'll use the first four arguments for `dojo.connect()`:

```
var fooObject =
{
  myHandler: function(event) {console.debug("myHandler fired", event);},
  myOtherHandler: function(event) ↵
```

```
  {console.debug("myOtherHandler fired", event);}
}
...
 dojo.connect(fooBtn, "onclick", fooObject, myHandler);
```

fooObject is passed in as the context argument, which means that myHandler will be called from that object. Don't over-think this too much. Remember, normally it's in the global scope on the this object. Now, however, I'm putting it as part of a different object and telling Dojo what that is by passing it as a context to the connect() function and the name of the function as the fourth argument. This is useful because you could have an object (or another class) that will handle the handlers.

You can attach as many events as you want to your objects. In addition, an event listener can fire off as many functions as you like. By doing this, you are keeping your code decoupled. Notice that you can use the same handler when either one of the connected elements becomes focused:

```
  dojo.connect(fooBtn, "onfocus", onfocus_handler);
  . . .
  dojo.connect(barLink, "onfocus", onfocus_handler);

var onfocus_handler = function(event)
{
  console.debug(event.target.innerHTML + " gained focus!", event);
}
```

That's because the function name was not only generic, but it had a generic API that both event listeners were able to abide by. Nothing in the logic of the event handler was specific to either the button or the link.

NotED

An **application programming interface** (API) is what defines how an application can interact with other libraries and services. The developer of the application doesn't need to worry about how the internals of the libraries work, just what input to give them and what to expect in return.

Listening for keyboard events

Traditionally, navigation and interaction with a web page were limited to the user moving their mouse and clicking stuff. Any keyboard interaction was limited to input boxes where the user was filling out a form. These days, websites have started catering to the computer power user by giving them the ability to perform actions on the site without ever touching the mouse. Run the demo called keyboardEvents.html for this chapter to see a simple example of using keyboard events.

LinkED

Two really great websites that demonstrate the use of keyboard navigation are the task management website Remember the Milk (http://www.rememberthemilk.com/help/answers/basics/keyboard.rtm) and the popular Google email service, Gmail (http://mail.google.com/support/bin/answer.py?hl=en&answer=6594).

Dojo provides a set of constants that represent keys on the keyboard. In plain JavaScript, these keys are actually represented by numbers, and it's a pain to figure out what they are manually. Dojo provides a special set of constants, dojo.keys, that you simply need to test against the event.keyCode property to see whether they are equal. The properties available on dojo.keys are as follows:

BACKSPACE	DELETE	NUMPAD_DIVIDE
TAB	HELP	F1
LEAR	LEFT_WINDOW	F2
ENTER	RIGHT_WINDOW	F3
SHIFT	SELECT	F4
CTRL	NUMPAD_0	F5
ALT	NUMPAD_1	F6
PAUSE	NUMPAD_2	F7
CAPS_LOCK	NUMPAD_3	F8
ESCAPE	NUMPAD_4	F9
SPACE	NUMPAD_5	F10
PAGE_UP	NUMPAD_6	F11
PAGE_DOWN	NUMPAD_7	F12
END	NUMPAD_8	F13
HOME	NUMPAD_9	F14
LEFT_ARROW	NUMPAD_MULTIPLY	F15
UP_ARROW	NUMPAD_PLUS	NUM_LOCK
RIGHT_ARROW	NUMPAD_ENTER	SCROLL_LOCK
DOWN_ARROW	NUMPAD_MINUS	
INSERT	NUMPAD_PERIOD	

Testing against this is quite easy. Take a look at the following code sample where I set up a basic keypress event handler and test for the Tab key:

```
var init = function(event)
{
  dojo.connect(null, "onkeypress", onKeyPress);
}

var onKeyPress = function(event)
{
  if(event.keyCode == dojo.keys.TAB)
  {
    console.log('The tab key was pressed');
  }
}

dojo.addOnLoad(init);
```

That was pretty easy; it's much better than looking up the numeric value of the Tab key and then putting that in the conditional statement. The following is the event handler from the demo you ran earlier.

NotED

*In programming, there is a special classification of variables called **constants**. They are regular variables but represent a constant value for the life of the application and are not meant to be changed. In fact, in many programming languages, you can't change the value once it has been set. Oftentimes a constant may represent special configuration, or in the case of these keyboard events, they represent the numeric value of event.keyCode and translate it to an easier to use English equivalent. It is a common convention to name constants in all caps to make it easier to distinguish them from other variables.*

```
var keypress_handler = function(event)
{
  var keys = dojo.keys;
  var num = dojo.byId('num');
  switch(event.keyCode)
  {
    case keys.UP_ARROW:
      num.value++;
      break;
```

```
    case keys.DOWN_ARROW:
      num.value--;
      break;
    default:
  }
}
```

The previous is the block of code representing the event handler keydown_handler that I used to listen for when the user was typing. I accept an argument that I named event, which is where I will get all kinds of information about the event. At the top of the function I defined a couple of variables. The first one is one you haven't seen before, dojo.keys. This will allow me to compare the numeric value that comes from the event to an English-readable variable, which is a constant in the event object. Next I have a switch case that allows me to compare the event keycode value to specific constants and determine which key was pressed.

NotED

You may have noticed a few new functions in the demo, switch *and* case. *This is known as a* **switch statement** *and is like a special* if *statement. Basically, you take one value, the one in the* switch *function, and compare it against any of the* case *statements. If you don't have a* break *statement at the end of a* case *block, it will continue to execute the other cases. The* default *block will be used if none of the cases match. You can learn more about the* switch *statement at W3Schools; see* http://www.w3schools.com/jS/js_switch.asp.

Listening to page events

The event that you will probably listen to most often when developing is the page load event. Because of the sheer frequency the onload event is connected to, Dojo has a special function built solely for connecting a function/event handler to it:

dojo.addOnLoad(obj:Object)

ExplainED

The page load event allows you to execute functions once the page has completely loaded. This is very useful for any functions that may modify the DOM. When they are executed, the DOM will be fully loaded and accessible.

By simply passing an anonymous function or a named function, Dojo will call those functions once the DOM has been loaded and all widgets on the page are instantiated. CSS and images may or may not be loaded at this time. Unfortunately, JavaScript doesn't provide an API to listen for when the CSS and images have finished loading.

You've already seen many examples of our use with this listener. Here is a stripped-down version of using it with an init() function to have a common place to initialize the page:

```
var init = function(event)
{
  console.debug(event);
  // put your event listeners and other setup statements here
}
dojo.addOnLoad(init);
```

This is a great approach to set things up for the page such as event handlers and listeners as well as making changes and adjustments to DOM elements. It's a good practice to follow to keep everything in one spot.

NotED

In addition to an onLoad *event for page, there are also* onUnLoad *and* onBeforeUnload *events that occur as the user is leaving your page. Dojo maps the* dojo.addUnLoad *event to* window.onBeforeUnload *and* dojo.addOnWindowUnload *to* window.onunload. *If you are considering modifying the DOM before the user leaves, it is better to use* dojo.addOnUnLoad *since the DOM may not be available at the point that the* dojo.addWindowUnLoad *event occurs.*

Please stop listening to me!

Just as you can connect to events and listen for them, you can also disconnect from events so that no further updates will be announced to your event handler. This is possible since dojo.connect() returns you a **handle** after the connection is complete. The handle is a simple array that contains information about the connection to the event. You don't need to concern yourself with the handle data. This handle is simply what you'll need to pass to the dojo.disconnect() function.

```
dojo.disconnect(handle:Object)
```

One of the generally accepted practices for doing this for many events is to keep an array of all the handles that are created:

```
var connections;
var init = function()
{
  var fooBtn = dojo.byId('fooBtn');
  connections = new Array();
  // connect button
  connections.push(
    dojo.connect(fooBtn, "onclick", onclick_handler),
    dojo.connect(fooBtn, "onfocus", onfocus_handler),
    dojo.connect(fooBtn, "onblur", onblur_handler)
  );

}
```

NotED

When you call the .push *function on an array, it allows you to insert one or more objects at a time to the end of the array. If you have more than one, simply separate each object with a comma.*

After one of those events has occurred, you may not have a desire to listen for the rest of the events any longer, in which case you want to disconnect all the events by looping through them inside the handler:

```
var onclick_handler = function(event)
{
  dojo.forEach(connections, dojo.disconnect);
}
```

You might be wondering why you would ever want to disconnect event listeners. One reason is that you may not want the user to perform an action again after they have already performed an event. This could be a case where they have submitted a form that is being sent via Ajax, and you want to disable the button and remove the event so that they cannot click it again to try to resubmit the request.

As you know, `dojo.forEach()` will automatically loop through all the elements of an array and send them to a specified function, which in this case is `dojo.disconnect`. Once you perform this, your event handlers will no longer get called when any of the events are dispatched.

What is the Dojo event object?

In my event handlers, I defined an argument called event (sometimes evt or even simply e). Although you can certainly handle events just fine without this special object, you'll probably find even more benefit in trying to use it when you can. The event object contains a wealth of information about the element that dispatched the event, how the user interacted with the element, and some other data that may help you when creating sophisticated user interaction of your site.

With normal JavaScript event connections, the event object that is passed isn't consistent from browser to browser. That's why Dojo provides a normalized event object, when `dojo.connect()` is used, to create your connections that contain a standard set of properties. Table 5-2 shows the attributes that are provided with the normalized event object.

NotED

As event handlers are being executed, the event listened for has not fully completed. This means that you can stop what is supposed to happen in favor of your own actions. You can use `dojo.stopEvent()` to prevent the default behavior. If you tried this on a link that would normally load a new page, this action would stop, and the user would stay on the same page.

Table 5-2. Attributes provided on Dojo's normalized event object

Attribute	Description
event.target	The element that dispatched the event (also the same one you referenced in the dojo.connect() method.
event.currentTarget	The current target.
event.layerX	The X position of the cursor where the event took place, relative to event.currentTarget.
event.layerY	The Y position of the cursor where the event took place, relative to event.currentTarget.
event.pageX	The X position of the cursor where the event took place, relative to the viewport.
event.pageY	The Y position of the cursor where the event took place, relative to the viewport.
event.relatedTarget	The object that the cursor is moving over and out for onmouseover and onmouseout.
event.charCode	The character code of the key being pressed for keyboard events.
event.keyCode	The code for nonprinting character keys in keyboard events (to be used with dojo.keys).
event.charOrCode	A normalized version of charCode and keyCode. This can be used for direct comparison of alpha keys and nonprinting keys together.

How do you listen for an event from multiple elements?

When you need to listen for the same event for multiple elements, there is an easy way to do it by coupling the dojo.query() method and dojo.connect(). If you recall, dojo.query() returns a NodeList containing many useful functions that will act on all the elements in a NodeList. dojo.connect() is one of the available methods, and since the NodeList is providing each element you are interested in, you don't need to specify the object to listen to. Simply type the event you want to listen to and the handler to execute when all the objects are getting connected. Take a look at the small demo named manyConnections.html for this chapter.

Surprise! I bet you didn't expect it to fade out, did you? Neither would your users, so please don't apply this example code in the navigation of any of your websites. You'll just end up with an online mob wanting to do bad things to you. Nonetheless, it's fun to provide a simple example to get the point across.

Looking at the code, notice how little it takes to add event listeners to every single navigation item:

```
var init = function()
{
  dojo.query('#nav li a').connect("onclick", nav_onclick);
}
var nav_onclick = function(event)
{
  dojo.fadeOut({node:event.target}).play();
}
```

Taking it one step further

What if you wanted to listen for more than just the onclick event? Well, since dojo.query() returns a NodeList, as do most of the functions that NodeList offers, you can chain as many event listeners as you like. Plus, to make it even easier, Dojo already provides a lot of the common events as method calls themselves, so you don't have to call .connect() and pass the method name in every time. You can play with manyConnections2.html to see this being used.

I use a common convention in the code that helps it be more readable when chaining these methods. This is generally accepted when chaining events:

```
var init = function()
{
  dojo.query('#nav li a').
    onclick(nav_onclick).
    onmouseover(nav_onmouseover).
    onmouseout(nav_onmouseout);
}
var nav_onclick = function(event)
{
  dojo.fadeOut({node:event.target}).play();
}
var nav_onmouseover = function(event)
{
  dojo.anim(event.target, {opacity:0.25}, 200);
}
var nav_onmouseout = function(event)
{
  dojo.anim(event.target, {opacity:1}, 200);
}
```

You can see the period at the end of dojo.query(), onclick, and onmouseover. This is simply a line break between statements. The JavaScript engine actually sees this as one long line instead. Also, notice that I'm not using anonymous functions here. Since it is likely you will come across anonymous functions if you review other developers' code or examples online, I'll show you what the previous code would look like using anonymous functions:

```
dojo.addOnLoad(function(event){
  dojo.query('#nav li a').
  onclick(function(event){
    dojo.fadeOut({node:event.target}).play();
  }).
  onmouseover(function(event){
    dojo.anim(event.target, {opacity:0.25}, 200);
  }).
  onmouseout(function(event){
    dojo.anim(event.target, {opacity:1}, 200);
  });
});
```

The code is a lot more compact at the cost of being slightly harder to read. This style is fine if you are only going to have a few statements in your handlers. However, if your handlers get larger (more than three lines), I recommend you break them into separate named functions.

Topical Events

A **topic-based event** is not something you are likely to hear about other JavaScript toolkits and frameworks supporting. It is unique to Dojo's topic system and is useful for anonymously publishing and subscribing to objects. This means that neither the receiver of the event nor the announcer of the event needs to know anything about each other or their internals. If you want an object to subscribe to these topical events, they simply start **subscribing** to a particular topic. Observe the following example code:

```
<script type="text/javascript">
var loggedin = false;
var init = function(event)
{
  var btn = dojo.byId('btnLogin');
  dojo.connect(btn, "onclick", btn_onclick);
  dojo.subscribe("user.loggedIn", userLoggedIn);
}

var userLoggedIn = function(data)
{
  console.log('User is logged in');
```

```
    dojo.byId('lblUsername').innerHTML = data.username;
}

var btn_onclick = function(event)
{
  console.log('Login button clicked');
  loggedin = true;
  if(loggedin)
  {
    var user = {
      username: 'foouser'
    };
    dojo.publish("user.loggedIn", [user]);
  }
}

dojo.addOnLoad(init);
</script>
<button id="btnLogin">Login the user</button>
Username: <span id="lblUsername"></span>
```

This is a login type example. Normally if you were to use this method, you would have an Ajax call to determine whether the user was logged in, but I am simply setting the loggedIn state to false when the page is loaded. When the user clicks the "Login the user" button, I set the loggedIn state to true and publish the user loggedIn event. The idea for this demo is that there is a function that I want to execute only after the user is successfully logged in. I don't care about anything else, so I'm going to tune into the topic user.loggedIn. When that topic is published, I'll receive its data, which will contain the username of the user who is logged in. Once I do, I set that value in the page and the lblUsername span to display it.

In this example, there is only one function that cares whether the user is logged in, but imagine a much larger page with many pieces that depend on that knowledge. It's nice to have a single point of notification that is broadcast to everybody on the page, but only those listening for that message will hear it and pick up the data that is sent. Let's go through the previous code.

dojo.subscribe()

dojo.subscribe() works similarly to dojo.connect(). The main difference is that you don't need a reference to a specific object to listen to; all you care about is the topic itself. With that, dojo.subscribe() needs only two arguments to be passed: a topic that's represented as a string and a function to call when the topic is published:

```
dojo.subscribe(topic:String, method:String|Function);
```

An alternative function signature is as follows:

```
dojo.subscribe(topic:String, context:Object, method:String|Function);
```

The latter is useful if the function that you want to call is inside another object. You would pass that object as the second argument and pass the name of the function as the third argument. This is just like the `dojo.connect()` function when you want to use a context. You can see the first usage in the small example earlier, which is explained next.

Beginning with the customary `init()` function, I want to listen for the login button, so I get a reference to it and create an event handler listening for the `onclick` event. In addition, this is the point where I subscribe the `userLoggedIn()` function to the `user.loggedIn` topic. Notice that the topic is simply a string. You can use any string you want here. I personally like to use dot notation to help categorize my topics. You could also use slashes, similar to a folder hierarchy: `user/loggedIn`. It's up to you and the style that you prefer, but since JavaScript uses dot notation for `namespacing` objects anyway, it makes sense to model topic naming convention in that manner as well.

The next function, `userLoggedIn()`, is the function that will execute when the `user.loggedIn` topic is published. I set it up to receive an object named `data`, but you can of course name it anything you want. I could have been more specific and called it `user`, but I chose `data`. In this function, I'm simply logging that the user is logged in and then setting the `innerHTML` of `lblUsername` to the username that is passed with the topic.

dojo.publish()

For anything listening for a topic, that topic needs to be announced. You do this with the `dojo.publish()` function. It takes only two arguments: a topic represented as a String (just like in `dojo.subscribe()`) and an array that contains the data you want to pass with the announcement. Its function signature looks like the following:

```
dojo.publish(topic:String, args:Array)
```

Although it is expecting to receive an array as that second argument, if you only wanted to send an object, you could just wrap your object variable name in a set of square brackets. That would create an array literal to be announced. In this example, I'm using the `dojo.publish()` function to announce to the page that the user is logged in. Read on for a more detailed explanation of this process.

After the userLoggedIn function, I define the btn_onclick handler. This should look similar to the handlers you've seen already where an event object is being passed. I'm not using the event for anything, but it's good to define the function to receive it; then, if you expand on it in the future, it is there ready to use. When the user clicks the "Login the user" button, this function gets executed and logs that the button was clicked. It then proceeds to set the loggedin global variable to true. After that, I have a conditional statement to check that the variable is true. Although this seems odd since I did just set it to true in the line before, I actually might have replaced that line with an Ajax call that would set the state to true if the user truly was logged in. For the sake of simplicity, I chose to set it myself. If they are logged in (loggedIn), then I create a simple object literal with a single property named username, where I set the value to fooUser. The next line is the point in which I publish the topic user.loggedIn and pass the data that will get passed to any of the subscribers that are listening for the topic. Note that the publish event needs to pass the data as an array. All you need to do is wrap whatever object you are going to publish in square brackets for this to work. You can, of course, send an actual array as well.

That's all there is to it! You may not see a need for this right away, but once you start to build more complex applications, there will be a point in which you will think of a use for the topic system.

dojo.unsubscribe()

Just like dojo.disconnect(), dojo.unsubscribe() allows you to easily stop listening to a topic. All you need is the handle that is returned to you from dojo.subscribe(), and you just pass it along as the only argument to dojo.unsubscribe(). Once you do that, the function that was listening for the topic before will not receive any more updates when they are announced or published.

LinkED

You can read about dojo.disconnect() *and how easy it is to stop listening to events earlier in this chapter in the "Please stop listening to me!" section.*

Summary

I hope you feel a little bit better about what an event is. It's actually not that hard of a concept to grasp. Just think of it as an envelope of data that gets pass to other objects about things that are going on in your page. In reality, there are actually many events occurring on the page; it is just a matter of whether you choose to listen to those events. Like anything else, the more you use them, the more they'll make sense. Don't forget to run console.debug(event) or console.debug(anyObject) as often as you can if you want to more about the objects that are getting passed around. I find that this is one of the most advantageous ways to learn about the data that I'm working with. By now, you should be familiar with the following:

- Creating event listeners
- Listening for the page load events
- Listening for user interaction events such as mouse and keyboard events
- Dojo's normalized event object
- Disconnecting event listeners
- Setting multiple listeners to a set of similar elements

Chapter 6

Make It Rich

Well, you've been working hard while learning what it means to build dynamic, responsive pages for your users. Now it's time to add a little spit and polish to give your pages and applications that special glean that users love, namely, smooth fades, animations, and the ability to drag and drop. Clicking and scrolling around a page is boring these days. Users want that little extra touch that makes the page complete.

> ## LinkED
>
> *Much of this desire for shiny, pretty graphics and smooth effects on a web page came from what some call Web 2.0. Although this style doesn't define Web 2.0, it really seems to be where it was introduced. Web 2.0 represents a friendlier, more approachable Internet that also provides a richer experience. Part of this rich experience has evolved into the social Web that we know and love. You can read more about Web 2.0 on Wikipedia; see* http://en.wikipedia.org/wiki/Web_2.0.

Spicing up your page encourages your users to interact with your website. That's really the point, right? Users spend a lot of time on the Internet these days, and you want to do what you can to attract them to your site while making them want to keep coming back. Just remember that a little polish can go a long way. You may want to overdo it once you learn all this cool stuff, but you should resist that urge.

What is a Dojo animation?

If you've ever tried animating something in JavaScript, you know it's not exactly fun or rewarding. It's usually difficult and definitely not something that you want to do just to add a little polish your site. It would take too much time and effort. Dojo has your back. It provides a great set of functions and classes that allow you to animate properties of an element and keep an eye on those animations via callbacks; it even provides some baked-in animation to help you on your way even quicker. Before moving on, take a look at the animations.html demo for this chapter's code download. The demo contains the examples for this chapter with exception of the Animation Events demo because of its specialized nature—it is included a separate demo.

LinkED

You can read more about animation events and play with the demo in the section "How do I execute other functions during phases of an animation?"

I hope you had a little bit of fun with that and you saw where you could use some of those effects in your web pages. All it takes is a little creativity and careful thought to recognize the right places to apply certain effects. Before I break down the demo, I'll talk about the key concept and class that is at the core of animations in Dojo.

Using the dojo.Animation class

Nearly all Dojo animation functions return an instance of the dojo.Animation class. It provides not only a set of functions that allow you to control the animation but also a set of callbacks that you can attach to functions when you set up an animation that will be executed during different phases of the sequence, such as starting, stopping, pausing, and so on.

NotED

*A **callback** is a special type of property that holds a reference to a function in a class. It gets its name because the class that you register a callback with is executing (calling back to) that function, which is located in your own code. Callbacks are similar to events in that they notify other code via a function about certain things that are happening. This is important when you want to execute code after something has occurred. For instance, if you wanted to fade out an element on the page that wasn't going to be used any longer, you could listen for the animation to complete and then execute a callback to delete the node reference from the page.*

The difference is that for each object that you can register a callback with inline with the creation of the object, you can only set a single function to be called when the callback is executed. Callbacks also provide other pieces of data specific to what is going on, which is more than an event would. If you choose not to assign any functions to a callback, then nothing happens in that phase. If you want to assign more than one function to a callback, you can use dojo.connect *after the object is created such as in the following code:*

```
// create the fadeOut animation
var fadeOutAnim =
  dojo.fadeOut({

    node: "slidingMoney",
    onEnd: function(o){
      dojo.attr("btnSendAway", {
        value:"You lost!"
      })
    }
  });

// setup first onEnd callback
dojo.connect(fadeOutAnim, "onEnd", function(evt){
  console.log('fadeOutAnim finished - 1st callback!');
});

// setup second onEnd callback
dojo.connect(fadeOutAnim, "onEnd", function(evt){
```

```
  console.log('I'm the 2nd callback and fadeOutAnim finished!');
});

// play the animation
fadeOutAnim.play();
```

Since this class is what controls the animation, when you create animations that are premade or using the dojo.animateProperty() function, you'll need to call the play() function on the returned object that you get in order to start playing the animation, as shown here:

```
var fadeOutFoobar = dojo.fadeOut('foobar');
fadeOutFoobar.play();
```

The previous could also have been written as the following:

```
dojo.fadeOut('foobar').play();
```

The Animation class is not really a tough concept to understand once you start to use the animation functions in Dojo.

Built-in animations

In this example, I wanted to fade out the button to only 40 percent opacity. For that, I had to use the animateProperty() function to have finer-grained control over what I wanted to happen. However, quite often you'll find that you don't need fine-grained control and you just need something quick and easy. Dojo has a few built-in animations that are simple to integrate with your existing code and will add some extra flair to your page.

LinkED

You can learn more about the animateProperty() *function in the section "How do you animate certain properties of an element?"*

Fading in and out

Two animations that are seen quite often are fade-ins and fade-outs. Dojo provides exactly two functions to do just this: dojo.fadeIn() and dojo.fadeOut(). Both require the same attributes to create their respective animation. You provide these attributes as an object literal to the first argument of the function:

```
dojo.fadeIn({node: 'fooBar', duration: '1000'});
```

Table 6-1 shows the attributes that you can use in the fade functions.

Table 6-1. dojo.fadeIn() and dojo.fadeOut() attributes

Attribute	Description	Required	Default value
node	domNode or ID of the element you want to fade out	Yes	--
duration	Number of milliseconds for the animation to span	No	350 (milliseconds)
easing	An easing function to apply	No	null

NotED

*In animation, **easing** makes certain animations look more natural by making it appear that the object is gaining momentum in the respective effect. Animations without easing are linear and would be represented by a straight diagonal line on a graph (from 0 to 1 over x amount of time), whereas animations with easing would be represented by a curved line. If you have an animation that eases out, it is said to start at the normal speed, but as it progresses to the end of the timeline, the effect occurs at a slower rate. To find out more about Dojo's built-in easing functions, go to* http://api.dojotoolkit.org/jsdoc/1.3/dojo.fx.easing.

You can see a demo of this easing effect in your local installation of the Dojo Toolkit by looking at the unit test in dojox/fx/tests/example_easingChart2D.html.

LinkED

To learn more about easing your animations, check out the section "Adding ease" later in this chapter.

As you can see in Table 6-1, a reference to a domNode or the ID of an element that you want to fade is all you need to implement it as quickly as possible:

```
dojo.fadeOut({node:'fooBar'}).play();
```

Note that you still need to call the play() method after you create a fading animation. If you want your fade effect to last longer than the default of 0.3 seconds, you can write your function as follows:

```
dojo.fadeIn({node:'fooBar', duration: 1000}).play();
```

This would make the fooBar element fade in over one second.

If you want an alternative way of fading out an element where you don't have to call the play() function, you can use dojo.anim(). This function has a different function signature:

```
dojo.anim(node:DOMNode|String, properties:Object, duration:Integer?,
easing:Function?, onEnd:Function?, delay:Integer?):dojo.Animation
```

Notice that the arguments for the animation are not passed as an object literal; rather, you pass in a element first, followed by an object literal of other properties, following by the duration, an easing function, an onEnd callback function, and a delay. The latter four are optional arguments. Once you call this function, you'll get a dojo.Animation back as usual, but it will already be playing, so you won't need to call the function play(). If you were to rewrite the previous fadeOut example using dojo.anim, it would like look the following:

```
dojo.anim("fooBar", {opacity:0});
```

It's even more concise because of many defaults that it implies when executing. However, it's up to you how and which animation functions you want to use. One thing to consider when choosing is that when you use dojo.anim, it immediately begins to play, which may not be a desired action.

Sliding

In one of examples from the demo, I used a sliding animation to bring in the picture of the $100 bill to the page from the left side of the screen. I then used sliding again to hide the bill by sliding it to the right while fading it out. The sliding function in Dojo is not part of the Dojo base functions like fadeIn() and fadeOut() are. Instead, it is part of the dojo.fx package to keep the base Dojo library light. The developers only wanted to include a couple of animations that were used often. However, anywhere you do want to use the other animation functions, you only need to call dojo.require('dojo.fx') to load the library and then call the appropriate animation function in your code.

The dojo.fx.slideTo() function will slide the element from its current position to a position that you specify. Keep in mind, however, that you don't use X and Y coordinates to specify the position; instead, you provide a left value and a top value. These values follow the same rules as the CSS that is applied to the element. This means that if the element has relative positioning, then the values are based on where the element is currently in the page. If it were absolute positioned, then they would be related to the browser boundaries. Again, this follows the same rules as in CSS. Table 6-2 shows the attributes you can provide to the slideTo() function.

Table 6-2. slideTo() attributes

Attribute	Description	Required	Default value
node	domNode or ID of the element you want to fade out	Yes	
left	Number of units to move the element to from the left	No	0
top	Number of units to move the element to from the top	No	0

NotED

You'll notice that the values for top *and* left *are expressed simply as integers with no suffix of a unit type such as* px *or* em. *The values are assumed as pixels since the underlying function for* slideTo *is* animateProperty, *which assumes pixels. You may notice in the documentation that you can provide a units property—this is actually not the case because pixels is the default. At the time of this writing, you are not able to choose an alternative unit.*

Just like the other animation methods, this one requires that you pass it an object with properties as well. In the case of my demo, I used the following:

```
dojo.fx.slideTo({
  node: "slidingMoney",
  left: 50,
  duration: 200,
  onEnd: function(o){
    dojo.attr("btnStartSlide", {value: "There it is!"});
  }
}).play()
```

I've used the onEnd callback for my slideTo to create an anonymous function that changes the value of the button. You can also pass an integer to the play() function when you call it to set a delay for the animation to start. If you wanted to delay the animation one second, you would call play(1000).

Looking at the CSS defined for my slidingMoney image, you'll see that I first set it up with a position of relative:

```
#slidingMoney{ position:relative;}
```

I also set its left position to -500px:

```
<img id="slidingMoney" src="100.jpg"
          style="left:-500px" />
```

Basically, this sets it to being -500px off the screen to the left. The slide function specified to move the money to the position of a positive 50 pixels from the left. This gave the money a grand entrance when you click the "Show me the Money" button.

LinkED

The attributes left *and* top *are related specifically to CSS positioning. This topic can be slightly confusing depending on how your elements are positioned on the page (for example,* absolute, relative, *and so on). W3Schools has some excellent tutorials and explanations on positioning elements using CSS; see* http://www.w3schools.com/Css/css_positioning.asp.

Wipes

If you wanted to specifically make an element grow larger (make it taller) on your page using animateProperty, you would need to know the desired exact ending height of the element in order for animateProperty to work correctly. Many times this won't be an issue, and simply using dojo.animateProperty() will work for your situation:

```
<div id="fooWidgetPanel"><!--widget contents --></div>
<button id="expandWidget">Expand</button>

<script type="text/javascript">
dojo.addOnLoad(function(evt){
  dojo.connect(dojo.byId('expandWidget'), "onclick", function(evt){
    dojo.animateProperty({
      node: "fooWidgetPanel",
      properties: {height:300}
    }).play();
  });
});
</script>
```

However, if you try to use animateProperty without an explicit height, don't get frustrated by the lack of a successful animation; there is a solution.

Let's say you had Frequently Asked Questions (FAQ) section on your site where you wanted to list all the questions, and when a user clicked a question, the answer would show up right below the question by sliding out. If you were to use animateProperty, you would need to know how long each of your answers was going to be and set that separately for every animation. This approach clearly does not make sense. When you add a new question and answer, you don't want to have to figure out what the height of the answer is going to be. The solution to this problem is dojo.fx.wipeIn and dojo.fx.wipeOut.

In my demo, you saw this very scenario in which there was a sample FAQ. Clicking the question yielded a smooth reveal of the answer. Clicking the question again reversed the animation and smoothly made it hidden. There is a small amount of setup for this type of operation. First here's the HTML:

```
<h3>Sample FAQ</h3>
<dl>
    <dt>
      <a id="faqQuestion" href="#">How do I cancel my account
      and stop receiving emails?
      (click this question to see the answer)</a></dt>
  <dd id="faqAnswer" style="display:none;">
  Lorem ipsum dolor sit amet...
  </dd>
</dl>
```

The hidden answer is identified by the ID faqAnswer. Notice that I set its display to none to hide it when the page loads. When the wipeIn animation plays, the display will switch to block, and the wipe will play. The second part of this example is the JavaScript:

```
dojo.connect(dojo.byId("faqQuestion"), "onclick", function(e){
  if(dojo.style('faqAnswer', 'display')=='none')
  {
    dojo.fx.wipeIn({
      node: "faqAnswer"
    }).play();
  } else {
    dojo.fx.wipeOut({
      node: "faqAnswer"
    }).play();
  }
});
```

This snippet of code is set up in a way that the same onClick handler can be used to either show or hide the answer. Since the main attribute of the answer that changes is the display setting, I simply checked to see whether it was either none or block. If it was none, I had to do a wipe in; if it was block, I had to do a wipe out to hide the answer.

ExplainED

As mentioned, the previous snippets are examples of inline and anonymous functions. If you were really going to design a FAQ page with this type of functionality, it would be best to make the code more reusable. This would entail moving the wipeIn *and* wipeOut *conditional statements into a separate function that might be called* toggleAnswer()*. In addition, every question link in the FAQ could have the same class name that you could call* dojo.query() *on, and adding an* onClick *listener to that would in turn call the* toggleAnswer() *method, probably passing in a reference to the answer element to be toggled.*

Adding Ease

Animations will look nice in and of themselves when applied correctly. However, sometimes they may appear too abrupt in their movement. You can mitigate this abruptness by applying a special layer to the animation known as **easing**. This is an algorithm that the animation will use to make the rate at which it changes the values of the properties it's modifying more dynamic, giving the illusion of a smoother, more realistic movement or transition.

In the easing example from the demo, the JavaScript code to move the red box and blue box is as follows:

```
// Easing with red and blue box
dojo.connect(dojo.byId("startEase"), "onclick", function(e){
  dojo.fx.combine([
    dojo.fx.slideTo({
      node: "redbox",
      left: 500 //px,
      duration: 5000 //ms,
      easing: dojo.fx.easing.sineOut
    }),
    dojo.fx.slideTo({
      node: "bluebox",
      left: 500 //px,
      duration: 5000 //ms,
      easing: dojo.fx.easing.linear
    })
  ]).play();
});
```

The HTML is as follows:

151

```
<button id="startEase">Start Animation</button>
<div id="redbox" class="easebox">Red Box</div>
<div id="bluebox" class="easebox">Blue Box</div>
```

I stared by connecting to the onclick event of the Start Animation button. This triggered a combined animation so that both boxes began moving at the same time. Each one was told to move 500 pixels from the left in a duration of 5,000 ms (5 seconds). Now you will notice that both have easing functions applied to them, but the blue box is using a linear function. This means it will go from point A to point B at a constant rate of speed. However, the red box uses a slideOut function, which will make it start fast and get slower as it comes to the end of the animation.

dojo.fx.easing

The magic behind the easing abilities of Dojo animations is thanks to the extensive library of easing functions available in dojo.fx.easing. This library contains more than 30 different functions to ease your animations in different ways. Table 6-3 describes all the functions that are available.

Table 6-3. Easing functions part of dojo.fx.easing

Function	Description
dojo.fx.easing.linear	The most basic easing function (and the default for animations); applies the effect linearly over time.
dojo.fx.easing.quadIn	A function to apply the rate of the effect by a power of 2 over time at the beginning. Starts slow and gets faster.
dojo.fx.easing.quadOut	A function to apply the rate of the effect by a power of 2 over time at the end. Starts fast and gets slower.
dojo.fx.easing.quadInOut	A function to apply the quad function at the beginning and end of the duration. Starts slow and gets faster and then gets slow again.
dojo.fx.easing.cubicIn	A function to apply the rate of the effect by a power of 3 over time at the beginning. Starts slow and gets faster.
dojo.fx.easing.cubicOut	A function to apply the rate of the effect by a power of 3 over time at the end. Starts fast and gets slower.

Function	Description
dojo.fx.easing.cubicInOut	A function to apply the cubic function at the beginning and end of the duration. Starts slow and gets faster and then gets slow again.
dojo.fx.easing.quartIn	A function to apply the rate of the effect by a power of 4 over time at the beginning. Starts slow and gets faster.
dojo.fx.easing.quartOut	A function to apply the rate of the effect by a power of 4 over time at the end. Starts fast and gets slower.
dojo.fx.easing.quartInOut	A function to apply the quart function at the beginning and end of the duration. Starts slow and gets faster and then gets slow again.
dojo.fx.easing.quintIn	A function to apply the rate of the effect by a power of 5 over time at the beginning. Starts slow and gets faster.
dojo.fx.easing.quintOut	A function to apply the rate of the effect by a power of 5 over time at the end. Starts fast and gets slower.
dojo.fx.easing.quintInOut	A function to apply the quint function at the beginning and end of the duration. Starts slow and gets faster and then gets slow again.
dojo.fx.easing.sineIn	A function to apply the rate of the effect by a sine function over time at the beginning. Starts slow and gets faster.
dojo.fx.easing.sineOut	A function to apply the rate of the effect by a sine function over time at the end. Starts fast and gets slower.
dojo.fx.easing.sineInOut	A function to apply the sine function at the beginning and end of the duration. Starts slow and gets faster and then gets slow again.
dojo.fx.easing.expoIn	A function to apply the rate of the effect exponentially over time at the beginning. Starts slow and gets faster.

Function	Description
`dojo.fx.easing.expoOut`	A function to apply the rate of the effect exponentially over time at the end. Starts fast and gets slower.
`dojo.fx.easing.expoInOut`	A function to apply the exponential function at the beginning and end of the duration. Starts slow and gets faster and then gets slow again.
`dojo.fx.easing.circIn`	A function to apply the rate of the effect circularly over time at the beginning. Starts slow and gets faster.
`dojo.fx.easing.circOut`	A function to apply the rate of the effect circularly over time at the end. Starts fast and gets slower.
`dojo.fx.easing.circInOut`	A function to apply the circular function at the beginning and end of the duration. Starts slow and gets faster and then gets slow again.
`dojo.fx.easing.backIn`	A function where the rate of change starts away from the target but quickly accelerates toward it.
`dojo.fx.easing.backOut`	A function where the end value actually goes past the end and then pops back to the end value.
`dojo.fx.easing.backInOut`	A function that applies both `backIn` and `backOut` to the animation behavior.
`dojo.fx.easing.elasticIn`	A function where the rate of change snaps elastically from the start value.
`dojo.fx.easing.elasticIn`	A function where the rate of change snaps elastically around the end value.
`dojo.fx.easing.elasticInOut`	A function that elastically snaps around the value, near the beginning and end of the animation.
`dojo.fx.easing.bounceIn`	A function where the rate of change "bounces" near the beginning value.
`dojo.fx.easing.bounceIn`	A function where the rate of change "bounces" near the ending value
`dojo.fx.easing.bounceInOut`	A function that "bounces" near the beginning and end of the animation.

Copyright (c) 2005–2009, The Dojo Foundation

Using any of these functions is just a matter of using `dojo.require('dojo.fx.easing')` to load the library and then from there calling any of the easing functions by name in the easing property of your animation function:

```
dojo.fadeIn({node:'fooBar', easing: dojo.fx.easing.bounceIn});
```

What I said for animations applies to easing, in that you shouldn't overdo them. Please use them tastefully. In other words, don't get ease crazy and start making everything bounce and be elastic. Feel free to let your creativity show by using them to complement the appropriate animations.

How do you animate certain properties of an element?

It would be nice if there was a function you could use to just say what DOM element you wanted to animate, followed by the name of a CSS property you wanted animated, and then provide a value that you want that property to be at by the end of the animation. Maybe it could be called *animateProperty()* or something obvious like that. You're in luck! There is a function in Dojo that does all that, and wait...it is called `dojo.animateProperty()`. Yes, it really is as easy as that.

LinkED

Opacity describes how opaque or transparent an element on the page is. Although not a CSS standard, opacity settings are available in all modern browsers and are described in values between 0.0 to 1.0 (0 to 100 percent). The smaller the percentage, the more transparent an element will be. With a value of 1.0, the element will be fully opaque. You can read more about how opacity is supported in different browsers at W3Schools; see http://www.w3schools.com/Css/css_image_transparency.asp.

In the Animations demo you saw for this chapter, the very first example was of a button that, when you clicked it, would fade down to about 40 percent opacity and then become disabled (preventing you from clicking it again). You may have thought I could have used a ready-made Dojo animation such as `dojo.fadeOut()`, but this would not have provided with what I needed, since that would have faded the button completely, making it invisible to the user. The effect I wanted to give in this instance was to tell the user that I received their click and that I was processing their request. I chose dojo.animateProperty() so that I could specifically configure the opacity to go down to only 40 percent transparency:

```
dojo.animateProperty({
  node: "fadeOutButton",
  properties: {opacity: 0.4}, // 40% opacity
}).play(); // start the animation
```

Passing arguments to the dojo.animateProperty() function is a little bit different from other functions. As you can see, I passed an object literal (noted by the curly braces) that contained the arguments for the function. It is best done this way because of the sheer amount of configuration that you can provide for the animations. This also makes it easy to put everything into one call. When using this style, the order of the properties does not matter.

NotED

Parts of the Dojo Toolkit use object literals to have the properties passed to the function. On the receiving end where the function is actually defined, the function looks something like function fooBar(obj). *Then inside the function block, the properties of the object are simply accessed as* obj.propertyA, obj.propertyB, *and so on. It's a simple concept—the only caveat is that the documentation needs to be stronger for that function since it doesn't get self-documented by having separate variables. It is important to state what properties are expected and can be used in the object that is being passed.*

You'll first need to provide the node reference of the element you want to animate; either it can be provided as a string that refers to the name of an ID of an element or you can pass a reference to the node as an object. If you fail to provide this, Dojo won't know what element to animate, and therefore the function will fail silently (without an error).

The next parameter that should be defined, again for consistency and for readability, is the properties object. Notice I said "object." This is another object because of its numerous possibilities of properties. With an animation, you can change the size, color, background color, opacity—the list goes on! In the previous example, I'm simply providing the property and its end value. Since animateProperty does not animate any specific properties, it needs to be provided with the CSS properties you want to change. Failure to do so will result in a failed animation that does nothing.

ExplainED

Opacity is always described in decimal format from 0 to 1. Don't make the mistake of trying to use 1 to 100 because your element will always be fully opaque in that transition.

After I defined the node and properties values in the object, I closed it up, as well as added the ending parentheses to close the call to the method. Then I called the play() function to immediately start the animation. Looking at the source code, you'll see that my animation does not look as simple as it did in the previous code. That is because I wanted you to focus on just the animation aspect. The following is the full excerpt of the code:

```
// fade out button
dojo.connect(dojo.byId("fadeOutButton"), "onclick", function(e){
  dojo.attr("fadeOutButton", {
    disabled: true,
    value: "processing..."
  }); // user can't click
  dojo.animateProperty({
    node: "fadeOutButton",
    properties: {opacity: 0.4}, // 40% opacity
    onEnd: function(o){
      o.blur(); // deselect the button
    }
  }).play(); // start the animation
});
```

The code in bold is what's different. Take a moment to look at it and see whether you can figure out everything that is going on; I've discussed pretty much all of it in previous chapters.

First, since I wanted this animation to occur upon the user clicking the button, I had to set up an event listener in the init() function of the page. You can see this because I start the block of code with dojo.connect listening for the *onclick* event, followed by a definition of an anonymous function. The anonymous function block is pretty much the container for this entire piece of code:

```
dojo.attr("fadeOutButton", {
    disabled: true,
    value: "processing..."
  }); // user can't click
```

NotED

Wondering what dojo.attr() *does to an element? Basically, it is a normalized way of setting values to properties of HTML elements. For example, a button tag can have an optional property called* disabled *defined, which determines whether it will be disabled on the page. I can set the value to that attribute using* dojo.attr, *as you can see in my example. What's nice about this method is that I can set multiple properties at a time since each property I'm setting is just another property with a value in the object literal that I pass to* dojo.attr().

This next part of the code is stuff you have seen before. I'm just setting some attributes of the fadeOutButton. I disable the ability for the user to click the button again, and I change the text of the button to processing...so that the user knows that I actually did receive their request and that they need to wait a moment (at least I hope they'll be patient and wait). For the demo, this button will always say *processing...* after you click it. If you were using this in a real-life situation, either you would be submitting a form and redirecting the user to another page, not needing to change the value again, or you could be sending an Ajax request, at which point you would change the value back to the default once the request was successful. If you want to reset this demo, you'll need to go up to your URL field in your browser and hit Enter/Return on your keyboard to do a fresh page load. If you try to hit Refresh, the button will remain disabled.

From there, the only thing that may look odd is the onEnd property within the animateProperty() method. Thinking back to the feature of Dojo animations, you can recall that they contain a list of callback properties that you can use to define functions that should be executed when certain events occur with your animation. In my case, I'm saying that I want to take the focus off of the button once the animation has completed. On a Mac, this removes the glowing halo around the button, and on a Windows machine it removes the dotted line that might be around the button. Technically, this command really could have been placed before the animateProperty() call, but I wanted to demonstrate how the callback functions worked. I'll touch on callbacks again later in the chapter.

NotED

By using anonymous functions for this one-off animation, I was able to keep my code more compact and concise without having to define a lot of other named functions. I'm not saying to do all of your code this way, but for this demo, it worked out really well. A general rule of thumb is that if you plan on reusing the functionality that you define in an anonymous function, you probably want to break it into a named function.

How can I play more than one animation at a time?

In the demo, after the money slid in, you were given the option to gamble it. Clicking that button caused the money to slide to the right and fade out:

```
// send the money away
dojo.connect(dojo.byId("btnSendAway"), "onclick", function(e){
  dojo.fx.combine([
    dojo.fx.slideTo({
      node: "slidingMoney",
      left: 150,
    }),
    dojo.fadeOut({
      node: "slidingMoney",
      onEnd: function(o){
        dojo.attr("btnSendAway", {
          value:"You lost!"
        })
      }
    })
  ]).play();
});
```

I didn't want to slide the money off the screen to the right because that would have made the effect too long. Users don't like to have to wait too long for things to happen. Just the right amount of special effects goes a long way. To help get rid of the money, I added a combination effect for the money to fade out at the same time as it was sliding away so as to provide a nice short slide while also fading it out of existence on the page. With that, I'll discuss a little bit about how that combine() animation function works.

dojo.fx.combine()

It is very simple to have multiple animations play at the same time in Dojo. All you need to do is provide an array of Dojo animation objects to dojo.fx.combine(). Once you have done that, call the play() method from dojo.fx.combine(), rather than the individual animations, and Dojo will do the rest for you. In the previous code snippet, all the code was written inline, but it could be more clearly expressed as follows. Note that I'm leaving out any callbacks for readability.

```
var slideMoneyOut = dojo.fx.slideTo({node: "slidingMoney", left: 150});
var fadeMoneyOut = dojo.fadeOut({node: "slidingMoney"});
dojo.fx.combine([slideMoneyOut, fadeMoneyOut]).play();
```

In the combine method, I provided the array notation using square brackets with a comma-separated list of animation objects.

dojo.fx.combine() returns an Animation object as well just like any other animation method. This of course means that you can register callbacks right on the combine animation, such as onEnd, onBegin, and so on. When doing this, be sure to use dojo.connect on the resulting object, as shown in the following code:

```
// create the combined animation
var combinedAnim = dojo.fx.combine([
  dojo.fx.slideTo({
    node: "slidingMoney",
    left: 150
  }),
  dojo.fadeOut({
    node: "slidingMoney",
    onEnd: function(o){
      dojo.attr("btnSendAway", {
        value:"You lost!"
      })
    }
  })
]);

// setup the onEnd callback
dojo.connect(combinedAnim, "onEnd", function(evt){
  console.log('combinedAnim finished!');
});

// play the animation
combinedAnim.play();
```

This does not limit you, however, to registering callbacks on the separate animations; you can still listen for the events separately of the combined animation.

How do I execute other functions during phases of an animation?

During an animation, you can execute code based on what phase an animation is in. I frequently like to know when an animation has completed to perform another action. In the case of the demo, you saw this in the submit button that faded out, where I disabled the button after the animation was complete. I also used it in the sliding money example to change the states and values of the buttons. This is all made possible thanks to callbacks provided by the dojo.Animation class.

dojo.Animation callbacks

Every animation that is created in Dojo allows you to hook into special internal events known as **callbacks**. These notify other parts of your code by executing the callback functions during certain phases of an animation. Pay attention to how each callback is executed, however. Like some of the callbacks, although their name may sound like they would represent the same thing, they execute the callback differently from the way their name would suggest.

A great example is the difference between onBegin and onPlay. By their names, you might think them to be synonymous with each other. However, looking at Table 6-4, you will notice that onBegin is called asynchronously and onPlay is called synchronously. Be sure you know which one is important for the type of execution that will be used. As an example, you might use onPlay if you wanted to simply alert the user that the animation has begun. On the other hand, if you wanted a method to be called after the animation starts, but that method has to finish executing before the animation can continue, you would use onBegin. The table lists the callbacks available for you to use. The first three callbacks in the table are listed in the order they execute after starting an animation by calling the function play().

NotED

In computing, processes can be described as being synchronous or asynchronous. **Synchronous** *means that two or more processes run in sync or at the same time as each other.* **Asynchronous** *is when two or more processes run one after the other. If one of the processes holds up, the next one will not execute until the former one is finished. These two types of executions are one of the things that separate a couple of the animation callbacks from one another.*

Table 6-4. Callbacks part of dojo.Animation

Callback	Description	Execution type
beforeBegin	Called before the animation begins.	Synchronous
onBegin	Called immediately after the animation begins.	Asynchronous
onPlay	Called after the animation begins.	Synchronous
onPause	Called when the animation is paused.	Asynchronous
onStop	Called when the animation is stopped explicitly.	Asynchronous
onEnd	Called immediately after the animation has completed.	Synchronous
onAnimate	Called after every step (or frame) of the animation. Passes an instance of dojo._Line containing the current value for the animation. When easing is used, it passes the value from _Line after it has been adjusted by the easing function.	Synchronous

In the code download for this chapter, you'll find another demo called animationEvents.html. Open this one and play with the fading of the black box. Notice the order in which events get fired when you do certain actions.

One thing to note is that the stop() function on an animation can receive an optional Boolean called gotoEnd The default is false, so if you don't provide it, the animation will simply stop in mid-animation, just like pause() would do. If you pass true into the function, it will set the animation to complete.

The code for this demo is very straightforward. First there are the buttons that control the animation, as well as a simple div that is styled to look like a black box:

```
<button id="btnStart" type="button">Start</button>
<button id="btnPause" type="button">Pause</button>
<button id="btnStop" type="button">Stop</button>
<button id="btnClear" type="button">Clear log
  </button>
<div id="blackbox">
  Black Box
</div>
```

The JavaScript to make all this function is as follows:

```
var anim = null; // stores animation reference
var init = function()
{
  // btnStart onclick, starts Animation
  dojo.connect(dojo.byId("btnStart"), "onclick", function(evt){
    anim = dojo.animateProperty({
      node: "blackbox",
      duration: 5000,
      properties:{opacity:0},
      beforeBegin: function(evt){
        logMsg('beforeBegin callback');
      },
      onBegin: function(evt){
        logMsg('onBegin callback');
      },
      onPlay: function(evt){
        logMsg('onPlay callback');
      },
      onPause: function(evt){
        logMsg('onPause callback');
      },
      onStop: function(evt){
        logMsg('onStop callback');
      },
      onEnd: function(evt){
        logMsg('onEnd callback');
      },
      onAnimate: function(evt){
        logAnimate('Opacity: ' + dojo.number.format(evt.opacity * 100,
          {places:1}) + '%');
      }
```

163

```
      }).play();
   }); // dojo.connect(btnStart, onclick)

   // btnPause onclick, pauses the Animation
   dojo.connect(dojo.byId("btnPause"), "onclick", function(evt){
      anim.pause();
   });

   // btnStop onclick, explicitly stops Animation
   dojo.connect(dojo.byId("btnStop"), "onclick", function(evt){
      anim.stop(true);
   });

   // btnClear onclick, clears the event log
   dojo.connect(dojo.byId("btnClear"), "onclick", function(evt){
      dojo.byId('log').value = "";
      dojo.byId('animateLog').value = "";
   });
} // init()

dojo.addOnLoad(init);
```

The code here is pretty straightforward and doesn't contain anything that you haven't seen before. In the init() function, I set up the various click handlers for the three buttons. The one for the start button is the most complex but still pretty easy to understand. I'm referencing the node that contains the black box, and then I set a duration for how long I want the animation to run. I specify that I want the animation to change the opacity of the box to zero over that period of time. Finally, the most verbose part of the setup of my animation is creating all the callback functions. Each one just basically adds a string to the log notifying you that the callback was fired. Use this demo again when you forget the order of which the events occur.

Registering a callback during creation

There are a couple of ways to connect to a callback on a returned Animation object. One way is to do it at the time you are creating an animation, such as I did in the demo:

```
...
dojo.fadeOut({
  node: "slidingMoney",
  onEnd: function(o){
    dojo.attr("btnSendAway", {
      value:"You lost!"
    })
  }
})
...
```

It's defined just like any other property. In this particular case, I used an anonymous function, but you could have just as easily set up the function separately and referenced it there.

Registering a callback using dojo.connect

In Dojo, the animation callbacks refer to internal events in the Animation mechanism; as such, they can be listened to in the same way as other DOM or Dojo events using dojo.connect. If you were to rewrite the previous code snippet to use a connect function, it might look like the following:

```
var moneyFadeOut = dojo.fadeOut({"slidingMoney"});
dojo.connect(moneyFadeOut, "onEnd", function(e) {
  dojo.attr("btnSendAway", {value:"You lost!"});
});
```

This should be a familiar style for you. It's always a good idea to remember to be consistent when you are coding so that when others look at your code (or you are looking at the code), there are certain expectations for how something is to be done. If you generally use dojo.connect() methods to set up event listeners, then that is probably what you should use to listen for callbacks.

How do you create simple drag-and-drop functionality?

Drag-and-drop (DND) functionality is a given on any modern operating system. However, within the constraints of the browser, websites have only recently begun to incorporate this type of advanced feature. It has typically been extremely difficult to support dragging and dropping of elements on a web page without the need of a very large amount of complex code. On the other hand, there are a lot of good (and poor) uses for such an interaction on modern websites. Not all sites have a use for it, but in certain situations it can prove to be extremely handy.

What can you do with drag-and-drop functionality?

To inspire yourself to think of ways where and how you could use drag-and-drop functionality, look around your operating system. The two most common types are reordering and dragging from a source and dropping on or into a target. Take an email application, for instance—you can drag emails that have been received from the inbox to another folder for archival. You can drag and drop files from folders to other folders, or even into applications for them to open the file.

Some creative things I've seen online are being able to drag items from a store into a shopping cart and reordering modules of content on a homepage such as news, games, and weather. In addition, I've also seen sites that offer task management to allow you to reorder your tasks easily by clicking one and moving it to a new position in the list. Think about a calendar application—you can easily move created events from one day or time to another simply by picking it up and dropping it.

LinkED

There are many sites online that you can visit to see examples of drag and drop. iGoogle (http://www.google.com/ig) and the BBC (http://bbc.co.uk) both have a customizable homepage approach that allows you to move modules or portlets of content around on the page so you can see the stuff that's more important to you right at the top. Google Calendar (http://calendar.google.com) exemplifies the concept of dragging calendar events from one day and time to another. Panic Software's web store (http://panic.com/goods/) is a great example of dragging store items into a shopping cart.

Drag and drop is a simple concept to understand as far as using it because it relates to real life in being able to pick up physical objects and place them somewhere. The programmatic implementation, however, is quite sophisticated. It gets even more interesting when you want to store the new positions for items after the user has dropped them so that when they come back to the page, the item is where they left it. If the latter is a requirement, you can make an Ajax request to a server-side application that will handle the storage and retrieval of those coordinates.

Setup

Before you can support drag and drop in your application, there are a few small prerequisites that you need on your page. First, there are some CSS styles that are provided by the toolkit that work as defaults to help you get up and running to make your drag and drop look nice and be intuitive to use. In the head of your page, put the following code:

```
<link rel="stylesheet"
```

```
href="http://o.aolcdn.com/dojo/1.3.2/dojo/resources/dnd.css"></link>
<link rel="stylesheet" href="dndDefault.css"></link>
```

The first CSS file is being pulled from AOL's CDN, so it is already available. The second file, however, is pulled from the unit tests for drag and drop and can be found in your Dojo installation under dojo/tests/dnd/dndDefault.css. I copied this file to the root of my demo to make it easy to refer to. However, if you intend to use the styles in the file, you may want to either reintegrate the rules in your existing style sheet or at least copy this one into your common CSS folder.

The second set of requirements are a couple of require statements that will give you some of the functionality you'll need for the next few snippets. Put the following snippet in your head as well:

```
<script type='text/javascript'>
  dojo.require('dojo.parser');
  dojo.require('dojo.dnd.Moveable');
  dojo.require('dojo.dnd.Source');
  dojo.require('dojo.dnd.Target');
</script>
```

I'll explain each of these in a bit.

The simplest form of drag and drop

Drag and drop is fun to play with, so I'm sure you are anxious to see the absolute minimum you'll need on your page so that an element can be dragged and dropped. First create a div:

```
<div id="dragMe">
  You can drag me around wherever you want!
</div>
```

I gave my div an ID so that I could style it quickly. Give it a background color and a definitive height and width so that it stands out on your page. Now, all you need to do to make this little div have the ability to be picked up and then dropped anywhere on the page is add the text in bold to your starting div tag:

```
<div id="dragMe" dojoType="dojo.dnd.Moveable">
  You can drag me around wherever you want!
</div>
```

That's it! When you run your page, you will be able to click the box and, while holding down your mouse button, drag around on the screen and drop it somewhere. That's fun for about a minute until you realize there is no real benefit of that type of feature to your users. But, hey, at least you didn't spend countless hours programming the functionality to figure that out. It's much more fun when it's this easy.

List reordering

Now that you have a simple way of allowing the user to pick up elements on the page and move them around, you can start to think of ways that you could actually make that be a beneficial experience for them. One of those ways that is actually quite common is the ability to reorder a list. It sounds simple enough since we take it for granted outside the browser. Again, this would normally be a very difficult and time-consuming task to program manually, but not with Dojo.

In drag and drop, there is a concept of a source and a target. The source is where a user might be pulling the elements from such as a list of online store items, and a target could be where they are dropping those items such as a shopping cart. In the case of the demo, the first list was the source, and the second one was the target. You were able to pick up and reorder items within the first list, but you were also able to pick up those same items and physically drop them into the second list easily.

Using Dojo markup, I set up the first list's HTML as so:

```
<ol id="todoList" dojoType="dojo.dnd.Source"
  class="container">
  <li class="dojoDndItem">Pick up milk</li>
  <li class="dojoDndItem">Take package to post office</li>
  <li class="dojoDndItem">Wash car</li>
  <li class="dojoDndItem">Fix leaky faucet</li>
  <li class="dojoDndItem">Take some time to relax</li>
</ol>
```

The ol is the source as noted by its dojoType. Note that dojo.dnd.Source is one of the items I included in the require statements earlier. Each of the list items also has a class of dojoDndItem. This denotes that the item can be used in the drag-and-drop feature. As a source, this list can be reordered simply by picking up any of the items and moving them to a different spot in the list. Dojo even provides special visual indicators to show exactly where the item will land when you drop it.

LinkED

Customizing the styles and layout of the visual indicators that Dojo provides when doing drag and drop is a somewhat complex topic and is not just a matter of changing some CSS styles. To learn more how to customize the drag and drop items, take a look at the "Customizing Item Creation" section in the article on SitePen at http://www.sitepen.com/blog/2008/06/10/dojo-drag-and-drop-1/. *You can learn more about the default "creator" in this introduction to drag and drop on DojoCampus.com; see* http://docs.dojocampus.org/dojo/dnd.

It is just as easy to provide a target that you would like to allow these items be dropped in:

```
<ol id="todoList2" dojoType="dojo.dnd.Target"
  class="container">
  <li class="dojoDndItem">Pick up milk</li>
  <li class="dojoDndItem">Take package to post office</li>
  <li class="dojoDndItem">Wash car</li>
  <li class="dojoDndItem">Fix leaky faucet</li>
  <li class="dojoDndItem">Take some time to relax</li>
</ol>
```

By simply calling this a dojoType of dojo.dnd.Target, you have instantly created a list that those other items can be dropped into but not taken out. If you want to be able to drag items out of each of the lists, then you simply label both with a dojoType of dojo.dnd.Source. This will allow you to freely move items from each list back and forth. With this basic knowledge, you should be excited about the possibilities of what you can start to do on your sites with drag and drop. Again, it is a great feature when used correctly. Don't attempt to make something drag and drop if it doesn't make the user experience better.

The topic of drag and drop can get very complex, and Dojo fully supports extremely complex interactions. This should be enough for now to get you started.

LinkED

If this whets your palate and you're very interested in drag and drop, SitePen has an excellent in-depth tutorial on some more drag-and-drop goodness; see http://www.sitepen.com/blog/2008/06/10/dojo-drag-and-drop-1/.

Summary

Adding that little bit of polish and frosting to your site is very easy with Dojo, as you discovered in this chapter. It doesn't take a lot of effort to pull in some simple effects and use them wisely to enhance the user experience. Always ask yourself when adding special effects, will this make my users happy and make for a more enjoyable experience? If you are not sure, it never hurts to ask family members and friends to play around with the user interaction as well.

I covered a lot of ground in this chapter, and by now you should know the following:

- What the `dojo.Animation` class is and how it fits into all the animation power of Dojo
- How to animate properties of an element
- How to use built-in animations that Dojo provides such as fades, slides, and wipes
- How to combine animations to play together
- How to listen for the different phases of animations and execute code during those phases
- How to create and operate basic drag-and-drop functionality

Chapter 7

Dynamic Data

In the early days of JavaScript, the concept of delivering dynamic data to a page was done only by special application servers that could interact with data on the server and render it into HTML for display in the browser. This suited web developers for a while, that is, until they realized that interacting with a website could be made a little easier for users if they did not have to wait for the page to load or reload every time they performed an action. In light of this issue, a technique known as **Ajax** was born.

ExplainED

Ajax is shorthand for Asynchronous JavaScript and XML. This means that a web request can be made on the page without refreshing the current page the user is on, which can lead to updating or refreshing only specific parts of the page that are affected by the web request. At the time of the conception of Ajax, XML was the primary data format the data that was returned from the server would be represented in. In actuality, Ajax functions can return any type of textual data (plain text, JSON, or XML).

What is Ajax anyway?

At the time that the technique we now know today as Ajax was first being used, it did not have a name. It was more simply processes that developers had devised as a way to get data from the server without refreshing the page. Primarily, this was achieved using hidden iframes that would load data in the page, and JavaScript would then read in that data and replace parts of the current page with that data. Figure 7-1 illustrates the concept behind Ajax.

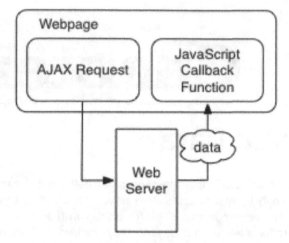

Figure 7-1. Basic concept of Ajax showing that without another page load, data can be sent and received from the server

Once the need for this type of server interaction was apparent, browsers introduced built-in JavaScript functions for calling special pages on the server that are meant to only return data in the background. A JavaScript function then interprets that data (usually formatted in JSON or XML) and uses it on the page by dynamically replacing values. The API that is used in most browsers, with exception to Internet Explorer 6 and older, is XMLHttpRequest (XHR). Don't be confused by the name since any textual data can be transferred through this protocol.

NotED

Internet Explorer 5 and 6 don't support the XMLHttpRequest *object. Instead, Microsoft implemented a special ActiveX object called* Microsoft.XMLHTTP. *If the user has IE 5 or 6, you have to instantiate this object as* var xmlhttp=new ActiveXObject("Microsoft.XMLHTTP"). *From there, most of the API is the same. With the release of Internet Explorer 7, Microsoft added support for the* XMLHttpRequest *object to be standard with all the other browsers. Personally, my prediction is that by 2010, we won't see a substantial number of users using Internet Explorer 6 to have to worry about this inconsistency any longer. Either way, Dojo will always help you mitigate these special cases by providing a simple and common API to its developers.*

As developers started to pile onto the Ajax bandwagon, many were discouraged by its unintuitive programming interface and were also unaccustomed to its workflow. It was around this time that JavaScript and Ajax libraries started to pop up all over the Internet, aiming to provide an easier-to-use API for working with Ajax. Dojo is no stranger to this trend and has the most powerful set of Ajax APIs, not to mention a very extensive set. Ajax sounds great, and it is, but let's look at the pros and cons so you have a clearer picture.

Pros of Ajax

The following are the benefits to using Ajax:

- You can load and submit content on the page without loading a whole new page.
- Data can be transferred in the background to allow the user to continue using the page.
- The data can be lightweight (the response is sending only data, not full HTML documents).
- Initial pages may also be lighter since the content is broken up.
- You can serve static HTML in lieu of server pages, cutting down page load time and server processing.

NotED

The major search engine companies such as Google, Yahoo!, and MSN are always researching ways to accommodate the indexing of dynamic Ajax-driven content. The Web needs to move forward with new technologies, and it is up to the search giants to make their tools compatible with what's in use. A developer should not have to sacrifice experience for search engine optimization (SEO).

Cons of Ajax

The following are the disadvantages of Ajax:

- At this time, search engine crawlers don't execute JavaScript on the page, so any content you write after the page is loaded will not be indexed.
- Page content is incomplete upon initial load (if loading data after page load).

- Ajax requires JavaScript to be enabled on the client (which may not work on mobile devices).

LinkED

Check out the "How do you stay search engine friendly?" section to learn why Ajax will work against you in getting your pages indexed by search engines unless you follow an important set of principles.

At the end of the day, the pros really do outweigh the cons in most situations. Some sites may require only one or two areas on a page to be powered by Ajax, whereas with others, you could create full applications using Ajax. Whichever it is, Dojo will support you no matter what route you go; with it, you can use basic operations or wield the enterprise power of Dojo to tackle the toughest and most complex problems.

How do you load external data?

External data is anything that is not part of the original HTML on a page. In this case, I am talking specifically about loading additional data, such as text and images that don't already exist on the page. There are many different ways of doing this, but first let's take a look at a brief demo. I've created a basic photo gallery whose actual contents don't get loaded with the HTML of the page. Rather, the content is filled in shortly after the original HTML is done loading. Run the gallery.html file from the downloaded code for this chapter. To ensure it is running correctly, when running it in your browser, it should look similar to Figure 7-2.

Figure 7-2. When you run the demo, this is what your page should look like.

In this example, the data was being loaded from a separate file named photos.json. This is a simple text file that contains a block of JSON with properties that refer to locations of images as well as the title and subtitle for the gallery.

My JSON file was relatively simple:

```
{
  "title": "FooBar Gallery",
  "subtitle": "Some photos that might be worth a few words",
  "images": [
    {
      "thumb": "images/thumb_1.jpg",
      "large": "images/large_1.jpg",
    },
    {
      "thumb": "images/thumb_2.jpg",
      "large": "images/large_2.jpg",
    },
    {
      "thumb": "images/thumb_3.jpg",
      "large": "images/large_3.jpg",
    },
    {
```

```
      "thumb": "images/thumb_4.jpg",
      "large": "images/large_4.jpg",
    },
    {
      "thumb": "images/thumb_5.jpg",
      "large": "images/large_5.jpg",
    }
  ]
}
```

NotED

JSON (pronounced as "jay-sun" or "jay-sahn") is a lightweight representation of a data model written in JavaScript object notation. It is well suited in JavaScript applications for external data because of its ease of use and implementation. It is this very type of syntax that you use to pass objects into Dojo functions such as the animation functions:

```
dojo.fadeIn(
  {
    node: dojo.byId('selectedImg')
  }
).play();
```

When loading external data, it doesn't always have to be a JSON file (though that is often preferred in JavaScript). It could also be an XML file or any plain-text file. Either way, it is read into the page as a separate process. If you were to develop this in plain JavaScript, the response that you get would be the raw data of the file, and you would need to parse it into something that you could easily use in the page. This type of operation is somewhat complex, which is why Dojo does all the dirty work for you.

Using dojo.xhrGet() to load external data

Before you look at the JavaScript, first take a look at the HTML in the body of the document when it first loads:

```html
<h1 id="title"></h1>
<h2 id="subtitle"></h2>
<ul id="thumbs" class="gallery thumbnails"></ul>
<div class="selected">
  <img id="selectedImg" />
</div>
```

I consider that fairly lightweight. Notice that there is not any JavaScript code in this part of the HTML either. That's because you do all that magic in the document's head! The best part about that is you've already learned 90 percent of the functions that I used. The only one missing is the function that performs the magic of loading data from an external location. The code in my init() function is what starts the whole chain of loading the gallery:

```
var fUri = "./photos.json"
var _images = null;
var _selectedImage = null;

var init = function(e)
{
  dojo.xhrGet({
    url: fUri,
    handleAs: 'json',
    load: galleryData_success,
    fail: galleryData_fail
  });
}
```

I set up a few global page variables that will need to be accessed from the other functions. fUri represents the URL/URI that you'll load the data from. The most common setup is to point to a URL that will build the data in the format you need and pass it on. You can also load from a simple static file that is stored on the server, which is what I did in this case. The latter is less likely to be used unless a separate background process updates it.

LinkED

*You already know what a URL is, but you are probably wondering what a URI is. First, a **uniform resource locator** (URL) is a type of **uniform resource identifier** (URI). The difference is that a URI simply identifies a resource that can be found on the Internet, whereas a URL identifies a resource as well as the mechanism for retrieving it. You can read more about URIs on Wikipedia; see* http://en.wikipedia.org/wiki/Uniform_ Resource_Identifier.

_images is simply an array that will store all the objects that contain references to the URLs to the thumbnails and large images. selectedImage will contain the currently selected image for the page, which will be the one that shows up as the large image.

Now jumping into the init() function, you can see the magical dojo.xhrGet() function. That looks pretty simple, right? It really is as simple as it looks. You pass an object to xhrGet() just like you did with the animation functions. Table 7-1 describes some of the properties you can use.

Table 7-1. Properties

Property	Description	Type	Required
url	URL to the data you want to load	String	Yes, unless the form property is used; then the action property from the form tag is used.
handleAs	Type of data Dojo should expect to load from the URL. It will automatically parse the data into a JavaScript object once it loads. Possible values are text (the default), json, json-comment-optional, json-comment-filtered, javascript, xml.	String	No
timeout	Maximum time to wait for the server to respond before throwing an error in milliseconds. If no value is provided, the timeout will defer to the browser.	Integer	No
load	Callback function to send the data to if it loads successfully. If no callback is provided, the request will be sent silently, and you won't be notified when it is complete.	Function	No
error	Callback function to call if an error occurs in the retrieval of the data, if an error occurs while parsing the data, or if an error occurs in the load callback function. If no callback is defined, when a fault occurs, JavaScript will throw an error.	Function	No

Property	Description	Type	Required
handle	Callback function that will be called at the end of the request regardless of it being successful. If the request is successful, the expected response data is passed to the callback; otherwise, an error object is passed. If no callback is defined, the same actions will occur in the case of load and error when no callbacks are defined.	Function	No
content	Data to send to the URL if required. If not defined, no extra content will be sent with the request.	Object	No

In my demo I told xhrGet() what URL to get the data from and that the data was going to be in the JSON format, and I passed in references to two functions to be called on either a successful request or a failed request.

Load callback

The load callback function requires a special function signature to ensure the proper delivery of your data. You simply need to define one argument: the response or data object. The response is the JavaScript object that Dojo parsed out of the external file. My load callback function is as follows.

> # NotED
>
> *In certain parts of the documentation for* xhrGet() *(see* http://docs.dojocampus.org/dojo/xhrGet), *you might see that the load callback function can also accept an optional second argument,* ioArgs. *This is an advanced argument that will allow you to inspect more information about the request such as the* statusCode *that the server provided. You can inspect this object in Firebug to see all the available data you can access. Also note that if you use the* dojo.Defferred(), *you will not receive an* ioArgs *object in your callbacks.*

```
var galleryData_success = function(data)
{
  setTitle(data.title);
```

```
    setSubtitle(data.subtitle);
    setImages(data.images);
    setSelectedImage(_images[0]);
}
```

Now that I have the data I need contained in the data object, I can start referring to properties inside that object. You can refer to my JSON excerpt from earlier to see what properties are available to use. When you start working with more complex JavaScript operations in your pages, you'll want to segregate your code into separate helper functions as shown here. This keeps it clean and easy to maintain.

```
var setTitle = function(title)
{
    dojo.attr('title', {innerHTML: title});
}

var setSubtitle = function(subtitle)
{
    dojo.attr('subtitle', {innerHTML: subtitle});
}

var setImages = function(images)
{
    _images = images;
    dojo.forEach(images,
    function(image, idx, array){
        var tmpLi = dojo.create('li');
        var tmpImg = dojo.create('img', {
        src: image.thumb,
            style: {opacity: 0}
        }, tmpLi);
        dojo.connect(tmpImg, "onclick", function(e){
            setSelectedImage(_images[idx]);
        });
        dojo.place(tmpLi,'thumbs');
    });
    dojo.query('#thumbs img').fadeIn().play();
}

var setSelectedImage = function(image)
{
    dojo.fadeOut({
        node: dojo.byId('selectedImg'),
        onEnd: function() {
            _selectedImage = image;
            dojo.attr('selectedImg', {src: image.large});
            dojo.fadeIn({node: dojo.byId('selectedImg')}).play();
        }
    }).play();
}
```

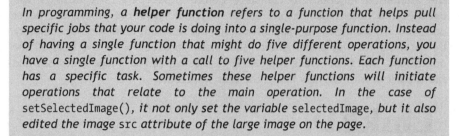

NotED

*In programming, a **helper function** refers to a function that helps pull specific jobs that your code is doing into a single-purpose function. Instead of having a single function that might do five different operations, you have a single function with a call to five helper functions. Each function has a specific task. Sometimes these helper functions will initiate operations that relate to the main operation. In the case of* setSelectedImage(), *it not only set the variable* selectedImage, *but it also edited the image* src *attribute of the large image on the page.*

The setTitle() function accepts a single String that is then used to alter the title h1 of the page. The beauty of this function (as well as the other helper functions) is that their functionality is not part of the success callback. You can call these functions independently of each other at any time that you want to use their functionality.

Next I have a setSubtitle() function that does the same thing as setTitle() but instead alters the subtitle h2 element in the page.

My setImages() function expects to receive an array of image information. It's labeled as images because this function is designed to work with the JSON data I'm getting back from the server, which is an array of image references, titles, and subtitles. I could have used a different name for this attribute, of course, but I chose not to because images is more compact. Within this function, I loop through the elements in the array using dojo.forEach. I define an anonymous function for forEach to pass each object into so that I can do further processing. In it, I create a list item element and an image element.

The image element creation is somewhat complex since I am not only setting properties of the image, but I'm also adding an onclick handler that when executed will change the current selected image on the page. I then place the newly created image element inside the list item element I created earlier using dojo.place.

Once the loop finishes processing all the elements, I use dojo.query to select all of them and fade them into the page as a nice effect.

Finally, the setSelectedImage function receives a single image object (based on the JSON data, not an actual image element). It proceeds to fade out the current selected image and uses an onEnd event listener for when the animation is completed. Once it is, it proceeds to set the passed image as the newly selected image and fades it back in. The reason I can't simply call a fade-out animation, set the selected image, and then call a fade-in animation and have it work correctly is because code doesn't stop executing to wait for the animation functions to complete before proceeding. The browser will execute the code much faster, and it will look as if the animations never occurred. To fix this, I wait specifically for the fade-out animation to complete by listening for the onEnd event, and then I proceed with the rest of the operations. The final effect is pleasing to the eye as the image fades out and fades back in with the new image the user selected.

LinkED

You learned how to loop through an array the Dojo way in Chapter 4's "How do you loop through a NodeList or an array?" section.

Error callback

If Dojo is not able to retrieve the data from the URL that you provided, if it is not formed correctly and it is not able to parse the data, or maybe if everything up to that point works but you have an error in your load/success callback, then the error callback is executed. This function is even simpler than load and simply needs a single attribute that will reference an error object. If the function ends up being called, the error object will contain codes and messages that better explain why the error occurred. Generally speaking, most of my error functions look like the following:

```
var galleryData_fail = function(error)
{
  console.log(error);
}
```

One of the common errors you'll get (most likely from mistyping the URL to load the data from) is a 404 error. You'll find this numeric value in error.status when the error callback gets called. The English message will be provided in error.message. This is just one example, though. Table 7-2 describes some common error messages you might receive.

Table 7-2. Common error messages

Error status	Error message	Explanation
400	Bad Request	The response from the server is malformed. This could be caused by your server not formatting the response data correctly.
401	Unauthorized	You don't have permission to access the URL or URI likely because of an invalid username or password.
404	Not Found	The URL or URI you are attempting to use does not exist. Double-check that you typed it correctly.
408	Request Timeout	This means that the server took too long to respond with your request. Sometimes this occurs when the server is overloaded and is not able to provide a response in time.
500	Internal Server Error	This occurs when the web server errors out. Check to make sure it is running properly.

That is to say, they look like that while I'm developing the JavaScript. In these functions, you should actually have other operations that notify the user that the data is not available at this time or do something that shows them they shouldn't be waiting for something to happen anymore. In my photo gallery example, the script may have had issues loading the JSON file, and instead of using console.log, I could have called my helper functions setTitle and setSubtitle to provide a message to the user that the photo gallery was unavailable:

```
var galleryData_fail = function(error)
{
  //console.log(error);
  setTitle("Photo gallery unavailable");
  setSubtitle("Please come back a little later");
}
```

Figure 7-3 shows the resulting error.

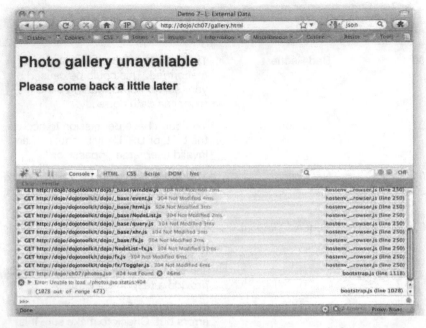

Figure 7-3. An example of what would show if an error occurred when attempting to load the external file

How do you submit a form using Ajax?

One of the most popular reasons that developers open a book on Ajax is to learn how to submit a form to the server without the need of the user sitting through a page refresh. View the demo simpleAdd.html to see a basic form in which you will input two numbers to add together. The arithmetic processing will not come from JavaScript but instead from a small PHP script that will handle the form post.

Note that you will need to have access to a server running PHP in order for this demo to work. Simply make sure that the HTML file and the PHP file are at the same folder level in order for it to process correctly.

LinkED

If you are not familiar with PHP, W3Schools has some great beginning tutorials on this popular dynamic language; see http://www.w3schools.com/php/.

Upon successful installation of the demo files, you'll see a screen that looks like Figure 7-4. You'll know for sure whether the PHP script is running when you receive a valid result, as shown in Figure 7-5.

Figure 7-4. If you loaded the page successfully, your screen should look like this.

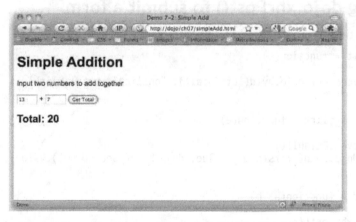

Figure 7-5. Upon inputting two numbers and clicking Get Total, you will see the result appear.

What do you think? I know it's an overly simplified example, but personally submitting forms via Ajax is one of my favorite things to do in JavaScript. It sounds absurd when there are so many things like animations and DOM manipulation, but there is just something righteous about submitting a form without having to wait for the page to reload. I think it has to do with the fact that this is one of the biggest things that makes a user's life on the Internet truly better and more efficient, which in turn creates a better experience. To be honest, I did not used to enjoy submitting forms with Ajax; it was only when I found Dojo that I enjoyed it. Let's go over the code, and you'll see why.

The following is the form:

```
<h1>Simple Addition</h1>
<form id="simpleAdd">
  <p>Input two numbers to add together</p>
  <input id="firstNum" name="firstNum" size="4" /> +
  <input id="secondNum" name="secondNum" size="4" />
  <input id="btnTotal" type="submit" value="Get Total" />
</form>
<h2 id="result">Total: <span></span></h2>
```

The form is very simple; it contains only two text fields and a submit button. The form tag itself is also stripped down to only a single attribute, id, which needs to be referred to in the Ajax call. Finally, there is an h2 to store the result from the server. If you are wondering why I have the empty span tag embedded in the h2, it's because I wanted to be able to refer to a location easily to place the single integer that is returned. I'll explain this more next when I cover the JavaScript portion.

Using dojo.xhrPost() to submit a form

Here is the JavaScript I used to submit the form:

```
var init = function(e)
{
  dojo.connect(dojo.byId('btnTotal'), "onclick", total_click);
}

var total_click = function(e)
{
  e.preventDefault();
  add(dojo.byId('firstNum').value, dojo.byId('secondNum').value);
}

var add = function(a, b)
{
  dojo.xhrPost({
    form: 'simpleAdd',
```

```
    url: 'simpleAdd.php',
    load: add_handle,
    handleAs: 'json'
  });
}

var add_handle = function(response, ioArgs)
{
  var total = response.simpleAdd.total;
  dojo.query('#result span')[0].innerHTML = total;
}

dojo.addOnLoad(init);
```

I start with the usual init() function to connect an event listener to the submit button in the form. That listener triggers the total_click() event handler. In this function, I call e.preventDefault() to discontinue the normal event from processing the form in the conventional manner. Even though there is not an action attribute in the form, the default processing page is the page the form resides on. After I stop the event, I call the add() function and pass in the two values from the text fields.

NotED

You can stop events from continuing their default actions by calling event.preventDefault *(assuming* event *is the name of the event variable) or* dojo.stopEvent(event). *This is useful if you want to override the functionality for an event. In the case of a mouse click on a hyperlink, for example, it would prevent the browser from loading the URL in the hyperlink.*

The add() function introduces the first use of dojo.xhrPost(), which is what works the magic of submitting the form data via Ajax to your PHP file. You should be impressed that it required a total of only five short lines to perform the post of an HTML form. First you need to provide a node reference to the form whose data you want to submit to the form attribute. The url attribute is passed the name of the file you want to post the data to. As in the example, this needs to be a server-side file such as Python, PHP, Java, and so on. The next two attributes should look familiar since they are the same ones we used in dojo.xhrGet(). They work the same way.

NotED

In functions such as add(), you would normally want to perform some validation on the values that are being passed in. With the add() function, I would validate that the values a and b were numbers by using the JavaScript function Number() or at least by ensuring that the values there passed are not null values. This helps prevent strange errors that could occur otherwise. Keep in mind, however, the validation performed in the browser is vulnerable to be compromised by the user, so it is best that you have the same validation on the server side as well. That means in your PHP file that processes the arithmetic, you would ensure that the values were not empty/null and that they were valid numbers.

LinkED

Unless you have seen how this is done in straight JavaScript (sans Dojo), this may be expected from Dojo. Let me show you what this same code would look like in regular JavaScript. Chris Root shows a great example of another simple form submission with plain JavaScript using Ajax; see http://www.devarticles.com/c/a/XML/XML-in-the-Browser-Submitting-forms-using-AJAX/5/.

Take note that with dojo.xhrGet() I'm only receiving data from the server; I'm not sending anything to it. With dojo.xhrPost(), not only does it expect you to send data to the server, but it has the ability to listen for a response from the server. The add_handle() function handles the response from the server whose data is formatted as a JSON string:

```
var add_handle = function(response, ioArgs)
{
  var total = response.simpleAdd.total;
  dojo.query('#result span')[0].innerHTML = total;
}
```

The following is an example of the JSON string you get back from the server:

```
{"simpleAdd":{"total":7}}
```

After I stored the total that I received from the server, I used dojo.query() to get a reference to the span in the result section. I simply set the innerHTML of that blank span to the total, and that's it. We have a real functioning Ajax simple addition calculator. You can conquer the world! By world, I mean this chapter, and by conquer, I mean you now nicely understand the concepts. Don't limit yourself, though, because these Ajax lessons can and most likely *will* completely change the way you build websites.

Making your code reusable

You might be wondering or at least had noticed that in my click handler for the total button, total_click(), I stop the event and then call another function that I pass the values of the text fields to. Why didn't I simply put the code for dojo.xhrPost() inside the total_click() function?

As your sites get more complicated with an increasing amount of JavaScript code, you want to try to eliminate how many times you duplicate similar operations. Be pragmatic about it; don't simply find every possible way to strip down a function to its most basic form. The idea is that if you have some common operations on your page, they should probably be created as separate helper functions, such as my add() function. add() is specifically used for performing addition on two separate numbers, whereas total_click() was specifically created to handle the click (or onclick) event of the total button. Had I put the code from add() into total_click() directly, any time I wanted to add two numbers together, I would have had to call total_click(). This doesn't make sense since I want to pass an event object to total_click() so that I can stop the form from processing.

How do you stay search engine friendly?

Wait, what do you mean? Do you mean to say that if I use Ajax to load data dynamically in my page after it has loaded, search engines won't see the data? The unfortunate truth is, yes. However, if you follow the principles of progressive enhancement, you can help mitigate this issue.

What is progressive enhancement?

At its core, **progressive enhancement** is the paradigm of focusing on the content when building the web page, not the browser. Content is the most important part of a website; without it, there is no point for the user to visit it. With this, you want to make sure that any user who attempts to access it and consume your content should be able to do so without serious issues. I'm not referring to just browser compatibility; it's a lot more than that.

Content

Many times web developers get so excited about the polishing features, how the site will look, or how it will function that they completely lose sight that users need content. When starting to architect your pages, start with the content. Lay it out using semantic standards-based HTML. Make sure that the user can get to all areas of your site with the most basic form of the HTML; this means that without any JavaScript or CSS, they should still be able to gain access to the content your site has to offer.

If you have plans for a hyperlink to do something fancy later when you click it using JavaScript, that's fine, but first make sure it has an actual href defined that points to the base content. You don't want users who have JavaScript disabled to be punished by not allowing them to access the content they came to your site for.

Presentation

Once you have established a solid foundation for your content in how it will be organized and architected for your site, you can then focus on making it look good. This is obviously done with CSS. More or less, this is the step where you'll start to be concerned with browser compatibility. You want to try to support as many browsers as possible to ensure you have and maintain a large audience of users.

Client-side scripting

Only after you have maintained good accessibility to your content and have presented it in a way that is pleasing to your user do you want to now ice the cake with some JavaScript goodness. It is at this time that you can add the special effects, Ajax, and other dynamic JavaScript integration into your site. Don't change the way your content links to itself; be sure to, instead, enhance it. For example, let's say you had a search page on your blog for the user to search the content of your website. In keeping with providing an awesome user experience, you've created an Ajax search so that as the user is typing, suggested queries pop up showing the user complete matches of what they may be searching for. Clicking one then yields the results of that search on the same page without even waiting for a new page refresh. However, this is not a great experience for the user who does not have JavaScript enabled. If you did not follow the guidelines for progressive enhancement, then you likely did not provide an alternative way to get the search results. This means if the user clicks Search, nothing will happen. The page will sit there since the user does not have JavaScript enabled to support your Ajax call.

The progressive enhancement way of doing this would be when you are designing the search form, you provide a form action property in the tag that points to a page that will process the search. Once that is set up and working, then you enhance the form so that if a user has JavaScript, the form will show the results via Ajax instead of a page refresh.

What about search engines?

With all this talk about the user and what the user will experience and see, what about search engines? Well, the examples and instructions provided in this chapter apply to search engines as well. I used users in the examples to put you into the mind-set that you are used to. If you follow the guidelines of progressive enhancement, then your site will be much more compatible and search engine friendly. Search engines will be able to crawl your site by using the normal HTML that you've embedded into the page, allowing them to gain access to the *content* without needing CSS or JavaScript.

Summary

Dynamic data can really improve the way a user perceives and interacts with a website. Although it can provide many benefits, it can also be dangerous if you don't follow some simple concepts of progressive enhancement. Remember that users' and search engines' main reason for coming to your website is because of your content; if you lose sight of that, you'll lose users and search engines. Once you have content, you can add the icing to your site by integrating what you learned in this chapter about working with dynamic data. You learned about the following:

- Loading and working with external data using the Ajax function `dojo.xhrGet`
- Working with callback functions when Ajax requests are successful or when they fail
- Common errors that can occur when making an Ajax request
- Posting a form using the Ajax function `dojo.xhrPost` to a server-side application
- Architecting your sites to follow the guidelines for progressive enhancement

Chapter 8

Widgets

"Genius is one percent inspiration, 99 percent perspiration."

—Thomas Edison

Throughout this whole book, I've demonstrated how Dojo saves you time by doing much of the dirty work of writing JavaScript for you, which in turn gives you more time to focus on your project's requirements. Dojo's library of prebuilt widgets and its widget framework, collectively known as Dijit, is no exception to this and will further enhance your productivity when it comes to building forms, layouts, containers, and applications on your websites.

How does Dijit promote code reusability?

There's a common saying that good programmers are lazy. I find this to be quite true. In the case of programming, lazy is not a bad attribute to have (well, until it becomes unethical). In the realm of web applications and rich Internet applications (RIAs), you want to try to reuse as much code as possible. At the same time, you want your users to be at home with your applications and should not be confused by how certain controls in your forms work.

Traditionally, providing "nice-to-haves" for the user, such as friendly notifications and easy-to-use inputs, meant that your web applications would cost more to develop. For example, if you've ever had to program a form that required client-side validation of the data, I'm sure you would be the first to agree that it is time-consuming and monotonous to write even the simplest validation algorithms. In addition, if you want your forms to be aesthetically pleasing, well, that's a whole other issue that involves good CSS styling.

NotED

Good programmers are lazy. They are constantly looking for ways to reuse existing code that they or somebody else has written before to accomplish the task at hand. If they see fit to write a function or class that will provide functionality to not only fix the current problem but future ones as well, they will. You should consider this especially if you see the possibility of the requirement coming up once again. For instance, form validation is a common requirement that websites have. Dojo provides reusable code in its form widgets to accommodate client-side validation for you using simple methods and techniques.

All of this is fine and would be expected in a well-developed web application. The problem is, this type of work takes your mind away from the real task at hand, which is developing the code for your client's requirements. I can't tell you how many times I personally have gotten distracted for numerous hours writing good client-side or server-side validation code. At the end, I still wasn't truly happy with my results.

The Dijit library was created to help, if not completely, solve all these issues. You see, widgets that are bundled with Dojo are all related to each other in that they all use a library of components that work together as a sort of a widget framework. This ensures that all the widgets that are created follow similar patterns and also can be packaged up easily and used anywhere on your site.

For example, let's say you had some sort of alert box that popped up notifying the user about something on a website; maybe it's an alert to update their profile. You'll most likely want to use that type of alert dialog box somewhere else on the site but with a different message, such as letting users know they need to be logged in before they perform an action. This code does not have to exist twice. Instead, you can create a widget that would have generic parameters for you to pass to it, and it will display the alert with those parameters. Examples of such parameters might be the title, message, icon, buttons, or something similar.

Accessibility

Built with screen readers and keyboard navigation in mind, Dijit has built-in accessibility for your users. With the support of high-contrast modes, widgets can still be used appropriately for those with visual disabilities. In addition, for the hearing-impaired users, screen readers will read Dijit components not as their tag name but by the name of the actual component.

LinkED

For a crash course on accessibility as it applies to the Web, check out A List Apart's article "What is Web Accessibility?" at http://www.alistapart.com/articles/wiwa/. *For the not so faint of heart, you can read the W3C's guidelines and articles on its Web Accessibility Initiative (WAI) website; see* http://www.w3.org/WAI/.

International support

Up to this point, the features provided in Dijit already save you countless hours of development; this next one is a biggie for the sites you build that need to reach users from around the globe. Dijit fully supports more than 100 languages and is completely internationalized. Not only does this mean that your international users will be able to read and understand what the widgets say, but it also means that cultural support and reading directions are built in to accommodate special cases, such as where calendars are different from the Gregorian calendar or where text is read from right to left, such as Hebrew.

With the complexity of Dijit and everything that it offers, you might be thinking that it is difficult to use. I would be misleading you if that was true. Dijit widgets are probably some of the easiest things to implement into your pages out of the whole Dojo toolkit.

How do widgets get implemented?

The term **widgets** is somewhat overused these days. However, most of the time it refers to a module that works like a mini-application. I use the term **application** loosely in this case, because a widget is often part of a much larger application. The idea, however, is that it encapsulates all of its functionality, styling, properties, and actions in a single module. That sounds a lot like a class, doesn't it? In Dojo, widgets are normal JavaScript classes.

Dojo is unique amongst JavaScript toolkits in that it allows widgets (especially user interface widgets such as form elements) to be created using HTML markup. This is in lieu of what some may see as a more complicated, albeit more standard, approach using JavaScript instantiation. They are certainly not limited to a markup approach because any widget is actually based on a JavaScript class and therefore can still be instantiated as such. Let's look at these options in more detail.

NotED

Instantiation is the term used to describe when you create a new instance of an object from a class. Remember, a class is like a blueprint for how an object should behave and what kinds of properties it should have. The actual structure of it is created when you create a new instance of the class.

Using HTML markup

Being able to instantiate JavaScript-based widgets via HTML is pretty unique to Dojo. The HTML tags that are used are still the standard HTML tags that you've always used. The difference is that you use a few new attributes depending on the widget that you want to use. An example of a widget in markup may look like the following:

```
<script type="text/javascript">
  dojo.require('dijit.form.ValidationTextBox');
</script>
<input id="firstName" type="text" name="firstName"
            dojoType="dijit.form.ValidationTextBox"
            trim="true"
            required="true"
            invalidMessage="Please provide a first name">
```

Even when you use HTML markup to instantiate classes and widgets, you still need to put a require statement somewhere in your code for the class that implements the widget; otherwise, Dojo will not be able to find it. In this example, I require *dijit.form.ValidationTextBox*, because this is what I'm using in the input element.

Even though you don't know much about widgets at this point, you can probably already guess some of the features this widget supports. dojoType and trim may be foreign to you, but required should give the clue that I want users to fill out this field before they submit the form. invalidMessage is the message I display to the user if the data entered is not valid according to the widget's rules. In this case, the only validation rules that I enforce on the user for the previous code is simply that they provide a firstName. You can see this is the case with the required attribute. However, required is only one validation. You can define other types of more complex validations by using the attribute regExp to provide a regular expression that the value adheres to.

NotED

Regular expressions are special patterns to compare text to see whether it follows that particular pattern. Most programming languages implement some sort of regular expression (or regex) evaluation; almost all of them that do implement the expressions in a very similar way, so you can likely look at one regex in one programming language and apply it to another with little changes. Regex formation can be very simple and also very complex. You can see some examples on Wikipedia; see http://en.wikipedia.org/wiki/Regular_expression_examples.

Before I discuss in more detail the nomenclature of widgets and how to use them, I'll go over how Dojo interprets these special attributes in the tags and magically creates rich, beautiful widgets.

The Dojo parser

The **parser** is a class that, when included and run on the page, will work out which HTML tags contain the special dojoType attribute. If a tag contains this attribute, then the parser will treat it as a Dojo-powered widget. What it actually does is match the widget up to a specific Dojo class based on the dot notation value in dojoType.

To bring the parser into a page and make it run after the page is loaded, you'll want to provide the attribute parseOnLoad and set it to true in the djConfig variable.

```
var djConfig = {parseOnLoad:true}
```

or

```
<script type="text/javascript" src="dojo.js"
  djConfig="parseOnLoad: true"></script>
```

After that, make sure you require the parser in your next script block:

```
dojo.require("dojo.parser");
```

ExplainED

The djConfig *variable is a JavaScript object literal that you define before the* script *tag that loads Dojo. It allows you to define a certain configuration for the toolkit so it knows how you want it to run on the page. You can do things such as put Dojo in debugging mode, parse the page for Dojo widgets, or set the locale, just to name a few. Don't forget that this doesn't have to be defined as a separate variable; you can also use the* djConfig *attribute to provide a comma-separated list of name-value pairs using a semicolon as well.*

Once the DOM has completed loading, the parsing engine will run and go through all the HTML tags on the page looking for the dojoType attribute. At this point, it uses the namespace and class name contained in the dojoType attribute of an element to search for classes with that name. Keep in mind that it will search for any class with this name, not just classes that are Dijit widgets. Once it finds a match for the class, it will instantiate it and pass the attributes of the tag to the class to be used as internal attributes. When the parser does this, it will also do some light datatype conversions to try to make sure the data getting passed is the same datatype that the widget is expecting. Figure 8-1 illustrates this. Every widget has an actual function that sets it up called the **constructor**. The widget itself may have certain properties that can be set. Whether those properties are Strings, Integers, Booleans, or similar, they should be set as such. The problem is, the only way you can pass those properties to the widget through HTML markup is via an attribute.

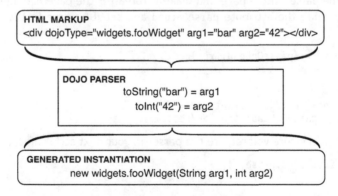

Figure 8-1. The process of light datatype conversions that the Dojo parser performs on widget properties when instantiating widgets

When the parser comes across a widget that it needs to create, it finds the widget class, inspects its properties, and determines what the datatype of those properties are in a very light manner. In other words, it will check for the simple datatypes such as Strings, Integers, or Booleans. Once it does that, it will take the values of the attributes you specified in the HTML markup and will attempt to convert those Strings into the requested datatype where appropriate. If the property should be a Number value, then the Dojo parser will convert the String to a Number, assuming you set it with a numeric value. Once it does this, it will pass these values to the widget constructor, create the widget, and display it on the page.

LinkED

The Dojo parser is even more complex than what I explain here. It would be advantageous for you to read more about how it works and what kinds of things it does in the background to truly gain a full understanding of its inner workings; see http://docs.dojocampus.org/dojo/parser.

Using JavaScript

Now you know that using markup is simply just making the parser do all the instantiation work of a JavaScript class. If you were to instantiate that same widget from the beginning of the "Using HTML markup" section using JavaScript, it would look like the following:

```
<script type="text/javascript">
var txtbox = new dijit.form.ValidationTextBox({
  trim: "true",
  required: "true",
  invalidMessage: "Please provide a first name"
}, "firstName");
</script>
<input id="firstName"></input>
```

In the case of instantiating widgets, you will notice that after I pass an object of attributes for the first parameter, the second parameter is a String. This is the ID of the node you want to replace with the widget. The node I wanted replaced is my input element with an ID of firstName and thus is the last argument of my instantiation code.

Pros and cons

There are of course pros and cons to each approach:

- The markup is easy to implement.
- The markup is comfortable for designers to work with without having to know JavaScript.
- JavaScript supports instantiating with more data types than just Strings.
- The markup technically does not validate with the HTML 4 specification.
- JavaScript instantiation enforces more programming-like principles of JavaScript object creation and is favored among programmers.
- JavaScript allows the widget to be instantiated in a separate JavaScript file outside the HTML file.
- The markup allows easy degradation for browsers that don't support JavaScript.

How do you create powerful forms?

Although Dijit offers so many different types of rich widgets, from this point on to the end of the chapter, I'll mainly focus on the ones that will be used often in forms (with a color picker thrown in for good measure). Figures 8-2 through 8-6 show a few others that are available. You can see all of these and more at http://www.dojocampus.com.

The HTML markup for an inline edit widget, as shown in Figure 8-2 and Figure 8-3, could look like this:

```
<span dojoType="dijit.InlineEditBox" editor="dijit.form.TextBox"
  width="250px" title="editableText">
    Click me, I'm editable!
</span>
```

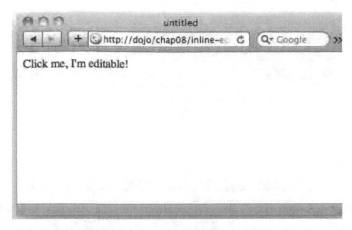

Figure 8-2. An inline editable text area before the user clicks to edit

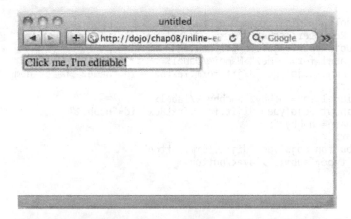

Figure 8-3. An inline editable text area after the user has clicked it to edit

The HTML markup for a tooltip widget, as shown in Figure 8-4, could look like this:

```
<button id="buttonId" dojoType="dijit.form.Button"
  style="position:relative;top:30px;">
    Longanimity
</button>
<div dojoType="dijit.Tooltip" connectId="buttonId" position="['above']">
    a <i>disposition</i> to bear injuries patiently :
    <b>forbearance</b>
</div>
```

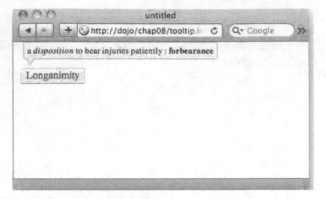

Figure 8-4. Tooltip widget. The tooltip is shown after the user clicks the button.

The HTML markup for a tooltip dialog box, as shown in Figure 8-5, may look like this:

```
<div dojoType="dijit.form.DropDownButton">
  <span>Register</span>
  <div dojoType="dijit.TooltipDialog">
      <label for="name2">Name:</label>
      <input dojoType="dijit.form.TextBox" id="name2" name="name2">
      <br>
      <label for="hobby2">Hobby:</label>
      <input dojoType="dijit.form.TextBox" id="hobby2"
       name="hobby2">
      <br>
      <button dojoType="dijit.form.Button"
        type="submit">Save</button>
  </div>
</div>
```

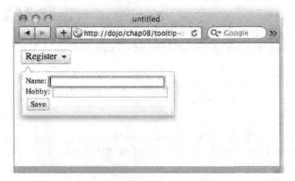

Figure 8-5. Tooltip dialog widget. This is a tooltip that allows you to place more than just text inside.

The HTML markup for a dialog widget, as shown in Figure 8-6, could look like this:

```
<div dojoType="dijit.Dialog" id="formDialog" title="Form Dialog"
execute="alert('submitted w/args:\n' + dojo.toJson(arguments[0],
true));">
    <table>
        <tr>
            <td><label for="name">Name:</label></td>
            <td>
                <input dojoType=dijit.form.TextBox type="text"
                 name="name" id="name">
            </td>
        </tr>
        <tr>
            <td><label for="loc">Location:</label></td>
            <td>
                <input dojoType=dijit.form.TextBox type="text"
                 name="loc" id="loc">
            </td>
        </tr>
        <tr>
            <td>
                <label for="date">Start date:</label>
            </td>
            <td>
                <input dojoType=dijit.form.DateTextBox
                 type="text" name="sdate" id="sdate">
            </td>
        </tr>
        <tr>
            <td>
                <label for="date">End date:</label>
            </td>
            <td>
                <input dojoType=dijit.form.DateTextBox
                 type="text" name="edate" id="edate">
            </td>
        </tr>
        <tr>
            <td>
                <label for="date">Time:</label>
            </td>
            <td>
                <input dojoType=dijit.form.TimeTextBox
                 type="text" name="time" id="time">
            </td>
        </tr>
        <tr>
            <td>
                <label for="desc">Description:</label>
            </td>
```

```
        <td>
            <input dojoType=dijit.form.TextBox type="text"
             name="desc" id="desc">
        </td>
    </tr>
    <tr>
        <td colspan="2" align="center">
            <button dojoType=dijit.form.Button
             type="submit"
             onClick="return dijit.byId('formDialog').isValid();">
                OK
            </button>
        </td>
    </tr>
</table>
</div>
```

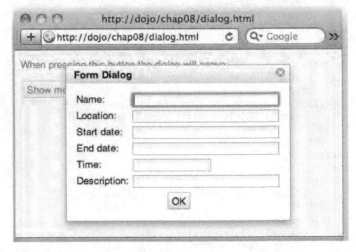

Figure 8-6. A dialog widget that opens after the user clicked a button. Notice the faded background and the pop-up window features.

The HTML markup for an editor widget, as shown in Figure 8-7, could look like this:

```
<div dojoType="dijit.Editor" width="150px" id="editor1"
onChange="console.log('editor1 onChange handler: ' + arguments[0])">
    <p>
        This instance is created from a div directly with default
toolbar and
        plugins
    </p>
</div>
```

Many of Dijit's widgets are based on standard form input elements but have been enhanced to provide the advanced functionality that I have discussed. As such, many of the base tags for using the widgets will be the same as the one you would use without using a Dijit widget. This is also a good thing, because if the JavaScript parser didn't load because of JavaScript being disabled, the form elements would still have their HTML base tags.

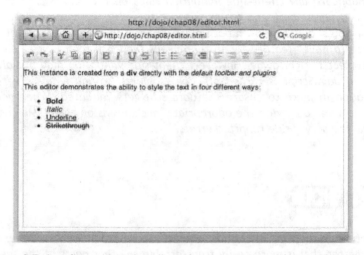

Figure 8-7. An editor widget that allows the user to enter rich text. The value is returned as HTML.

Let's first take a look at an example of various widgets with some simple validation. Open widgets.html from the code download for this chapter. You'll be presented with a few tabs. Each one represents a step in a multistep fictitious form. This simply helps mitigate overloading the user with too much information at one time. The user could click the next tab on their own, but it is more intuitive to provide a *Next* button that will advance to the next tab. Try entering some values in the fields to see how some of them validate.

ExplainED

Any time the user has to input data into your system, you should validate it both on the client side and on the server side. The rule of thumb is that you duplicate any client-side validation rules on the server side as well with a dynamic back-end technology such as PHP, Python, or Java. The reason you should have it in both places is because client-side validation is a "nice to have" feature for instantaneous feedback for the user so they can correct it right away. However, client-side validation may not always work (if JavaScript is turned off, for example), so you need server-side validation in place to ensure the data still gets validated. When you do this, be sure to provide the appropriate mechanisms on the HTML page to handle the server-side reported errors.

NotED

*Sometimes data from an application needs to be combined with other data in a matter that is more easily transferrable to other parts of the system. **Serialization** is a method for doing this. It basically takes a regular data type and converts it to something almost any data system can read or at least be able to move around easily. For instance, a JavaScript object may not be able to be recognized by many systems, but XML could be. A JavaScript object could be serialized into an XML document for easy transferring. Serializing form fields into URL parameters may also be a method of serializing data.*

Standard Dijit form controls

The following are some of the Dijit form controls you'll likely use.

LinkED

Dijit includes built-in themes for all of its widgets as well. You can learn more about them in the "What are widget themes?" section.

- `dijit.form.Form`: This is the form container used to wrap all the Dijit elements. You can use this with a standard form tag to help with validation as well as serializing and deserializing data.

- `dijit.form.Button`: This is similar to an `<input type="button">` or `<button>` element.

- `dijit.form.CurrencyTextBox`: This is a text input box meant to show the data formatted as a valid currency. It's flexible for country-specific currencies.

- `dijit.form.DateTextBox`: This is a special text input box that when clicked provides a pop-up calendar allowing the user to easily find a date and select it.

- `dijit.form.NumberSpinner`: This is a text input box meant specifically for displaying numbers that can be changed with a set of up and down arrows.

- `dijit.form.ValidationTextBox`: This is a basic text box that will validate its data whether it's required or also based on an expression to determine whether the data is valid.

- `dijit.form.TextArea`: This is just like a regular text area except that the height will grow based on the user's input for easier editing.

- `dijit.form.ComboBox`: This is a special select box that allows the user to enter a value if it is not available in the list. The list will autofilter as the user types.

- `dijit.form.FilteringSelect`: This is a special select box that allows the user to enter a value to filter the list, making it easier to find the option they are looking for. It does not allow the user to use a value that is not already in the list.

- `dijit.form.CheckBox`: This is a standard checkbox that offers the styling of the chosen Dijit theme.

- dijit.form.RadioButton: This is a standard radio button that offers the styling of the chosen Dijit theme.
- dijit.layout.TabContainer: Although not a form element per se, TabContainer is an excellent choice to break up forms into mini-steps for the user so as not to overwhelm them.

From the names of the different components, it is usually self-explanatory what that component is used for. The exceptions might be with the ones that are named dijit.form.ComboBox and dijit.form.FilteringSelect. When you read the descriptions in the documentation about what each one does, it sounds like they do the same thing. If you look closer, though, you'll notice that when a user uses FilteringSelect, they can only enter values that already exist in the list. If they were to type a value that is not in the list, the select box would render invalid. This is unlike what ComboBox does, which still allows the user to filter data based on what they type, but if an option is not in the list, the box allows to them to use any value.

dijit.form.Form

A Dijit form works much like any other form, except that it has a few extra pieces of functionality to ease the trouble that forms usually cause in regard to data validation as well as data submission. The following is what I used in my demo for the form:

```
<form id="widgetsForm" dojoType="dijit.form.Form">

  <script type="dojo/method" event="onReset">
      return confirm('Press OK to reset widget values');
  </script>

  <script type="dojo/method" event="onSubmit">

      if(this.validate()){
          return confirm('Form is valid, press OK to submit');
      } else {
          alert('Form contains invalid data.  Please correct first');
          return false;
      }
      return true;
  </script>
<!-- the rest of the form code -->
</form>
```

If you come from a JavaScript background, the previous statement may seem unconventional. However, if you don't, then you actually might feel comfortable with the previous statements. I'll explain the special script tags next, but here I'm setting up a new Dijit form and creating two event handlers for the events of resetting and submitting the form. The confirm function used in both the script blocks is a built-in JavaScript function that will display a dialog box to the user with a message as well as a set of two buttons, *OK* and *Cancel*. If the user clicks *OK*, the confirm function will return true; otherwise, it will return false.

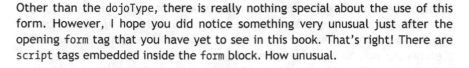

NotED

An alternative that you could provide in such a situation where the user does not have JavaScript enabled in their browser but you still want them to be able to use the form is to use the noscript tag. You could put a duplicate version of the form with normal form tags and input elements between a block of the noscript tags. This would show a standard form and normal submission capabilities to the user. The difference is that you would have to provide server-side validation (which you should do anyway) on the data that is coming in since you won't be able to perform any client-side validation.

Other than the dojoType, there is really nothing special about the use of this form. However, I hope you did notice something very unusual just after the opening form tag that you have yet to see in this book. That's right! There are script tags embedded inside the form block. How unusual.

Scoped script tags

Following 9.420the innovative trends that Dojo lends, the developers created an out-of-the-box solution for constructing a more natural way of handling events. These are special script tags that don't contain the usual type="text/javascript" attribute and value that you are used to seeing. Instead, they contain a dojo/method type. Dojo handles these script blocks just like actual methods as if they were part of the widget's own code. In addition, by providing the event attribute, these tags automatically hook up these methods to the appropriate event you want to listen for on this widget.

If you were to rewrite the onSubmit method for that form in purely JavaScript, it would have looked like the following:

```
<script type="text/javascript">
  var init = function(e)
  {
    dojo.connect(dojo.byId('widgetsForm'), "onsubmit", function(e)
```

```
    {
      if(this.validate()){
          return confirm('Form is valid, press OK to submit');
      } else {
          alert('Form contains invalid data.  Please correct first');
          return false;
      }
      return true;
    });
  }
  dojo.addOnLoad(init);
</script>
```

Although this is good form and everything, the script slightly loses its context with the form. By using a context or scoped script tag, you can clearly see that the JavaScript you write in those dojo/method tags are meant solely for that form and will act upon the data in that form. Plus, they really are scoped with the form so that when you use the this variable, it refers to the form, not the document.

NotED

*JavaScript **scope** refers to where the JavaScript engine looks to find variables and functions that you are calling. For instance, if you create a global variable on a page called* foo, *you could access that variable elsewhere on the page by using* this.foo. *However, if the variable was declared inside a function, it would not be available in the* this *scope; instead, it is available to the scope of the function, and you can access it only when you are executing the function. Putting* script *blocks between HTML elements on the page makes the JavaScript inside execute from the scope of that element. You could add an* onClick *handler to a button in the same manner I did with the form. In that case, the scope would be the* button, *so this would refer to the button DOM element.*

Form validation

Validating form data in the past has always been somewhat of a pain in JavaScript. With Dijit forms, it is made incredibly simple, especially for the simple need of requiring data during input.

Single element validation

The most basic Dijit widget that you'll need to require the user to input data is one of dojoType dijit.form.ValidationTextBox. If you were to use simply dijit.form.TextBox and set the attribute required to true, it would not validate since the Dijit does not inherit the appropriate base Dojo validation classes. You must either use ValidationTextBox or use another widget that inherits ValidationTextBox (such as Number or Currency). This is an example of a simple textbox that requires input:

```
<input id="firstName" type="text" name="firstName"
  dojoType="dijit.form.ValidationTextBox"
  required="true">
```

If the user gave focus to this element by tabbing to it or using their cursor to select it and then left it without entering any data, the color of the box would change and a warning icon would be displayed to notify them that they had invalid input, as you can see in Figure 8-8. At this point, the user could submit the form anyway, ignoring the errors. The only way you can prevent them from doing so is by putting logic in the onSubmit event handler that checks to see whether the Dijit form is valid. If you are using a Dijit form, this is simply done by saying form.validate(), where form is a DOM reference of your Dijit form.

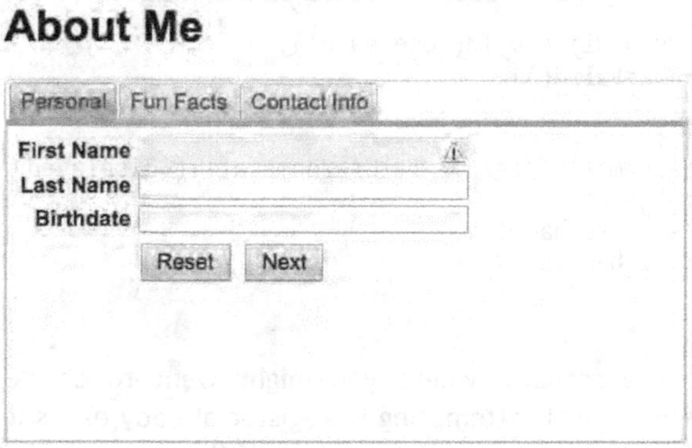

Figure 8-8. A ValidationTextBox notifying the user of an invalid entry (blank input when required)

If you want to provide a message to the user when they clicked the warning icon, then you would modify your code like so:

```
<input id="firstName" type="text" name="firstName"
  dojoType="dijit.form.ValidationTextBox"
```

```
required="true"
invalidMessage="Please provide your first name.">
```

Figure 8-9 demonstrates this type of action.

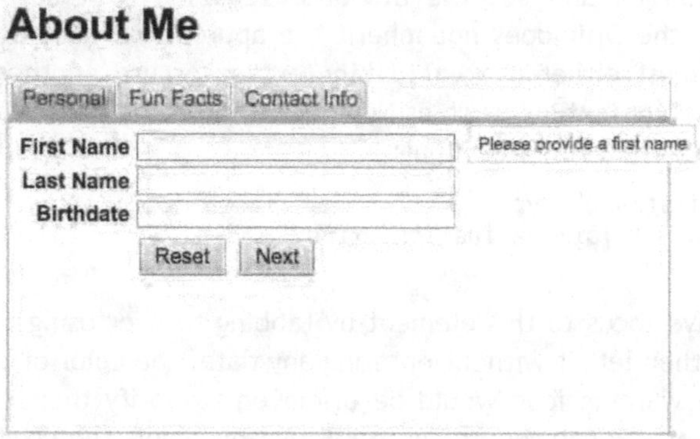

About Me

| Personal | Fun Facts | Contact Info |

First Name		Please provide a first name
Last Name		
Birthdate		

Reset   Next

Figure 8-9. A ValidationTextBox displaying a message to the user when they click the warning icon

If you want to see whether this textbox is valid from JavaScript, you can easily do that as well using the isValid() method on the widget:

```
var txtUsername = dijit.byId('username');
if(txtUsername.isValid())
{
  dojo.xhrGet({
    url: '/username/exists/' + txtUsername.attr('displayedValue');
    handleAs: 'json',
    success: success_handler,
    error: error_handler
  });
}
```

The previous is a scenario where you might want to check whether the username that the user is attempting to register already exists in your system. However, you don't want to send the request if the username is not valid. You first check for its validity, and then you proceed with the Ajax call to see whether the username already exists.

Note that I used dijit.byId() instead of dojo.byId() to get a reference to the widget. This is because I'm getting a reference to a widget and not a DOM node. Widgets are separate from the DOM and contain extra functions and properties. Dojo and Dijit keep track of these instances of widgets automatically, which is why when you call dijit.byId(), you get a reference to the actual Dijit instance, with all the methods and properties available, instead of simply getting the DOM node that is in the document.

Full form validation

By the same token, if you wanted to check whether all the fields in a form are valid, it is as simple as executing the isValid() method on the form widget:

```
var formValid = dijit.byId(' widgetsForm').isValid();
```

This will return a Boolean on the validity of all the form fields. What this will not do, however, is show the user any special messages that indicate whether it was valid. To automatically receive a Boolean and display individual warnings for any invalid fields, simply run the validate() method from the form widget, and any field that is not valid will gently notify the user of their mistakes:

```
var formValid = dijit.byId('widgetsForm').validate();
```

I hope you are seeing the true value of this automated validation. This actually makes programming forms fun.

Validating with regex

It's almost just as simple to validate using regular expressions. You can do this in two ways:

- Supply your own regular expression string to the attribute regExp on a Dijit widget
- Provide a reference to a function that returns a regular expression to the attribute regExpGen on a Dijit widget

The former is what I use for the email address validation on the third tab of the example:

```
<input id="email" type="text" name="email"
  dojoType="dijit.form.ValidationTextBox"
  trim="true"
  regExpGen="dojox.validate.regexp.emailAddress"
  required="true"
  invalidMessage="Invalid email address">
```

Since the function used was external to this file, I had execute the following before this widget:

```
dojo.require("dojox.validate.regexp");
```

You can write your own regular expressions if you are familiar with how to do so. The following is a simple example of a ValidationTextBox using a regular expression:

```
<label>Input a value with letters only</label>
<input id="foo" dojoType="dijit.form.ValidationTextBox"
       regExp="[a-zA-Z]+"/><br/>
<input type="button"
  onclick="alert('Foo is valid: ' + dijit.byId('foo').isValid())"
  value="Submit">
```

The regular expression is the value of regExp, and it is saying to allow any letters A-Z, uppercase or lowercase. Let's say you wanted to allow uppercase letters only; you could modify the regular expression like so:

```
<input id="foo" dojoType="dijit.form.ValidationTextBox"
       regExp="[A-Z]+"/>
```

As soon as the user types in this textbox, it will begin to validate and will show a tooltip error if they are typing invalid data.

If you are not up to writing your own regular expressions, it is best to use the ones that are provided in dojox.validate.regexp or gather some that are provided on the Internet. The following is an example of using one of the validators from dojox.validate.regexp:

```
<label>Input an email address</label>
<input id="foo" dojoType="dijit.form.ValidationTextBox"
       regExpGen="dojox.validate.regexp.emailAddress"/><br/>
<input type="button"
  onclick="alert('Email is valid: ' + dijit.byId('foo').isValid())"
  value="Submit">
```

The functions in dojox.validate.regexp basically generate regular expressions on the fly for the function to use to determine validity. This way, you don't have to be concerned with the actual regex itself and can use a method that is familiar to you. You still need to use dojo.require('dojox.validate.regexp') to load the class that generates those just like you would do anywhere else.

Table 8-1 shows a few others that are available in the dojox.validate.regexp class.

Table 8-1. Regular expression validation functions available in dojox.validate.regexp

Generator	Description
dojox.validate.regexp.emailAddress	Builds a regex that matches an email address.
dojox.validate.regexp.emailAddressList	Builds a regex that matches a list of email addresses.
dojox.validate.regexp.host	Builds a regex that matches a network host. A host is a named host (A-z0-9_ but not starting with -), a domain name, or an IP address, possibly followed by a port number.
dojox.validate.regexp.ipAddress	Builds a regex that matches an IP address. Supports five formats for IPv4: dotted decimal, dotted hex, dotted octal, decimal, and hexadecimal. Supports two formats for IPv6: standard IPv6 and hybrid IPv4/IPv6.
dojox.validate.regexp.numberFormat	Builds a regex to match any sort of number based format. Look at the documentation for this at http://api.dojotoolkit.org/jsdoc /1.3.2/dojox.validate.regexp.num berFormat.
dojox.validate.regexp.url	Builds a regex that matches a URL.

LinkED

Mozilla's Developer Center has a good article on regular expressions as they apply to JavaScript; see https://developer.mozilla.org/ en/Core_JavaScript_1.5_Guide/Regular_Expressions. *In addition, you can find a JavaScript regex tester at* http://regexpal.com/.

What are widget themes?

You probably noticed how slick my demo looked even before testing any of the controls. This is because the elements in my demo were skinned according to a Dijit theme. In this case, the name of the theme is Soria.

All the widgets that are included in the Dijit library are fully compatible with the included themes, and as of this writing, there are three themes. Well-designed widgets should be able to be skinned very easily to make them as flexible as possible for any environment. The beauty of the themes that are included with Dojo is that they are beautiful. Don't take my word for it; see for yourself using the Dijit Theme Tester: http://download.dojotoolkit.org/ release-1.0.0/dojo-release-1.0.0/dijit/themes/themeTester.html. Note that you will only be able to test two of the three themes there: Soria and Tundra.

Once you load that page, look near the bottom, and you'll see a tab named *Alternate Themes*. Clicking this tab will give you the option to choose other built-in themes to test.

Where do I find the theme assets?

All the themes are created simply by a group of image and CSS assets, just like in regular HTML. You can find these pieces for the included themes under dijit/themes/[theme-name] where [theme-name] is either nihilo, soria, or tundra. Figure 8-10 shows a sampling of the CSS files that are used in the Soria Dijit theme.

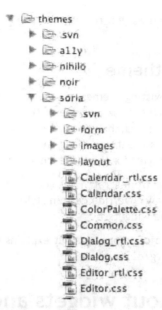

Figure 8-10. A partial listing of the CSS files used in the Soria theme

Using themes

Themes are not used in your code by default. You need to explicitly point to the appropriate theme CSS file and apply a class to your body.

Import the theme CSS file

Just like any other CSS file you are going to use in your page, point to the one for the desired theme:

```
<link rel="stylesheet"
  href="../dojotoolkit/dijit/themes/soria/soria.css" />
```

Apply the class name

So as not to override other styles, you need to explicitly set the body's class to the same name of the theme. This way, the appropriate styles will be used:

```
<body class="soria">
```

That's it. Now all your widgets that you use on the page will automatically inherit the styles of that theme. If you want a new look, all you need to do is change the path in the CSS location and swap out the class name in the body.

Once you've done that, as soon as you refresh the page, you'll see the new style instantly applied.

Creating your own theme

Although you can modify the existing themes or create your own from scratch, that is not within the scope of this book because of the complexity of creating a high-quality theme. Keep in mind, however, that making themes for Dijit components actually just means creating CSS styles. But to make your theme look good, you need to create styles for the different states of a given widget.

If you don't want to create one from scratch yet you are not quite happy with the ones provided, you can always override certain styles by creating new class names and applying them to the widgets.

There is a great resource on DojoCampus.org that explains how to get started; see http://docs.dojocampus.org/dijit-themes.

How do you lay out widgets and other elements?

The Dijit library provides everything you need to create a well-constructed web application. This includes additional widgets that help bypass the complexities and specifics of dealing with laying out components on a page. Dijit includes a package of advanced layout widgets called dijit.layout. Some of these are featured in Table 8-2.

These containers don't need to be used individually; in fact, most of the time they are used in conjunction with each other. In the example form, I needed to use ContentPane with TabContainer to create my tabs, as you'll see next.

Table 8-2. A few layout widgets provided in Dijit

Widget	Description
ContentPane	The most basic of the layout widgets, ContentPane is used to hold content and other widgets as well as display them correctly when used with a TabContainer, BorderContainer, AccordionContainer, and the like. You can kind of think of it like an iframe without it actually being a frame in the page and containing a lot more functionality. This commonly uses a title attribute that parent containers use to label the widgets when displayed on the page.
BorderContainer	This widget is great for creating the skeleton high-level layout of a widget, allowing you to partition its space into five regions: left (leading), right (trailing), top, bottom, and of course, center (which is required). From here, each region can contain any other HTML content as normal.
AccordionContainer	This uses the title attribute from a set of AccordionPane widgets to display a layout resembling that of an accordion. One pane is showing at a time with the others *rolled up* to show only their titles. When the user clicks a title, the previously shown pane rolls up, and the clicked pane rolls out.
TabContainer	This displays a layout container with a set of tabs that represent a set of ContentPane widgets. A tab's label corresponds to the title of a ContentPane, similar to the AccordionContainer and AccordionPane. A single pane is shown at a time based on the selected tab. The user can change the focus of a pane by simply clicking any of the tabs. The focus of a tab can also be set programmatically using the functions in TabContainer, such as forward() or back().

Using dijit.layout.TabContainer

As a developer of websites and applications, you should always be on the lookout for ways to make usability as good as possible. Most users don't like filling out forms, but one of their only motivations is that they will be getting something in return, whether it be a newsletter, an order, or a question answered. However, that doesn't mean you shouldn't put some extra thought into making forms more interesting or at least less confusing and overwhelming for them. A great way to achieve this is to use a tabbed form. In Figures 8-11,

8-12, and 8-13, you'll see three different states that my TabContainer can have based on the tab the user has selected. Note that when a tab is selected, the widget is updated immediately to reflect the change and show the elements in that tab without a separate page refresh.

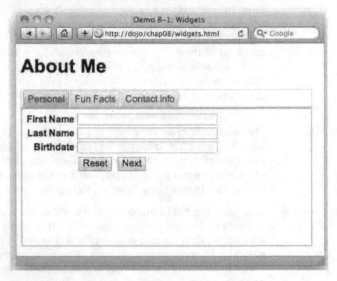

Figure 8-11. The first tab of my multipart form

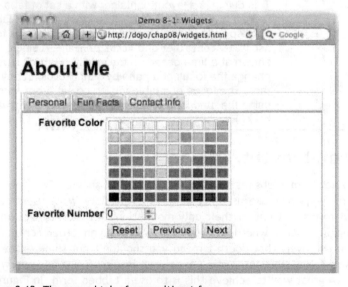

Figure 8-12. The second tab of my multipart form

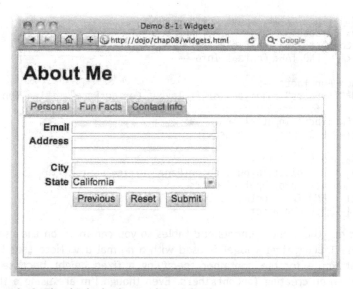

Figure 8-13. The third tab of my multipart form

Tabs are beneficial in a couple of ways. First, they allow you to categorize the type of data that is being entered, thereby further clarifying to the user the type of data that is expected. This pretty much fills the same role as a fieldset would in a form. The second thing tabs are good for is breaking up the fields into manageable, byte-sized pieces (pun intended). As always, don't overuse the tabs. Be sure to think about some high-level categories beforehand that your form elements could fall into. Don't force the use of tabs either if your form is small; they are best used to break up larger forms with multiple categories of data.

LinkED

Fieldsets are special tags that help group form elements into categories that are easier for the user to understand the type of data that is to be entered into the forms. Different browsers have different styles for the fieldsets. You can read more about how to use them and legends at W3Schools.com; see http://www.w3schools.com/TAGS/tag_fieldset.asp.

The following is my TabContainer source code:

```
<div id="tabs" dojoType="dijit.layout.TabContainer"
  style="width: 500px; height: 270px; border: 1px solid #ccc;">
```

```
<div dojoType="dijit.layout.ContentPane"
 title="Personal">
 <!-- Contact info input elements -->
</div><!-- END TAB: Contact Info -->

<!-- TAB: Fun facts -->
<div id="funFacts" dojoType="dijit.layout.ContentPane" title="Fun
Facts">
 <!-- Fun facts input elements -->
</div><!-- END TAB: Fun facts -->

<!-- TAB: Contact Info -->
<div dojoType="dijit.layout.ContentPane" title="Contact Info">
 <!-- Contact info input elements -->
</div><!-- END TAB: Contact Info -->
</div><!-- Tab Container -->
```

I've left out the input elements and tables so you can focus on the use of the tabs. The TabContainer widget is used with a normal div. Note that I have a style attribute for the container specifying a fixed height because this is required when creating TabContainers. Even though I'm are using a theme, I chose to also give it a single-pixel border around the container to separate it from the rest of the page.

Next, I defined a set of three tabs using the ContentPane widget that I mentioned in the table at the beginning of this section. Each ContentPane utilizes the title attribute that will be displayed on the tabs themselves as labels. Also, note that the order of the tabs is reflected in the order they are placed in the TabContainer. The first ContentPane in the TabContainer will be the leftmost tab. The last ContentPane in the TabContainer will be the rightmost tab. Once you have decided on the placement and order of your tabs, it's time to fill them up with actual content. This can be anything that you would place in a div. In my demo, I'm creating a form so each of the panes contains form elements and data input widgets laid out in small tables to keep everything looking tidy.

In another scenario, let's say you were not creating a form but some other feature of the website where the tabs were going to hold a lot more content than just a few elements. You could certainly use the other layout containers inside each tab for an even more controlled layout experience.

> Some would disagree with using tables in a form to lay out form elements since, semantically speaking, tables should have tabular data in them. However, I find for complex forms that require specialized accurate layout of form elements, tables work really well. I would not say the same, however, for laying out entire websites with them.

Using dijit.layout.BorderContainer

Earlier I told you that a BorderContainer is great for laying out the skeleton of a section of your page, or a whole page if you are doing a full-page Ajax web application. Its strength not only lies in the outer skeleton but also in its ability to truly give you control over specialized layouts in your ContentPane. To see what I mean, run the bordercontainer.html demo for this chapter. When you do, you'll notice a very complex layout that gets generated on the page. Figure 8-14 shows you what the demo will look like when it is done loading.

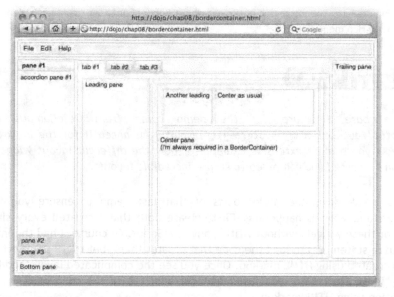

Figure 8-14. A complex layout demonstrating the power of the Dijit layouts and widgets as well as how they can all be used together

Figure 8-15 highlights a MenuBar and some rich MenuBarItem widgets that not only contain a label as normal but also an icon to the left just as you might see in a traditional desktop application.

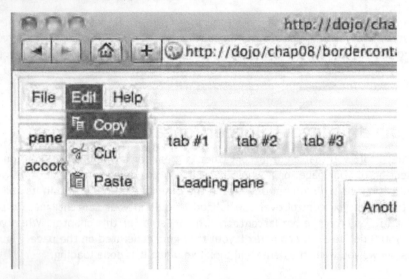

Figure 8-15. The top region of the outermost BorderContainer contains a MenuBar with rich menu items.

LinkED

The base structure for the demo came from DojoCampus at http://docs.dojocampus.org/dijit/layout. *I enhanced it for the book to show you a more extensive example of how the different layout widgets can be nested and combined to create incredible layouts.*

Let's break down the major parts of that last demo to ensure you fully understand what is happening. First, please note that I created every single one of these widgets without writing any JavaScript. Of course, I had the initial require statements to load the code that creates them, but every single widget was created using HTML markup. Once you see the complicated layout and how easy it was to create, you just might get addicted to the concept of widget creation using HTML markup.

After you have loaded the appropriate theme CSS library and the Dojo library, you need to provide the require statements in the head that will load all the components you want to use in the page:

```
<script type="text/javascript">
    dojo.require("dijit.layout.BorderContainer");
    dojo.require("dijit.layout.TabContainer");
    dojo.require("dijit.layout.AccordionContainer");
    dojo.require("dijit.layout.ContentPane");
    dojo.require("dijit.MenuBar");
    dojo.require("dijit.Menu");
    dojo.require("dijit.MenuItem");
    dojo.require("dijit.PopupMenuBarItem");
</script>
```

There is nothing out of the ordinary here. You already know that when these are executed, Dojo loads the appropriate libraries based on what you pass to require.

When you start your body tag, you must make sure to add the name of your theme as the body class; otherwise, the theme won't load. This is a common mistake when you are first starting out with widgets and themes. You'll load the page and work for 15 minutes trying to figure out why you don't see any styling. Most of the time, it's simply because you forgot to put that class name in the body:

```
<body class="tundra ">
```

Next you create the outermost BorderContainer widget that is going to be the exoskeleton of the page:

```
<div dojoType="dijit.layout.BorderContainer"
        style="width: 100%; height: 100%;">
```

It doesn't look like much by itself. But let's take a look at a bird's-eye view of this container with its first-level children:

```
<div dojoType="dijit.layout.BorderContainer"
  style="width: 100%; height: 100%;">
    <div dojoType="dijit.MenuBar" region="top">
      ...
    </div>
    <div dojoType="dijit.layout.AccordionContainer"
      region="leading">
      ...
    </div>
    <div dojoType="dijit.layout.TabContainer" region="center">
      ...
    </div>
    <div dojoType="dijit.layout.ContentPane" region="trailing">
```

```
        Trailing pane
      </div>
      <div dojoType="dijit.layout.ContentPane" region="bottom">
        Bottom pane
      </div>
</div>
```

The BorderContainer widget can hold other layout containers in its main layout. As long as you provide the attribute region and specify either top, leading, center, trailing, or bottom, you'll be good to go. Remember, no matter what regions you use in the BorderContainer, you must always use a center. I used a Dijit MenuBar as the top region since this is where the user will expect to find this type of functionality. The leading or left side of the BorderContainer is created using an AccordionContainer where you have a set of panes that expand and collapse to reveal content. The center pane is a TabContainer that will host a set of three tabs. The trailing or right region uses a simple ContentPane that simply contains the text *Trailing Pane*. And finally, the footer, or bottom pane, is a simple ContentPane as well.

This default setup will actually give you a really good start to creating an intuitive interface for your users. Plus, you have not had to write any JavaScript to create this or write a single line of CSS (well, besides the style of the BorderContainer, but that doesn't count).

Let's take a look at the nifty MenuBar widget:

```
<div dojoType="dijit.MenuBar" id="menu" region="top">
  <div dojoType="dijit.PopupMenuBarItem">
    <span>File</span>
    <div dojoType="dijit.Menu" id="fileMenu">
      <div dojoType="dijit.MenuItem"
        onClick="alert('New File!');">New</div>
      <div dojoType="dijit.MenuItem"
        onClick="alert('Open File!');">Open...</div>
      <div dojoType="dijit.MenuItem"
        onClick="alert('Close File!');">Close</div>
      <div dojoType="dijit.MenuItem"
        onClick="alert('Quit application');">Quit</div>
    </div><!-- fileMenu -->
  </div><!-- popupMenuBarItem -->
  <!-- the edit and help menus go here -->
</div>
```

The root widget of a MenuBar is a dijit.MenuBar. In this case, you also apply the region attribute of top so as to position it at the top of your BorderContainer. From here, for each new menu you want to create, you need to create a new PopupMenuBarItem widget. This is the container that will hold all the individual items. Use the `label` attribute to provide the text that will be the name of the menu, such as File, Edit, Help, and so on.

Between the `div` tags for the `dijit.PopupMenuBarItem` is a set of `MenuItem` widgets that are wrapped in a `dijit.Menu` widget. This combination creates the actual menu content itself. Each `MenuItem` div contains the text that you want to display in the menu. These work just like any other interactive elements on the page and therefore can have event handlers registered to listen for clicks or mouseover events. In my case, I'm simply listening for the `onClick` event to alert the user that they clicked that item.

NotED

MenuItem will also accept an attribute called `iconClass` *where you can provide the appropriate CSS classes that will show an icon for that item. You can see an example of this in the demo source code for the Edit menu.*

The `MenuItem` widgets can also be disabled so the user can't click them. For instance, if there is nothing to save on the page, you could disable the Save `MenuItem` by setting its `disabled` attribute to true.

Moving on to the `AccordionContainer`, the following is the source code:

```
<div dojoType="dijit.layout.AccordionContainer"
  region="leading">
    <div dojoType="dijit.layout.ContentPane" title="pane #1">
        accordion pane #1
    </div>
    <div dojoType="dijit.layout.ContentPane" title="pane #2">
        accordion pane #2
    </div>
    <div dojoType="dijit.layout.ContentPane" title="pane #3">
        accordion pane #3
    </div>
</div>
```

Again, you'll see that since this is one of the children of the main `BorderContainer`, you provide a `region` attribute to specify that you want this `AccordionContainer` to be positioned on the left side of the container. Creating the individual "ribs" of the accordion is quite easy. For every rib you want, simply provide a new `ContentPane`; it's that simple. The same rules applied as for the `TabContainer`, and the order you provide the `ContentPanes` is the order they will appear in the `AccordionContainer`. Provide a `title` attribute to give a textual value of each rib so the user knows what they are going to expand.

One of the cool attributes of this particular widget is an attribute that you can add to the AccordionContainer called persist. If you set this to true, the selected pane will persist even if you leave the page and come back. It does this by setting a cookie in the user's browser that maintains the state. The beauty of this is that you don't have to write the code to manage the cookie; you simply tell it to persist or not.

Next I'll focus on the TabContainer, which renders the center region of the main BorderContainer:

```
<div dojoType="dijit.layout.TabContainer" region="center">
    <div dojoType="dijit.layout.ContentPane" title="tab #1">
        <div dojoType="dijit.layout.BorderContainer">
          <div dojoType="dijit.layout.ContentPane"
            region="leading" style="width:25%">
            Leading pane
          </div>
          <div dojoType="dijit.layout.ContentPane"
            region="center">
            <div dojoType="dijit.layout.BorderContainer">
              <div dojoType="dijit.layout.ContentPane"
                region="top" style="height:25%">
                <div dojoType="dijit.layout.BorderContainer"
                  <div
                    dojoType="dijit.layout.ContentPane"
                    region="leading">
                    Another leading
                  </div>
                  <div
                    dojoType="dijit.layout.ContentPane"
                    region="center">
                    Center as usual
                  </div>
                </div>
              </div>
              <div dojoType="dijit.layout.ContentPane"
                region="center">
                Center pane<br/>
                (I'm always required in a BorderContainer)
              </div>
            </div>
          </div>
        </div>
    </div>
    <div dojoType="dijit.layout.ContentPane" title="tab #2">
        tab pane #2
    </div>
    <div dojoType="dijit.layout.ContentPane" title="tab #3">
        tab pane #3
    </div>
</div>
```

This may seem like a lot of code, but if you look over it, it shouldn't be unfamiliar to you. When you first start out with Dijit's layout components, you may have to start with your most basic layout, test it in your browser to see what it looks like, and then work on implementing the next part of it. Otherwise, if you try to implement the entire layout and all the subpieces in one shot, the code will get confusing, and you might have a hard time visualizing it. Once you get real good at working with the layouts, you'll be able to visualize what each piece is doing. This is one of the things I like about creating these layouts via markup because it is easier to visualize how each piece is nested in each other vs. gazing at awkward JavaScript code to create these complex layouts. Trust me, you don't want to go there.

The ContentPane widgets inside a TabContainer work just like they do inside the AccordionContainer. Each new ContentPane that is a child of TabContainer becomes a new tab. Provide a title for the ContentPane to display a label in the tab informing the user the subject of that tab.

The first tab in the previous code has a rather complex layout compared to the other tabs. I wanted to demonstrate how you can nest layouts inside of layouts inside of layouts, and so on. On this tab, I create another BorderContainer that has a leading region and a center region. Inside the center region I have another BorderContainer that has a top region and a center region. Inside that top region I have yet another BorderContainer that defines a leading region and a center region. Although this layout may seem absurd, it's actually not out of the ordinary for larger applications that have a lot of moving pars, figuratively speaking.

Refactoring your layout

After coding the previous demo, I realized that I did not write my layouts in the most efficient way for the first tab of the TabContainer. Instead of fixing it and showing it to you fixed, I decided to run through how you can check your layouts to see whether refactoring could optimize them. Refactoring is simply taking something and changing it a bit, ideally for the better. Before we proceed, take a look at the previous code again and see whether you notice what I could change.

Did you see it? Well, as you saw in the main exoskeleton BorderContainer, you can use other layouts besides just ContentPane widgets to create the different regions of the BorderContainer. With that, it's obvious that I could have done this in the layout for the first tab. In my original example, I was creating ContentPanes for each region and then putting BorderContainer widgets inside the ContentPane. The issue here is that I have extra outer containers that I don't need. I'll give you a simpler example. The first BorderContainer that I put inside the tab currently has two ContentPane widgets defined. Inside the center region ContentPane, I define another BorderContainer. Instead of defining the center region as a ContentPane, I should have implemented a BorderContainer. This is the first refactoring. The original code looked like this:

```
<div dojoType="dijit.layout.ContentPane" title="tab #1">
    <div dojoType="dijit.layout.BorderContainer">
      <div dojoType="dijit.layout.ContentPane"
        region="leading" style="width:25%">
        Leading pane
      </div>
      <div dojoType="dijit.layout.ContentPane"
        region="center">
        <div dojoType="dijit.layout.BorderContainer">
        ...
        </div>
      </div>
    </div>
</div>
```

The new, refactored version looks like this:

```
<div dojoType="dijit.layout.ContentPane" title="tab #1">
    <div dojoType="dijit.layout.BorderContainer">
      <div dojoType="dijit.layout.ContentPane"
        region="leading" style="width:25%">
        Leading pane
      </div>
      <div dojoType="dijit.layout.BorderContainer"
          region="center">
...
      </div>
    </div>
</div>
```

With this refactoring, I saved two lines of code that I don't need. That's not a big deal in itself, but when you write verbose code like this many times in the page, it creates an unnecessary complicated sea of tags. Continuing with this same effort, I will go ahead and refactor the deeper nested ContentPane widgets that contain BorderContainer widgets for the BorderContainer widgets to be the regions and not the extra ContentPane.

When all is said and done, the final refactored code is as follows:

```
<div dojoType="dijit.layout.BorderContainer"
 title="tab #1">
  <div dojoType="dijit.layout.ContentPane"
    region="leading" style="width:25%">
    Leading pane
```

```
    </div>
    <div dojoType="dijit.layout.BorderContainer"
        region="center">
      <div dojoType="dijit.layout.BorderContainer"
        region="top" style="height:25%">
        <div
          dojoType="dijit.layout.ContentPane"
          region="leading">
          Another leading
        </div>
        <div
          dojoType="dijit.layout.ContentPane"
          region="center">
          Center as usual
        </div>
      </div>
      <div dojoType="dijit.layout.ContentPane"
        region="center">
        Center pane<br/>
        (I'm always required in a BorderContainer)
      </div>
    </div>
```

It may not look like I shaved off much, but in total I removed six additional HTML tags that did not need to be there. This includes me using that BorderContainer that was inside the tab #1 ContentPane and making it the actual container for tab #1.

Summary

The Dijit widget library is a huge asset to the Dojo Toolkit. It provides so many great and powerful features that many JavaScript libraries cannot match. Combine that with the ease of implementation by using HTML markup, customizable layouts, and beautiful themes, and you've got yourself an incredible platform for creating advanced Ajax applications and websites. In this chapter, you learned about the following:

- How Dijit promotes code reusability by allowing you to create encapsulated widgets

- How the Dojo parser brings widgets into your page via HTML markup

- Dijit's extensive form element library and framework that includes easy hooks into prefabricated validation and support for custom validation using regular expressions

- How Dijit themes can make boring HTML forms and widgets looks sparkly and fresh
- How to lay out widgets and other HTML elements using the library of Dijit layout widgets
- How to refactor your layout widget code

Chapter 9

Where to Go from Here

I hope this has been a great journey for you and you have learned how to rethink the way you design and develop for the Web. Leveraging the Dojo Toolkit in your projects will help you develop modern, rich websites that your users will enjoy revisiting and using.

Everything you have learned in this book has given you a great foundation and understanding of JavaScript and Dojo. This will certainly allow you to do a lot and enhance your web projects. However, if you are willing to invest the time, there is even more to learn about Dojo. The upcoming concepts are not for the faint of heart. They cover advanced programming concepts and technologies. That's not to say that the chapter is dull; in fact, these topics are some of my favorite to talk about. I'll cover the following:

- Techniques for optimizing your code before it goes live
- Creating JavaScript classes the Dojo way
- Extending Dojo widgets
- A brief introduction to DojoX, the future of Dojo
- Deploying desktop applications powered by Dojo and Adobe AIR
- Server-side projects that bundle Dojo, such as Spring, Django, and Zend PHP Framework

How do I optimize my JavaScript code?

When users visit a site, all they see is a page loading before their eyes. They may notice individual graphics loading as well, but that's about it. Most users don't understand that so much more is being loaded and downloaded from the server at the same time, such as CSS and JavaScript files. Combine these files with the HTML, images, SWFs, or whatever else is on your page—the more files you have, the longer the page is going to take to finish loading.

You are likely already familiar with optimization techniques for images in that if you are working with a JPEG file, you can make it download faster by reducing its quality, changing the size of the image, and using other techniques. In the same manner, you can also optimize the JavaScript code to make it download more quickly from the server. In regard to JavaScript (and CSS), this process is known as **minification**.

JavaScript minification

Although not an exact science, you can perform minification in a couple of ways depending on the tool you use to minify your code. In addition, most tools offer configurations to choose what it will do to your code to minify it. Dojo provides a tool called ShrinkSafe to achieve a few main things:

- Remove all whitespace (except for line breaks)
- Shorten variable names
- Remove comments
- Do all this without hurting your code so that it will still work

During development, we as programmers use the elements removed by ShrinkSafe to make it easier for other humans or programmers to read the code. Once you deploy your JavaScript to an actual web server, there is no need to make your JavaScript readable by humans anymore, only by the browser. By doing this, you can greatly compact the size of your JavaScript source files. This brings up an additional point: automated minification can be applied only to JavaScript source files (files ending with .js). It cannot be easily applied to JavaScript that is inline with your web page—such as the JavaScript between script tags. This is a good practice to follow anyway. If you can, try to have as much JavaScript code in external files as you can. Not only will this help in this process, but it is good practice to separate your page logic from your page view.

The following is an example of a standard JavaScript statement that is unminified:

```
var keydown_handler = function(event)
{
  var keys = dojo.keys;
  var num = dojo.byId('num');
  // switch case to determine the
  // key that was pressed
  switch(event.keyCode)
  {
    case keys.UP_ARROW:
      num.value++;
```

```
        break;
    case keys.DOWN_ARROW:
        num.value--;
        break;
    default:
    }
}
```

The following is what that same code looks like once it has been minified. In the file itself, this code is actually all on one line. I had to break it up to make it fit on the book's page:

```
var keydown_handler = function(_1){var _2=dojo.keys;var
_3=dojo.byId("num"); ↵
switch(_1.keyCode){case _2.UP_ARROW:_3.value++;break;case _2.DOWN_ARROW: ↵
_3.value--;break;default:}}; ↵
```

Quite a bit is going on here. First you will notice that all the internal variables of the function keydown_handler have been renamed to much shorter names such as _1, _2, and so on. You may be wondering why the keydown_handler name was not renamed; this is because it is a global name, and had it changed, all your references to the function call would have broken as well. Another thing you will notice is that all the code is one continuous line.

NotED

Although not required in JavaScript, it is good practice to end all your statements with a semicolon. Failure to do so would cause the previous minified code to break since the statements would be seen as one statement. With semicolons, the JavaScript engine understands the separation of the statements.

Not only does ShrinkSafe shorten variable names, but it even removes the comments in the code. Then the Dojo build comes by and also removes the line breaks to make the output extremely compact. The previous doesn't really show you the true benefits of this process, where file sizes are often decreased by one third; it is simply an illustration of what occurs. With that in mind, you should always try to minify your code to shorten the download time for the user's browser. In addition, timesaving techniques such as gzipping and caching should not be overlooked.

Minifying a JavaScript file with ShrinkSafe

You can send your files through ShrinkSafe in a couple of ways. The first is the easiest and most straightforward but is not efficient if you plan on doing a lot of files or doing the process often.

Online

Over at http://shrinksafe.dojotoolkit.org/, simply upload a few files and click "shrink em!" (see Figure 9-1). The files will then be combined and downloaded.

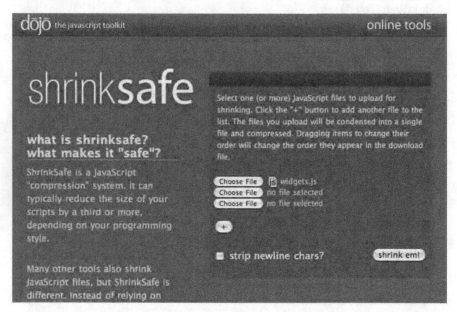

Figure 9-1. ShrinkSafe online upload

Locally

If for some reason you don't like the idea of uploading your code to the server, you can always download your own copy of ShrinkSafe and run a list of files through yourself. The instructions for installing and setting up ShrinkSafe have already been detailed at http://docs.dojocampus.org/shrinksafe/. The reason I won't cover the steps for going this route is because in the next section I talk about how ShrinkSafe is already part of the larger Dojo build system, and you might want to use it there instead.

Dojo build system

ShrinkSafe is a tool in and of itself, but in the Dojo development community, you will see and hear about ShrinkSafe being most often used as one of the pieces of the Dojo build system. If you download the full source of Dojo, you will get the necessary tools to run a build. This basically runs through defined sets of files and not only minifies them but also combines files where defined to do so. I'll provide some high-level explanations of a couple main features that the build system provides.

LinkED

To get a more detailed look at how to use these features, it is best to take a look at the online documentation on this topic at http://docs.dojocampus.org/build/.

Profiles

When you do a build of Dojo, you don't simply pass a list of files for it to process the way you would with ShrinkSafe. Instead, you use what are known as **profiles**. These are JSON files that define certain parameters for how you want your build to be run. Before moving on, I'll explain the concept of **interning**. It is the process of taking the contents of a file and injecting them to a specific point in another file. A great example is with widgets; when they use separate HTML files as their template, the contents of that HTML file get interned into a string variable within the widget's JavaScript code.

Using the build parameters, you can specify whether to have CSS files interned, you can make your JavaScripts cross-domain compatible, you can intern widget HTML template strings, you can optimize options (such as ShrinkSafe), you can strip console statements and comments, and you can build your djConfig settings right into the main file—just to name a few. The profile is also where you define how you want your layers to be built.

Interning your djConfig settings into the build is useful for a couple of reasons. First, it is cleaner to not have your configuration settings inline with the HTML on the page. Second, you don't have to worry about having the same settings on every page since they will already be included in the built Dojo file.

LinkED

You can learn more about build profiles at DojoCampus.org; see http://docs.dojocampus.org/build/profiles.

One of the most useful features of Dojo's build system is the concept of **layers**. A layer is basically a simple JavaScript file that contains a list of dojo.require() functions of things you might commonly need throughout your site. When the build runs, it will take that file and intern all the JavaScript classes for each dojo.require() method directly into a single file.

The top reason to use layers is to limit the amount of extra remote calls Dojo needs to make to fetch classes by way of the dojo.require() method. The concept is fairly simple, but actually implementing it is a bit more complex and requires a good look at the online documentation.

LinkED

There are a couple of great resources that talk about creating layers for a Dojo build. The first is a video demo by Peter Higgins at DojoCampus.org; see http://dojocampus.org/content/2008/05/26/dojo-build-201-layers-and-css-optimizing-builds/.

The second is referring to the build, but it also talks about layers; see http://docs.dojocampus.org/build/.

Cross-domain support

In JavaScript, you can make XHR calls to a script or resource that exists on the same domain that the calling script is from. However, if you attempt to make a call to a resource at a different domain, browser security regulations prevent you from doing this, unless you use an alternative approach, such as calling that resource from inside a script tag on the page. Within a Dojo build, you can choose whether to do a cross-domain (XD) build. If you do, the XHR functions you've been using don't change, but Dojo will automatically make them work by using the script tag method behind the scenes and transparently to you, the developer. It's pretty slick. Once you do that, you'll be able to access resources on another server without an issue.

Creating your own classes

Throughout this whole book you have been working with premade JavaScript classes. Many features, such as most of the Djit library, come from a class. It is important to understand this concept because it is a fundamental of object-oriented programming. As you develop more complex pages and functionality for your sites, you are going to want to put that functionality into classes to group it together and make it easier to reuse.

Prototype-based programming

JavaScript is a prototype-based programming language. It is still considered to be an object-oriented language, but unlike languages such as C#, C++, or Java, there is no class keyword to define a class. Instead, to create a class in JavaScript, you simply create a function, since classes are functions. To create methods on those classes, you add them to the prototype object in a class to ensure proper inheritance.

ExplainED

The keyword class *is actually a future reserved JavaScript feature and therefore cannot be used as an identifier or a variable name.*

```
var Car = function(type)
{
  this.type = type;
  this.running = false;
}
Car.prototype.start = function()
{
  this.running = true;
  alert("The car started");
}
Car.prototype.stop = function()
{
  this.running = false;
  alert("The car stopped");
}

var ferrari = new Car('Ferrari');
ferrari.start();
```

NotED

If you wanted to clean up the previous code using dojo.extend, *you could fairly easily. Simply define your base class as so:*

```
var Car = function(type)
{
  this.type = type;
  this.running = false;
}
```

You'll notice that I only defined the simple class of Car *without any methods. Then, using* dojo.extend, *I define the different functions by passing in the same of the class I want to extend, followed by an object literal of function definitions:*

```
dojo.extend(Car, {
  start: function() {
  this.running = true;
  alert("The car started");
  },
  stop: function() {
  this.running = false;
  alert("The car stopped");

  }
}
```

As in my plain JavaScript example, this works by extending an object's prototype.

LinkED

You can read more about the prototype-based programming paradigm and how it compares with class-based models (as well as the languages that use this methodology) on Wikipedia at http://en.wikipedia.org/wiki/Prototype-based_programming. *Also, the Mozilla Developer Center (MDC) has a great article comparing this paradigm,* https://developer.mozilla.org/en/Introduction_to_Object-Oriented_JavaScript.

dojo.delcare

Although the plain JavaScript method for declaring a class is compact and straightforward, if you are wanting to perform some of the more common OO operations and wanting to have some extra value added, then dojo.declare is what you want. declare helps you easily create a class and have it be declared a little more the way you might expect if you are coming from other languages. If you were to rewrite the previous class using Dojo, it would look like the following:

```
dojo.declare("Car", null,
{
  constructor: function(type)
  {
    this.type = type;
    this.running = false;
  },
  start: function()
  {
    this.running = true;
    alert("The car is running");
  },
  stop: function()
  {
    this.running = false;
    alert("The car is stopped");
  }
}
```

It appears to be very close to the same amount of code. What you don't see are the extra pieces that Dojo adds for you to make it more natural to perform standard object-oriented procedures, such as inheritance and encapsulation. Although this may add a little bit of weight to the file size of your application, it's nominal and worth it if you desire a higher level of organization and packaging. For starters, the constructor is separated into its own function to be more explicit. Second, the second parameter of dojo.declare is used to provide an array of classes that you can extend using inheritance. However, in my example, I didn't want to extend any classes, so I provided null since this attribute is required. This makes it incredibly easy to have high-level generic objects and create more specific ones as you go. Additionally, if you are using inheritance, normally in programming you would expect that the superclass's constructor would get called as well before the subclass's did, and with Dojo it does do this for you automatically.

There are many other benefits that Dojo's class declaration functionality provides you that I won't cover here. I highly recommend you read the article at http://docs.dojocampus.org/dojo/declare on DojoCampus.org.

Extending Dijit widgets

ExplainED

If you recall from Chapter 8, Dijit is Dojo's widget library and infrastructure for building widgets, and an incredibly powerful one at that. Dijit components are geared toward being reusable components that you can use in your web applications and sites. At development time, the business logic and view are separated so as to ease development, such that the view can be a separate HTML file referenced by the JavaScript class that the Dijit is represented by. At the time of deployment to production, running a Dojo build will combine these two files into a single JavaScript class, as you learned at the beginning of this chapter.

An understanding of classes as they relate to JavaScript and Dojo is a requirement before you look at extending Dijit widgets. That's because widgets are classes, and as such, their functionality is completely encapsulated. Each widget's class contains internal properties and methods that make it function properly. Additionally, the thing that makes a class a widget is that it specifically inherits the dijit._Widget class. This special class also has internal methods and properties that are specific to widget instantiation, setup, and DOM placement. When any JavaScript/Dojo classes inherit this class, they become widgets since they inherit the Dojo widget properties and methods. In addition, they are registered with the Dijit registry, which is where you'll have access to the set of widgets on a page, as well as convenience functions for manipulating the widgets in bulk.

LinkED

You can use the Dijit registry to manipulate all the Dijit widgets on a page where Dijit is used. You may read more about it on DojoCampus.org via http://docs.dojocampus.org/dijit/registry.

Since you can give any class additional functionality by extending another class, you can extend widgets as well because they are classes. In fact, many of the widgets included in the Dijit library already do this. For instance, dijit.form.TextBox is a simple form input textbox that provides a small amount of additional functionality. However, it doesn't provide any validation of the data that was entered. This is a good thing because if you don't require validation for your form, there is no sense in downloading larger files that enable it. If you do need validation, then you can use dijit.form.ValidationTextBox. This is a perfect example of a widget that has extended another widget. If you open the ValidationTextBox source code, you will see the following statement near the top:

```
dojo.declare(
  "dijit.form.ValidationTextBox",
  dijit.form.TextBox,
  {
    ...
```

This declares a new class of type dijit.form.ValidationTextBox, but the next line below it shows that it is going to inherit dijit.form.TextBox, another Dijit widget. This is an obvious form of code reuse. The developer didn't have to rewrite properties and methods to work with and create a form textbox. They were simply able to use an existing class and add functionality to it, such as validation.

If you needed a special widget or form element that was similar to a Dijit widget but it didn't quite do what you wanted, you could extend it in the same way and create a new widget with all the existing functionality, and you could just start building your new features. For instance, currently there is not a TextBox in the Dijit library that supports placeholder text functionality such as you see in some forms where an example value is shown for that field. Upon the user clicking inside the textbox, the placeholder text is removed, and the user can start typing the actual value. Since it is not available in Dijit already, I've decided to roll my own custom TextBox that supports this. Read the following code line by line, and try to digest as much as possible. You'll probably be surprised how much you can understand and figure out:

```
dojo.provide("com.hayes.form.TextBox");

dojo.require("dijit.form.TextBox");

dojo.declare("com.hayes.form.TextBox",
             [dijit.form.TextBox],
{
  placeholder: "",
  placeholderColor: "#999",
  textColor: "#000",

  /**
   * Ensure there is not already a value in the field
   * before setting the placeholder
   */
  setPlaceholder: function()
  {
```

```
    if(this.attr('displayedValue').length == 0)
    {
      this.attr('style', 'color:' + this.placeholderColor);
      this.attr('displayedValue', this.placeholder);
    }
  },

  /**
   * Upon the textbox gaining focus
   */
  _onFocus: function()
  {
    this.unsetPlaceholder();
    this.inherited(arguments); // call super
    this.focus();
  },

  /**
   * Upon the textbox losing focus
   */
  _onBlur: function()
  {
    if(this.attr('displayedValue').length == 0)
    {
      this.setPlaceholder();
    }
    this.inherited(arguments); // call super
  },

  /**
   * Drops the placeholder text and returns the textbox
   * to normal
   */
  unsetPlaceholder: function()
  {
    this.attr('style', 'color:' + this.textColor);
    this.attr('displayedValue', '');
  },

  /**
   * Once this widget is created, determine if the placeholder
   * should be set
   */
  postCreate: function()
  {
    if(dojo.trim(this.placeholder).length > 0)
    {
      this.setPlaceholder();
    }
    this.inherited(arguments); // call super
  }
});
```

I'll cover a couple of advanced pieces in this code, so get ready! Before I get into the code, I'll tell you at a high level how I'm going to provide this functionality. One thing I know for sure is that I don't want to create a basic TextBox widget from scratch; I want to use and extend the one that already exists in the Dijit library, dijit.form.TextBox.

Since dijit.form.TextBox is a class, I can extend it by creating a subclass that will inherit all of its functionality in addition to the functionality I will write. With that, dojo.declare is what I want to use since it provides a solid infrastructure for extending classes for accomplishing things such as inheriting properties, methods, and the ability to call the superclass's functions as well. Once I have inherited the TextBox class, I'll override the functions that TextBox has for certain events and drop in my own code to handle the placeholder logic; then I'll call those functions again from the superclass to ensure everything gets set up the way the original class developer intended it. This will make more sense when I explain the code.

After I've done all this, I will have a new class that I can create TextBox widgets from. I'm going to store it in my own namespace called com.hayes.form.TextBox so as not to interfere with the original TextBox in the dijit.form namespace. Without further ado, I'll break down the code from the previous example.

Here are the first few lines:

```
dojo.provide("com.hayes.form.TextBox");
dojo.require("dijit.form.TextBox");
dojo.declare("com.hayes.form.TextBox",
          [dijit.form.TextBox],
{
  ...
```

The first is dojo.provide and basically registers this class with Dojo to handle the loading of the code when needed. This also defines the namespace your class will live in and should be the same value that you use for the first argument of dojo.declare. The second line is the dojo.require statement that you are familiar with. You have to use it to load the TextBox class since you will be extending it. Immediately after this you use the dojo.declare function to define the new class, com.hayes.form.TextBox. The first argument is the name of the class with the full namespace. The second argument is an array of classes that you want to extend. I'm only extending TextBox so my array literal contains only a single class reference. Finally, the third argument is a very large one because it is another object literal where you define all the properties and methods for the class. The next three lines are as follows:

```
placeholder: "",
```

```
placeholderColor: "#999",
textColor: "#000",
```

This is a list of local properties that you want to use in your class. This is the data model for the class. There isn't much here because it's not a very big class. Keep in mind, however, that you will inherit all the properties from the TextBox class as well. In this class you need to store the text that you want as the placeholder. In addition, you store the color of text when the placeholder is shown, as well as the color of text when the user types in the field. The next few lines define the first function for this class.

NotED

You can set the properties defined at the top of a class through tag attributes when a widget is instantiated inline with the HTML via a dojoType *attribute. For instance, if you were to instantiate your placeholder* TextBox *widget using HTML, it would look like the following:*

```
<input dojoType="com.hayes.form.TextBox" placeholder="Your first
name" />
```

If you don't pass a value to a property, the default will be used as defined in the class. For instance, since you didn't pass textColor *in as an attribute, the default of* #000 *would be used instead.*

LinkED

You can see all the methods and properties that a class has in the Dojo API at http://api.dojotoolkit.org/jsdoc/1.3.2/dijit.form.TextBox.

```
**
 * Ensure there is not already a value in the field
 * before setting the placeholder
 */
setPlaceholder: function()
{
  if(this.attr('displayedValue').length == 0)
  {
    this.attr('style', 'color:' + this.placeholderColor);
    this.attr('displayedValue', this.placeholder);
  }
},
```

My setPlaceholder function first checks to make sure there is not already text in the field so it doesn't overwrite it, and if there isn't, it shows the value of the placeholder property. In addition, it also sets the color of the text to the value of placeholderColor, which in this case is gray. The next set of functions is shown here:

```
/**
 * Upon the textbox gaining focus
 */
onFocus: function()
{
  this.unsetPlaceholder();
  this.inherited(arguments); // call super
  this.focus();
},

/**
 * Upon the textbox losing focus
 */
onBlur: function()
{
  if(this.attr('displayedValue').length == 0)
  {
    this.setPlaceholder();
  }
  this.inherited(arguments); // call super
},
```

Any time you see a function name starting with the word *on* followed by something like *Click, MouseOver, Focus,* and others, it means it is an event handler for the event of that name. Since we are concerned only about a single input type, we will have only one event handler for each type of event. In the previous code, these event handlers are actually set up by the superclass, dijit.form.TextBox. In fact, the listeners are created in the constructor of the superclass, as well as the actual functions to handle the event. You must be wondering, then, why do I have them defined as well? The simple reason is that I want to intercept the events to add some functionality in working with the placeholder text. For instance, when the user clicks the textbox, I don't want the placeholder text to be there anymore so the user can edit it without having to delete the placeholder text first. To accomplish this, I need to perform an action upon the user focusing the textbox with the mouse or Tab key. The only way to do this is through the onfocus event.

It's convenient that this event is already being listened to from the superclass, so instead of creating a new event listener for onFocus, I've decided to piggyback on the existing one. The way you do this is to simply write the function the way you would normally but then at some point call the method this.inherited(arguments). What this does is it then calls the superclass's _onFocus method as well to ensure everything gets set up correctly in the way it is supposed for the TextBox widget. By passing in arguments, I'm simply passing the default array of arguments that get passed to a function on to the superclass method.

ExplainED

All JavaScript functions have an arguments array. Whether that array is empty depends on whether any variables were passed in. Each argument that gets passed is a new element in the arguments array.

Inside my _onFocus function, I call the unsetPlaceholder() function to hide the placeholder. Then I call the superclass _onFocus function via this.inherited(), and finally I give the TextBox focus since at some point when I was testing this, the TextBox would lose focus.

Finally, the _onBlur event handler will get executed when the TextBox *loses* focus. That could be from the user tabbing to the next field or from them using their mouse to click out of the field. Either way, when that occurs, you want to show the placeholder text again if the field is still empty. To do that, you check the attribute displayedValue to ensure its length is equal to zero, and if it is, you show the placeholder again. Otherwise, you keep the value that is already in there. Any time I was working with the value that was being shown to the user, you'll notice I was checking the property displayedValue as opposed to just value. This is because the widget dijit.form.TextBox has set up this property to be consistent so that when you get this value or set this value, it will reflect in the value of the TextBox. I know that may not make a lot of sense, but because of the order of operations that the widget provides and the native value element is not part of the widget's data model, a widget-created displayedValue needs to exist for better control. Whenever I set or get the value of the TextBox, I need to use displayedValue, not value. If you run the PlaceholderTest.html demo included in the code for this chapter, you'll be able to see this TextBox work. The code that I used to instantiate in my test is as follows:

```
<input dojoType="TextBox" placeholder="Your first name"/>
```

I didn't use a full namespace to call the TextBox in dojoType because I had the source .js file sitting at the same level as the test. Figure 9-2 shows the widget with the placeholder text showing, and Figure 9-3 shows the widget after I entered some text.

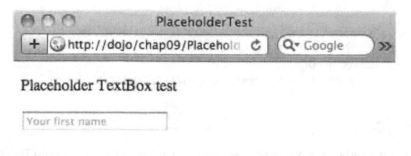

Figure 9-2. Placeholder TextBox test showing the placeholder text

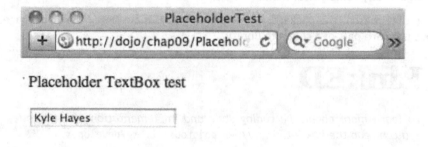

Figure 9-3. Placeholder TextBox test showing an entered value

You'll want to read more about creating widgets from scratch before learning to extend them. Here are a couple of links to help you get started:

- Writing Your Own Widget:
  http://docs.dojocampus.org/quickstart/writingWidgets

- Dissecting Dijit:
  http://www.sitepen.com/blog/2007/11/13/dissecting-dijit/

DojoX

DojoX is another one of the libraries that is included with the full Dojo Toolkit. It also includes special utility functions, classes, packages, and widgets. Why aren't they integrated into the other libraries? It's because the files that are part of DojoX are fairly new and are considered to be experimental and have not been fully tested to comply with Dojo's strict standards for stability and scalability. At the same time, the community still may want to use this functionality if it works well enough for them. In addition to new code, DojoX is used as a place for plug-ins that other developers have created to work with Dojo and don't have a place to live in the other libraries. Also, widgets that don't comply with A11y standards will be placed in here as well since Dijit widgets fully comply with them.

For that reason, the packages are included in the main Dojo Toolkit package, but they are part of a separate library.

LinkED

To learn more about the coding style and implementation of Dojo code, you can read the links at http://www.dojotoolkit.org/developer.

Now that you are familiar with Dojo, you'll find it quite fun and interesting to start exploring through the code that's available in DojoX. You can do this by simply going through the files that in the /dojox folder from the download and opening them to see what's inside. This folder should be at the same level of your dojo and dijit folders.

The other way to see what's available is by checking out DojoCampus on the topic of DojoX; see http://docs.dojocampus.org/dojox/.

As of this writing, some of what you can find in DojoX is as follows:

- Charting
- Cryptography
- Offline data
- Templating based on Django's templating language
- Special animation effects
- Live JavaScript graphics
- Utilities for working with images
- Layouts
- Validation
- More widgets
- XML utilities
- And much more than I can list here

You can find a lot about DojoX classes simply by going to Google and searching for *DojoX*. You'll also find that if you ask a question in the forums or on the IRC channel such as "Can Dojo do this...?" and it's not available in the core libraries, it may be available as part of DojoX.

Adobe AIR

A few years ago, Adobe Systems saw the need for coupling the power of the Internet and everything it has to offer with desktop applications. Adobe did what Java tried to do in the early phases of the Internet with Java applets and created the Adobe Integrated Runtime (AIR) that allows you to write code in languages you are already familiar with, such as Flash, Flex, ActionScript, or HTML/Ajax, as applications that will run on your user's desktop.

However, don't think that it is just mini web browsers displaying specific web pages. You are able to work with local resources such as file manipulation, drag and drop, local databases, and network detection, just to name a few—all with the power of accessing resources from the Internet. This enables you to build powerful, engaging, and rich applications that will install easily on your user's Mac, Windows PC, or Linux desktop with a single installer.

Since AIR allows you to use existing technologies, it's easy to drop in the Dojo Toolkit with your project and use the same API you are already familiar with. You still work with it in a normal HTML file as always, so it should be easy to get started.

Getting started

Personally, my favorite way to develop AIR apps using HTML and Ajax is with the free Aptana Studio IDE, but you can also use Adobe Dreamweaver or any other IDE/text editor. You can get this full-featured workspace from http://www.aptana.com/studio. If you don't have an existing version of Eclipse, then I recommend you download the Aptana Studio stand-alone version. Otherwise, grab the Aptana Studio plug-in version.

Once you've downloaded and installed Aptana Studio and run it for the first time, it will ask you about some additional Aptana plug-ins you would like to install.

You'll need the *Aptana Adobe AIR 1.5 Development* under *Desktop*, as shown in Figure 9-4.

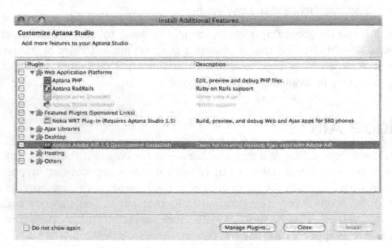

Figure 9-4. Select *Aptana Adobe AIR 1.5 Development* under the *Desktop* category.

You'll also need to choose *Dojo* under *Ajax Libraries*, as shown in Figure 9-5.

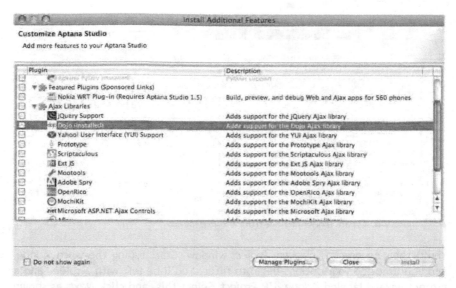

Figure 9-5. Select *Dojo* under the *Ajax Libraries* category.

Once you have completed these steps, the application will go through a series of screens in which it will download the software it needs to install those items. At one point it will prompt you to accept the terms and conditions for installing and using the software, in which you need to agree to proceed. Once you do, it will install the plug-ins and need to restart. Confirm the restart.

Once Aptana restarts, it will pop up the window asking you whether you want to install any plug-ins as it did previously. You can choose to not show this anymore when you start up by selecting the check box at the bottom left of the window, or you can simply close the window.

Creating a desktop project

At this point, Aptana should be up and running. To create a new project, go up to the top menu and choose *File* ➤ *New* ➤ *Project*, as shown in Figure 9-6.

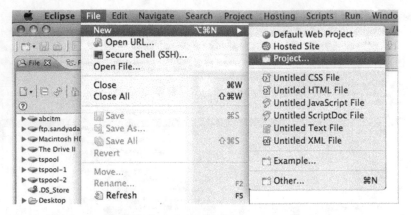

Figure 9-6. Create a new project from the *File* menu.

You'll then be greeted by *New Project* window. Start typing the word *Adobe*, and you'll notice your options begin to filter. You'll be left with a folder and a project wizard labeled *Adobe AIR Project*. Select this, and click *Next*, as shown in Figure 9-7.

Figure 9-7. Choose *Adobe AIR Project* from the *New Project* window.

On the next screen, give your project the name *HelloWorldAIR*, and click *Next*. From here, keep all the defaults on the subsequent screens, and click the *Finish* button at the end. Your new Adobe AIR project will be created, and the main HTML file will open in the editor.

From this point, you can already run the project by going to the *Run* menu and choosing *Run*. Optionally, you can click the play icon in the top toolbar.

The resulting application is a demo provided by Aptana to show you how to execute certain AIR-specific operations such as remote calls and reading local files, as shown in Figure 9-8.

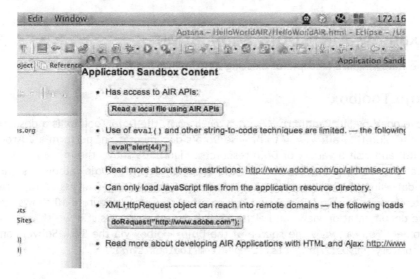

Figure 9-8. Demo AIR Ajax application

You can close the application by normal means on your operating system. When you go back to editing the file, you'll notice it is just simple HTML and JavaScript like you are used to. The only difference is that a special JavaScript file is brought in called AIRAliases.js. This is an API to open up the special desktop operations to your application.

When you created this project, you chose to include the Dojo libraries. To add them to the HTML file, again it is just like before only you'll refer to them as if your project is your root path. To do this, your script tag should look like the following:

```
<script type="text/javascript"
  src="lib/dojo/dojo.js"></script>
```

That's it! You can now work with the Dojo Toolkit in the manner you are familiar with.

LinkED

You'll want to read up on some documentation that is specific to Ajax AIR applications such as what is available at Adobe (http://www.adobe.com/devnet/air/ajax/) and Aptana (http://www.aptana.com/air#content_learn;).

Example AIR + Dojo applications

The following are a couple of existing AIR applications that use Dojo.

Dojo Toolbox

Developed by SitePen (http://www.sitepen.com), the Dojo Toolbox is a desktop application that allows you to browse Dojo's documentation, perform a custom build, and visit a variety of Dojo resources. Figure 9-9 shows the menu for Dojo Toolbox, which allows you to view the documentation for Dojo (albeit it's out-of-date since it covers up to 1.2 at the time of this writing), access a graphical interface for the Dojo Build, and link to other resources. Figure 9-10 shows you the documentation view, and although it is out-of-date, it's still worthwhile to look at. You can view the source of the Dojo Toolbox via the SVN (Subversion) repository (https://projects.sitepen.com/toolbox/svn/).

Figure 9-9. Main menu for the Dojo Toolbox

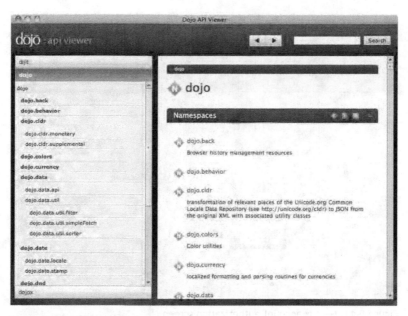

Figure 9-10. API Viewer of the Dojo Toolbox

Queued

Also developed by SitePen, Queued is a desktop application that enables you to easily view and update your Netflix queue (you need to have a Netflix.com account for this application to work). It showcases the use of the Django Template Language support in the Dojo widget system. The application looks very nice and works very well. Figure 9-11 shows the account authorization screen. Netflix (as well as other websites with an open API such as Facebook and Twitter) allows you to interact with the service via clients other than a web browser, but it does require you, the account holder, to authorize that application to access your account for security purposes.

Figure 9-11. Netflix account authorization screen

Figure 9-12 shows the Netflix Top 100 movies and presents a very user-friendly interface for simply adding movies to your queue. All you need to do is click *Add*, and that movie instantly gets added to your queue without ever leaving this screen. Finally, in Figure 9-13 you can see your current queue of movies. In addition, I also show you what it looks like when I roll over the links for any movie—a description and cover art pops up, making it easy for you to see what the movie is about without ever leaving the screen you one. The whole application uses this anywhere you see a link to a movie. You can of course click the link to see a more detailed movie page.

You can download and install the Queued application via http://sitepen.com/labs/queued/.

Figure 9-12. Queued Netflix Top 100 screen

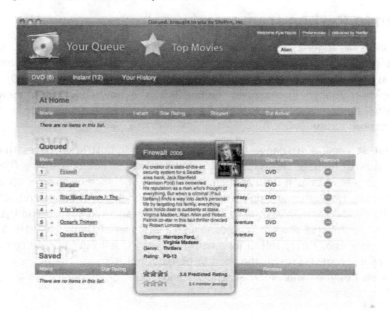

Figure 9-13. Queued queue screen showing the movies in your queue

Server-side frameworks

The Dojo Toolkit has not only been loved by front-end web developers and designers but also has been adopted as an official Ajax library of choice by the Django and Zend frameworks. This means that when any developer downloads either one of these frameworks, they'll get Dojo bundled with it as well.

Zend PHP framework

This popular PHP framework is robust, is stable, and supports popular Web 2.0 technologies. One of the ways it does this is with its strong support and integration with the Dojo Toolkit. Zend Framework provides special methods in the form of a PHP API. When the PHP processor renders the pages for display to the browser, it turns the PHP methods directly into Dojo, JavaScript, and HTML. This helps PHP developers harness the power of Dojo using a language they are already familiar with.

You can download Zend Framework at http://framework.zend.com/. The documentation for using Dojo within Zend Framework is available at http://framework.zend.com/manual/en/zend.dojo.html.

Django Python framework

Python is a general-purpose, object-oriented programming language. It is flexible enough to provide a great API for desktop application development as well as web application development. The latter is emphasized with the Django framework. Django (pronounced "jang-goh") is a powerful web framework allowing Python developers to build well-structured database-driven MVC applications easily.

The latest version of Django utilizes Dojo in its administration pages that it generates to manage the data in the applications. In addition, many Django developers have chosen Dojo as their Ajax library of choice because of its ease in creating rich Internet applications while also being a reliable and stable toolkit. By the same token, many Dojo users have adopted Django and Python as their server-side stack of choice. When I discovered Django a little more than a year ago, I truly fell in love with how easy it is to get up and running. Much of its greatness seems too good to be true, but it's not. The framework is very well designed and enforces strong standards of programming while being efficient and scalable.

To learn more about Django, http://www.djangoproject.com has a plethora of resources and tutorials to get started. Remember, Django is a framework for Python. It is not a language itself.

LinkED

The next section, "Third-Party Extensions," will discuss a Django application that bundles Dojo with it for use on your projects and easy tie-in to the Dojo Toolkit from Django.

Third-Party Extensions

Dojo has so much to offer with its package, and its goal is not to be an end-all solution to every requirement you'll ever have for a project. What it does provide you with is a lot of out-of-box functionality in addition to a great toolkit to create just about anything you'll need for JavaScript development. With that, other developers have created projects that extend or build on top of the Dojo Toolkit. Oftentimes these projects are made to be open source and freely available to use in your own projects. I'll cover just a few hear: Plugd, Dair, and Dojango.

Plugd

Plugd is a natural extension, actually namespace, to the Dojo Toolkit. Although there are no plans to ever bundle it with Dojo, it's great for developers who might be coming from another JavaScript toolkit such as jQuery and are used to using familiar syntax and coding styles. For that reason, it's kind of known as the missing APIs for Dojo. Although the jQuery default function names clutter up the global namespace in your JavaScript, a lot of developers don't care about this and just prefer the more concise syntax. Take heed, however, because just as I mentioned with the chaining capabilities of Dojo.NodeList, the chaining powers of Plugd can be just as detrimental to your code. You want to be careful not to do too much in these chain blocks because your code can become more difficult to maintain in the long run as it becomes harder to read.

The following is an example of a style of code you can write with Plugd but not normal Dojo:

```
$("p.baz")
  .appendTo("body")
  .addClass("bar")
```

```
.onclick(function(e){
  e.target.innerHTML = "Wow, JavaScript";
});
```

In this example, you can think of the $() function as synonymous with the dojo.query() function. As such, it will return a dojo.NodeList that you can act upon in a chain block where you chain one function after another to perform operations on the selection of elements that are returned from the $() function. This function will return all paragraph elements with a class name of baz and append them to the body tag. It will then add the class name of bar to all of them as well as an onclick event listener that will set their contents to "Wow, JavaScript" when clicked.

There is a "Getting Started" guide for using Plugd available at http://code.google.com/p/plugd/wiki/GettingStarted. The project's homepage is hosted on Google Code at http://code.google.com/p/plugd/.

Dair

You saw earlier in this chapter how Dojo can work well with Adobe AIR. Dair makes it even easier to use the Adobe AIR API using Dojo. By wrapping much of the AIR patterns in constructors that you are familiar with in Dojo, this project will help you build an AIR app faster than ever. It's still a very new and early version of the project (0.1 at the time of this writing), but it's worth taking a look at if you are interested in building a desktop application using Dojo and Adobe AIR. The project is also hosted on Google Code at http://code.google.com/p/dair/, where you will also find a sample application and a module overview to see what's available in the project. In addition, they offer a quick-start guide to get you up and running quickly; see http://code.google.com/p/dair/wiki/QuickStart.

Dojango

Mix Django and Dojo together, and you get Dojango! This reusable Django application is built and distributed for you to quickly get started with a new Django project that is already hooked into Dojo as well. It provides the ability to easily choose how you want to load Dojo into your pages (whether via a CDN or your own storage), it offers many utilities to help with making rich Internet applications and web pages, and it makes your own build easy and straightforward.

If you have a desire in looking at this project, you'll need to know Python and Django before doing so. The Django project website (http://www.djangoproject.com) provides a lot of great entry-level tutorials on getting up and running. In addition, *Dive into Python* (available at http://diveintopython.org/) is a book that is distributed absolutely free and can help you get to know, understand, and write Python in no time.

Dojango is a natural project for you to look at if you are interested in creating dynamic and rich websites using a solid web framework and JavaScript toolkit. The project is hosted with Google Code at http://code.google.com/p/dojango/.

Summary

Dojo's flexible, scalable, and stable architecture are what make it the best Ajax/JavaScript library a developer can choose. It can be used as simply and as small as you like by only using the Dojo base functionality, or you can ramp it up with advanced and complex logic by extending it to its fullest using Dijit, DojoX, or a server-side framework.

My desire is that this book would encourage you to build rich interfaces and web applications for your users to enjoy, providing them with smooth animations, transitions, and easy Ajax integration, all on top of a scalable, reusable architecture. In addition, Dojo's community is friendly, approachable, and always willing to help out fellow developers.

I hope you found this book to be a useful and solid introduction to JavaScript development with the Dojo Toolkit and that it will serve you will as you solidify your understanding. Feel free to drop by http://startdojo.com and ask questions or submit bugs from the code.

Appendix A

Setting Up a Local Web Server

It'll be much easier for you to run the examples in this book if you run them on a local web server. One reason for this is because of a security sandboxing feature that Internet Explorer has for running HTML files that contain JavaScript in them; the other is to replicate the manner in which you will be using Dojo for a real website or web application.

Although the Mac OS X operating system includes a built-in web server as do some versions of Windows, I will be going through, step-by-step, how to install a local web server that will serve HTML, JavaScript, and PHP files. You won't be using the included web servers built into your operating system because of the complex configurations. Instead, you will be using a turnkey solution, one for the Mac called **MAMP** (which stands for Macintosh, Apache, MySQL, and PHP) or one for Windows known as **XAMPP** (the *X* is for the four operating systems it supports; the other letters stand for Apache, MySQL, PHP, and Perl). These two products are great because they give you an extremely easy and straightforward method for quickly setting up a local web server that not only supports serving static files such as HTML and JavaScript files but also supports PHP and database connectivity. The best thing about both of these tools is that they are completely free to download and use.

If you are on Windows, you'll want to skip the next section and jump to "XAMPP on Windows."

MAMP on Mac OS X

The latest version of MAMP supports Snow Leopard (OS X 10.6) and older. In addition, it supports both the Intel and PowerPC processors for excellent backward compatibility. Although MAMP is completely free to use, it doesn't support as many features as MAMP PRO, albeit enough for the purposes of this book. You can see the differences between the two products on the MAMP website at http://www.mamp.info/en/mamp-pro/features/matrix.html. I run MAMP PRO on my Mac because I need its advanced features, and I've been very happy with the product. With that, let's get on to installing it!

Installation

Follow these steps for installation:

1. Visit http://www.mamp.info/en/downloads/, and click the *MAMP and MAMP PRO* link below the *Downloads* page header, as shown in Figure A-1, to begin downloading MAMP and MAMP PRO. *Note: When downloading MAMP, you'll also be downloading a 14-day trial of MAMP PRO, but you won't need to install it.*

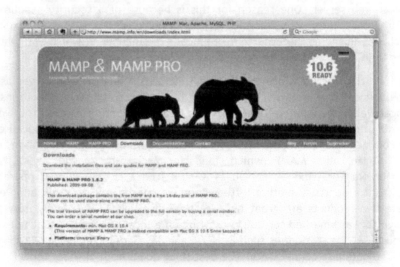

Figure A-1. Download screen for MAMP and MAMP PRO from http://www.mamp.info

2. Once the download has completed, if you have your browser set to automatically open the file, you'll be presented with a screen like Figure A-2, which shows the license agreement for installing and using MAMP and MAMP PRO. If the download did not open for you automatically, then double-click the DMG file that you downloaded in step 1, and you should see the screen in Figure A-2.

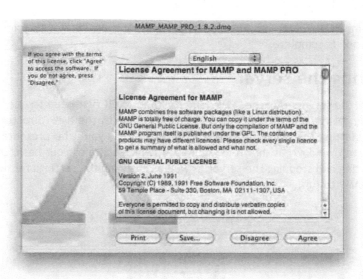

Figure A-2. License agreement for MAMP and MAMP PRO

3. If you agree to the license, click *Agree*.

4. A new Finder window will open, showing you a simple install screen, as shown in Figure A-3. Simply drag the MAMP folder into the Applications folder.

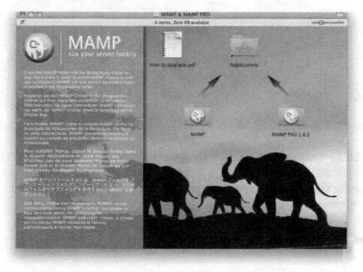

Figure A-3. Finder window showing the contents of the MAMP disk image

After the MAMP folder has finished copying to the Applications folder, the installation is complete.

Starting the server

To start the servers (Apache, PHP, and MySQL), you'll first need to open MAMP by going to the Applications directory, then going to the MAMP directory, and finally starting the MAMP application. When you do, you'll be presented with the startup window, as shown in Figure A-4, which contains your basic controls for starting and stopping the server as well as changing the settings for how you want MAMP to run.

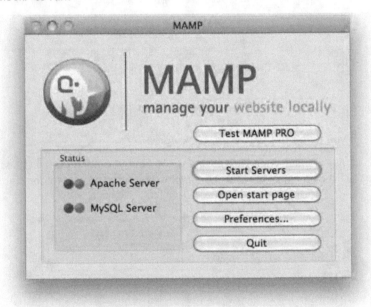

Figure A-4. Control panel for MAMP

It's probably obvious, but to start up the servers, click *Start Servers*. The first time they start, it will take a little time to complete. You'll know that they've successfully started when your screen looks like Figure A-5 with green "lights" on the left status panel.

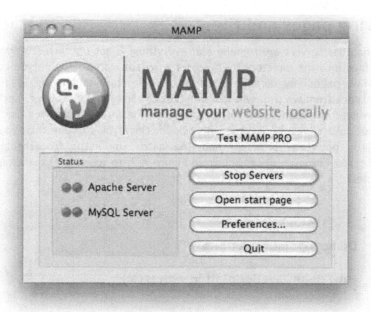

Figure A-5. The *Start Servers* button will change to *Stop Servers* when they have finished starting.

Once they have started, you can click *Open start page* to verify that your server got set up correctly and is running. Your screen should resemble Figure A-6. You can browse around these pages to learn a little bit about what is set up on your servers. Read on to find out how to serve pages and files.

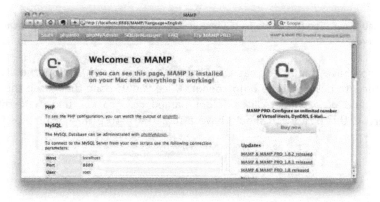

Figure A-6. MAMP start page that can be started from the MAMP control panel

Serving pages and files

Now that the servers are running and everything is set up correctly, you can move files into the directory the web server reads from to enable you to view the HTML pages. By default, MAMP has a directory under /Applications/ MAMP/htdocs from which it will look for files to serve to the browser. Let's test it. Download the demo code for this book from http://friendsofed.com. Copy the ch01 folder into the location mentioned. Once you've done this, you'll be able to open a browser and navigate to http://localhost:8888/ ch01/introductions.html, as shown in Figure A-7, to see one of the Chapter 1 examples.

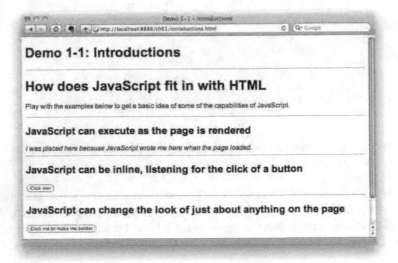

Figure A-7. The first demo from Chapter 1 running from the newly set-up local web server

Once you have confirmed that the Chapter 1 demo works, follow the steps in Chapter 3 to download the Dojo Toolkit. Once you've done that, drop the dojo, dijit, and dojox folders in a folder named dojotoolkit under the htdocs folder. At this point, you should have a folder structure that resembles Figure A-8.

Figure A-8. Folder structure for dojotoolkit in htdocs

Once you copy the Dojo Toolkit files to the web server, you are ready to run the other examples. Copy the rest of the demo folders from the different chapters to the htdocs folder as well. After this is completed, test one of the examples such as Chapter 4's dojoQuery.html, which should look like Figure A-9.

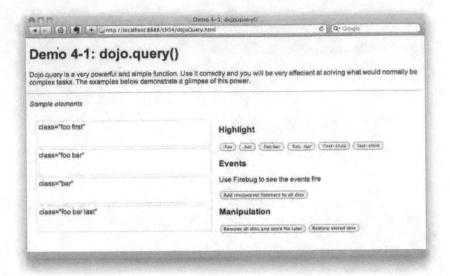

Figure A-9. Chapter 4's Dojo Query demo running on the local web server

This concludes the setup and configuration for MAMP on Mac OS X. The next section will cover setting up XAMPP on a Windows operating system. Unless you plan on setting up a local web server on Windows as well, you can skip that section.

XAMPP on Windows

Apache Friends' XAMPP is an excellent way to quickly set up a local web server environment on your Windows PC. It is completely free to use and includes Apache, MySQL, and PHP, along with a few other server products all configured and ready to run once installed. Let's begin.

Installation

Follow these steps for installation:

1. Visit http://www.apachefriends.org/en/xampp-windows.html#646, and click the *EXE* link (as shown in Figure A-10) to download XAMPP Lite. Note that XAMPP Lite is a considerably smaller download than the full version since it contains only a subset of what XAMPP provides. It will, however, completely suffice for your needs in running the demos for this book.

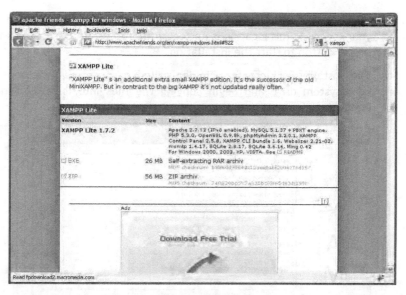

Figure A-10. Apache Friends website showing the download links for XAMPP Lite

2. Find the EXE file you downloaded, and double-click its icon to start the installation, as shown in Figure A-11.

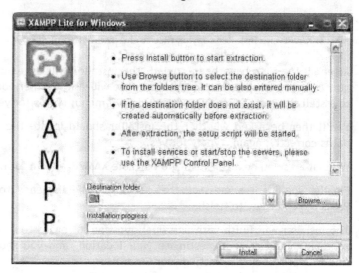

Figure A-11. Initial installation screen for XAMPP Lite

3. The installer defaults to the root of your system drive (in most cases, your C drive). This location is perfectly fine, so leave it as is. Click the *Install* button to start the installation.

4. The installer will create a folder called xampplite in the root of your system drive and begin copying the files into it, as shown in Figure A-12.

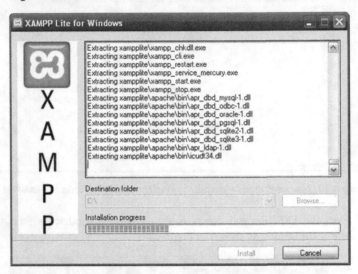

Figure A-12. XAMPP Lite installer copying files to the installation directory

5. After all the files have been copied, the installer will ask you a few questions to complete the install. The first will ask whether you want to install shortcuts to your desktop and *Start* menu; type y for yes.

6. You'll then be asked whether the installer should locate the XAMPP paths correctly; again, type y for yes.

7. When it asks you next for making a portable XAMPP, type n for no.

8. Finally, you'll get a message that states "XAMPP is ready to use." Press the Enter key to finish.

9. The installer will finish with one final question in regard to your time zone. It should correctly estimate your location, and you should be fine with proceeding by hitting your Enter key.

10. When your screen shows a menu like Figure A-13, type x, and press Return; or simply close the window. The installation of XAMPP Lite has completed.

```
C:\WINDOWS\system32\cmd.exe                                    _ □ ×

############################################################################
# XAMPP Lite 1.7.2 - Setup                                                 #
#--------------------------------------------------------------------------#
# Copyright 2009 Carsten Wiedmann (FreeBSD License)                        #
#                                                                          #
# Authors: Carsten Wiedmann <carsten_sttgt@gmx.de>                         #
#          Kay Vogelgesang <kvo@apachefriends.org>                         #
############################################################################
1. start XAMPP Control Panel
2. relocate XAMPP
   (current path: C:\xampplite)
3. disable HTTPS (SSL)
4. disable Server Side Includes (SSI)
5. enable IPv4 only (current: IPv4/6 (auto))

x  Exit

Please choose (1-5/x):
```

Figure A-13. A menu screen that shows once XAMPP Lite has finished installation. You may close out of this.

Starting the server

To start the servers, you'll want to open the XAMPP control panel by double-clicking the icon that installed on your desktop, as shown in Figure A-14. Once you do, the XAMPP control panel will open, displaying quite a few options and buttons, as you can see in Figure A-15.

Figure A-14. XAMPP Control Panel icon on the desktop

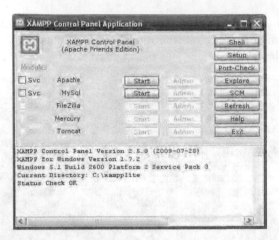

Figure A-15. XAMPP control panel

To start the Apache server, simply click the *Start* button to the right of the *Apache* label. Once the server has successfully started, the *Start* button will change to say *Stop*, and the *Admin* button to the right of it will become enabled. Additionally, a status message will display just to the right of the word *Apache*, and if your server started successfully, it should read as *Running*, as shown in Figure A-16.

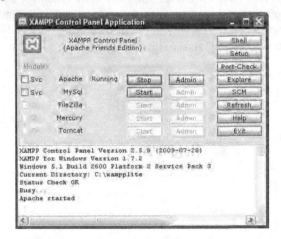

Figure A-16. Main control panel screen after the Apache server has successfully started

After you start the server, click the *Admin* button, which will open your default web browser. The first time you do this, a screen, as shown in Figure A-17, will ask your preferred language. Once you've selected a language, you won't be prompted with this screen again when you launch the Admin page. You should now see a screen similar to Figure A-18 that provides you with a welcome page as well as navigation on the left side. If you don't see this, go back through the previous steps to ensure that you performed all the steps correctly.

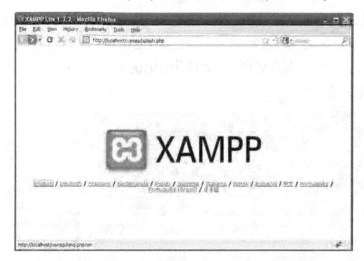

Figure A-17. Language selection screen for the XAMPP admin page

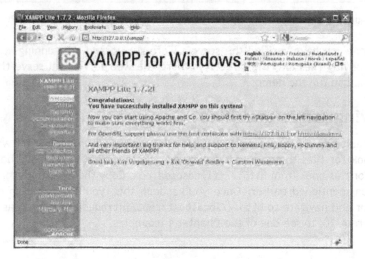

Figure A-18. XAMPP admin welcome page showing a successful installation

To verify everything else is running well, click the *Status* option in the navigation to see a status of the running servers. Your screen should look like the one in Figure A-19 with at least PHP reporting as *Activated*. If this is not occurring, go through the previous installation steps to double-check that you did everything correctly.

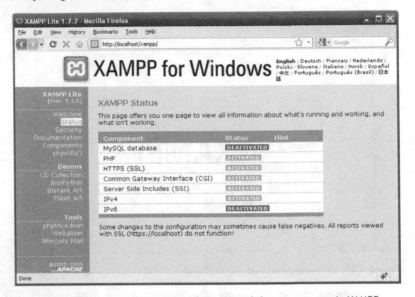

Figure A-19. Status screen reporting the status of the components in XAMPP

Now that you have verified the servers were set up and are running, you can start copying files into the directory where the web server will serve them so that you can run the demos.

Serving pages and files

By default, XAMPP has a directory under C:\xampplite\htdocs from which it will look for files to serve to the browser. Let's test it. Download the demo code for this book from http://friendsofed.com. Copy the ch01 folder into the location mentioned earlier. Once you've done this, you'll be able to open a browser and navigate to http://localhost/ch01/introductions.html, as shown in Figure A-20, to see one of the Chapter 1 examples.

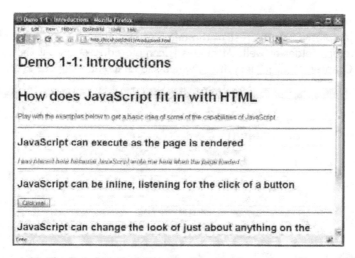

Figure A-20. The first demo from Chapter 1 running from the newly set-up local web server

Once you have confirmed that the Chapter 1 demo worked, follow the steps in Chapter 3 to download the Dojo Toolkit. Once you've done that, drop the dojo, dijit, and dojox folders in a folder named dojotoolkit under the htdocs folder from earlier. At this point, you should have a folder structure that resembles Figure A-21.

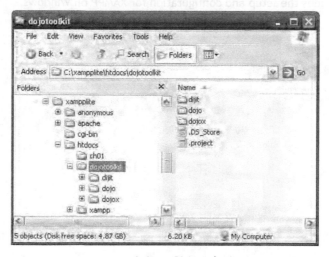

Figure A-21. Folder structure for dojotoolkit in htdocs

Once you copy the Dojo toolkit files to the web server, you are ready to run the other examples. Copy the rest of the demo folders from the different chapters to the htdocs folder as well. After this is completed, test one of the examples such as Chapter 4's dojoQuery.html, which should look like Figure A-22.

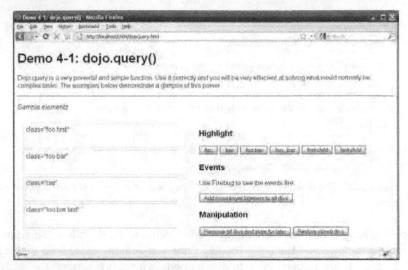

Figure A-22. Chapter 4's Dojo Query demo running on the local web server

This concludes the setup and configuration for XAMPP on Windows.

Appendix B

Dojo Base Quick Reference

This appendix compiles all the functions and constants available to you in Dojo Base. Use this guide as quick reference for function signatures. If you are unsure what a function does, you can look it up in the online documentation at http://api.dojotoolkit.org/.

Document Life Cycle

```
dojo.addOnLoad(obj, functionName)
dojo.addOnWindowUnload(obj, functionName)
dojo.addOnUnload(obj, functionName)
```

DOM Manipulation

```
dojo.clone(o)
dojo.body()
dojo.byId(id, doc)
dojo.destroy(node)
dojo.place(node, refNode, position)
dojo.create(nodeType, attrs, refNode, pos)
dojo.empty(node)
dojo.query(query, scope)
dojo.query('.nodes').empty()
dojo.query('.nodes').place(queryOrNode, position)
dojo.query('.nodes').orphan(simpleFilter)
dojo.query('.nodes').adopt(queryOrListOrNode, position)
dojo.query('.nodes').query(queryStr)
dojo.query('.nodes').addContent(content, position)
dojo.query('.nodes').destroy()
dojo.query('.nodes').clone()
```

DOM Attributes

```
dojo.isDescendant(node, ancestor)
dojo.setSelectable(node, selectable)
dojo.marginBox(node, box)
dojo.contentBox(node, box)
dojo.coords(node, includeScroll)
dojo.hasAttr(node, name)
dojo.attr(node, name, value)
dojo.removeAttr(node, name)
dojo.query('.nodes').attr()
dojo.query('.nodes').coords()
dojo.query('.nodes').val(value)
```

Language Helpers

```
dojo.eval(scriptFragment)
dojo.isString(it)
dojo.isArray(it)
dojo.isFunction(it)
dojo.isObject(it)
dojo.isArrayLike(it)
dojo.isAlien(it)
dojo._toArray(obj, offset, startWith)
dojo.trim(str)
new d.Deferred(canceller)
```

Arrays

```
dojo.indexOf(array, value, fromIndex, findLast)
dojo.lastIndexOf(array, value, fromIndex)
dojo.forEach(arr, callback, thisObject)
dojo.every(arr, callback, thisObject)
dojo.some(arr, callback, thisObject)
dojo.map(arr, callback, thisObject)
dojo.filter(arr, callback, thisObject)
dojo.query('.nodes').slice()
dojo.query('.nodes').splice()
dojo.query('.nodes').indexOf()
dojo.query('.nodes').lastIndexOf()
dojo.query('.nodes').every()
dojo.query('.nodes').some()
dojo.query('.nodes').concat(item)
dojo.query('.nodes').map(func, obj)
dojo.query('.nodes').forEach(callback, thisObj)
dojo.query('.nodes').filter(simpleFilter)
dojo.query('.nodes').at()
```

Event System

```
dojo.connectPublisher(topic, obj, event)
dojo.disconnect(handle)
dojo.subscribe(topic, context, method)
dojo.unsubscribe(handle)
dojo.publish(topic, args)
dojo.connectPublisher(topic, obj, event)
dojo.fixEvent(evt, sender)
dojo.stopEvent(evt)
dojo.query('.nodes').connect()
```

Nodelist Events

```
dojo.query('.nodes').onblur(a, b)
dojo.query('.nodes').onfocus(a, b)
dojo.query('.nodes').onchange(a, b)
dojo.query('.nodes').onclick(a, b)
dojo.query('.nodes').onerror(a, b)
dojo.query('.nodes').onkeydown(a, b)
dojo.query('.nodes').onkeypress(a, b)
dojo.query('.nodes').onkeyup(a, b)
dojo.query('.nodes').onload(a, b)
dojo.query('.nodes').onmousedown(a, b)
dojo.query('.nodes').onmouseenter(a, b)
dojo.query('.nodes').onmouseleave(a, b)
dojo.query('.nodes').onmousemove(a, b)
dojo.query('.nodes').onmouseout(a, b)
dojo.query('.nodes').onmouseover(a, b)
dojo.query('.nodes').onmouseup(a, b)
dojo.query('.nodes').onsubmit(a, b)
```

Effects

```
new d._Animation()
dojo.fadeIn(args)
dojo.fadeOut(args)
dojo.animateProperty(args)
dojo.anim(node, properties, duration, easing, onEnd, delay)
anim.duration
anim.repeat
anim.rate
anim.play(delay, gotoStart)
anim.pause()
anim.gotoPercent(percent, andPlay)
anim.stop(gotoEnd)
anim.status()
```

Package System

```
dojo.require(moduleName, omitModuleCheck)
dojo.provide(resourceName)
dojo.platformRequire(modMap)
dojo.requireIf(condition, resourceName)
dojo.requireAfterIf(condition, resourceName)
dojo.registerModulePath(module, prefix)
dojo.requireLocalization(moduleName, bundle- Name, locale,
availableFlatLocales)
dojo.moduleUrl(module, url)
dojo.load()
```

Objects OO (Object-oriented)

```
dojo.mixin(obj, props)
dojo.setObject(name, value, context)
dojo.getObject(name, create, context)
dojo.exists(name, obj)
dojo.extend(constructor, props)
dojo.hitch(scope, method)
dojo.delegate(obj, props)
dojo.partial(method)
dojo.declare(className, superclass, props)
dojo.query('.nodes').instantiate(declaredClass, properties)
```

Ajax

```
dojo.xhr(method, args, hasBody)
dojo.xhrGet(args)
dojo.xhrPost(args)
dojo.rawXhrPost(args)
dojo.xhrPut(args)
dojo.rawXhrPut(args)
dojo.xhrDelete(args)
```

JSON

```
dojo.fromJson(json)
dojo.toJsonIndentStr
dojo.toJson(it, prettyPrint, _indentStr)
dojo.formToObject(formNode)
dojo.objectToQuery(map)
dojo.formToQuery(formNode)
dojo.formToJson(formNode, prettyPrint)
dojo.queryToObject(str)
```

Styles

```
dojo.boxModel
dojo.getComputedStyle(node)
dojo.style(node, style, value)
dojo.hasClass(node, classStr)
dojo.addClass(node, classStr)
dojo.removeClass(node, classStr)
dojo.toggleClass(node, classStr, condition)
dojo.query('.nodes').style()
dojo.query('.nodes').addClass()
dojo.query('.nodes').removeClass()
dojo.query('.nodes').toggleClass()
```

Colors

```
new d.Color(color)
dojo.blendColors(start, end, weight, obj)
dojo.colorFromRgb(color, obj)
dojo.colorFromHex(color, obj)
dojo.colorFromArray(a, obj)
dojo.colorFromString(str, obj)
```

Sniffing

```
dojo.isBrowser
dojo.isKhtml
dojo.isWebKit
dojo.isChrome
dojo.isMoz
dojo.isMozilla
dojo.isFF
dojo.isQuirks
```

Advanced Scope

```
dojo.global
dojo.doc
dojo.setContext(globalObject, globalDocument)
dojo.withGlobal(globalObject, callback, thisObject, cbArguments)
dojo.withDoc(documentObject, callback, thisObject, cbArguments)
```

djConfig

```
djConfig.parseOnLoad
djConfig.requires
djConfig.isDebug
djConfig.debugAtAllCosts
djConfig.baseUrl
```

Miscellaneous

```
dojo.config
dojo.locale
dojo.version
dojo.experimental()
dojo.deprecated()
dojo.baseUrl
```

Key Constants

```
dojo.keys.BACKSPACE
dojo.keys.TAB
dojo.keys.CLEAR
dojo.keys.ENTER
dojo.keys.SHIFT
dojo.keys.CTRL
dojo.keys.ALT
dojo.keys.PAUSE
dojo.keys.CAPS_LOCK
dojo.keys.ESCAPE
dojo.keys.SPACE
dojo.keys.PAGE_UP
dojo.keys.PAGE_DOWN
dojo.keys.END
dojo.keys.HOME
dojo.keys.LEFT_ARROW
dojo.keys.UP_ARROW
dojo.keys.RIGHT_ARROW
dojo.keys.DOWN_ARROW
dojo.keys.INSERT
dojo.keys.DELETE
dojo.keys.HELP
dojo.keys.LEFT_WINDOW
dojo.keys.RIGHT_WINDOW
dojo.keys.SELECT
dojo.keys.NUMPAD_0
dojo.keys.NUMPAD_1
dojo.keys.NUMPAD_2
```

```
dojo.keys.NUMPAD_3
dojo.keys.NUMPAD_4
dojo.keys.NUMPAD_5
dojo.keys.NUMPAD_6
dojo.keys.NUMPAD_7
dojo.keys.NUMPAD_8
dojo.keys.NUMPAD_9
dojo.keys.NUMPAD_MULTIPLY
dojo.keys.NUMPAD_PLUS
dojo.keys.NUMPAD_ENTER
dojo.keys.NUMPAD_MINUS
dojo.keys.NUMPAD_PERIOD
dojo.keys.NUMPAD_DIVIDE
dojo.keys.F1
dojo.keys.F2
dojo.keys.F3
dojo.keys.F4
dojo.keys.F5
dojo.keys.F6
dojo.keys.F7
dojo.keys.F8
dojo.keys.F9
dojo.keys.F10
dojo.keys.F11
dojo.keys.F12
dojo.keys.F13
dojo.keys.F14
dojo.keys.F15
dojo.keys.NUM_LOCK
dojo.keys.SCROLL_LOCK
```

Appendix C

Plug-ins

By now you should have at least a cursory understanding of the tools available in the Dojo Toolkit. Although Dojo seems to contain a built-in component for nearly every conceivable situation in JavaScript, the reality of it is a bit less euphoric. Sometimes, a component or function behaves nearly perfectly, just as you would imagine or are comfortable with. However, sometimes a function or component simply doesn't exist publicly, and you need to expand the core functionality with your own concoction, giving you full control over the desired behavior.

At the risk of going beyond the scope of a StartED series book, I'm presenting this appendix on plug-ins. Some of the concepts are best explained in the form of "pure JavaScript" and may be more difficult to grasp than the standard syntactic sugar Dojo provides. Rest assured—at the end of the day, Dojo is *just* JavaScript. Understanding how elegantly self-healing JavaScript is as a language will open doors leading to your own customized mini-library of reusable functionality built on top of Dojo. This appendix begins you on a journey into the "next step" of your JavaScript enlightenment. Beyond the stock, cookie-cutter functionality of Dojo is a powerful language ready to be harnessed. Consider this a jump start.

In this appendix, I'll cover a lot of interesting material. You'll learn about the various extension points exposed explicitly for augmentation, some of the theories behind how Dojo "plugs" itself, how to utilize JavaScript's dynamic nature to best accomplish this, and some of the great functions Dojo already has built in to make these extensions incredibly easy.

Dojo is ready out of the box to be "plugged" in any way imaginable. Dojo's dedication to backward compatibility ensures the code that your plug-in augments will never go stale, and Dojo's commitment to providing fast and stable APIs means you have a bit of breathing room in the performance department to add the magic where you see fit with a minimal cost. Keeping the magic out of the core functionality is Dojo's way of providing a sane, stable foundation from which to build. You are free to add as much magic as you like.

What is a plug-in?

The term **plug-in** by itself is rather generic, commonly used in numerous software packages to describe some third-party component that augments, patches, or otherwise complements the original intent of the software author. For example, web browsers such as Mozilla's Firefox have "add-ons" you can download that provide an additional layer of control over the chrome. Anything you can imagine your browser accomplishing can be achieved by writing these add-ons using Mozilla's documented and exposed API for doing just this. Dojo is no different.

Ultimately, a plug-in is just a function (or a series of functions) that is property loaded in to augment code. These functions can do anything...they are meant to be as generic as the term **plug-in** itself. The Don't Repeat Yourself (DRY) principle says, "If you repeat any bit of functionality (or have a pattern used throughout your code) more than once, you will probably be better served by reducing it to the most common case." Once your repeated functionality is reduced, you have created a plug-in for yourself—something you can use over and over again with no additional overhead.

As you are probably already aware, Dojo has a package system designed to pull in your own code simply by issuing a `dojo.require()` call that points to some JavaScript file on your local system. By loading any code that isn't already provided by Dojo, you are "plugging in" functionality. Though this is by far the loosest definition of a plug-in available, or rather the broadest, it is a great place to start.

Two basic forms of "plug-ins" apply to Dojo: functional plug-ins and NodeList plug-ins. As the chapter progresses, you will realize how they are ultimately one in the same, though NodeList plug-ins carry a limited meaning and are not reflective of how powerful a language JavaScript can be. A third, more advanced, form of plug-in involves object inheritance (commonly referred to as **subclassing**), though again, they are all ultimately one in the same. JavaScript is just cool like that. I'll cover all three in this appendix, explaining the differences and theories behind each. You will feel like a JavaScript ninja once you start comprehending how powerful these concepts are.

What is a NodeList?

Dojo provides a class named dojo.NodeList. All calls to dojo.query() return an instance of this NodeList class, so you are using it often, typically without directly creating it. A NodeList is a "subclass" of a standard array, meaning it looks and acts like a plain JavaScript array though is "decorated" with additional helper functions that act upon each element in the list. dojo.query() executes a CSS3 selector on the document, finding nodes and creating this super-array with the found nodes. Later, when you make a dojo.query() plug-in, really you will be extending the dojo.NodeList class, which is something worth remembering.

The dojo.NodeList class has a function called style() that works identically to dojo.style(), though it iterates over every node in the NodeList rather than a single node, as shown here:

```
// set all nodes with class="classes" text color "red"
dojo.query(".classes").style("color", "red");
```

Typically, you can chain calls from one NodeList function to the other, which is a standard practice with working with dojo.query():

```
// set the color blue AND register an onclick in one line:
dojo.query("#someId").style("color", "blue").onclick(function(e){/*click
handler*/ });
```

The big secret here is each NodeList function typically returns itself to allow this chaining. You can chain indefinitely if each call successfully returns the NodeList over and over again.

The truth of the matter is that whenever a function returns anything, that anything is accessible as the next dot-accessible item. Consider the following example:

```
var n = document.createElement("div");
var a = document.createElement("a");
a.innerHTML = "The Link";
n.appendChild(a); // add the <a> to the <div>
```

The return value from the createElement() call is the newly created div node. You save this return value into the variable n. You then create an anchor tag, saving it into a variable a. You access the anchor's innerHTML, giving it new content, and then append the anchor to the div node. You could do this all inline with a single line by utilizing the return values in place:

```
var x = document.createElement("div").appendChild(document.createElement("a"));
x.innerHTML = "The Link";
```

The return value from the appendChild() call is the newly appended node (in this case, the anchor you created directly within the appendChild() call). By storing that to x, you can set the inner value of the anchor by accessing x.innerHTML.

NodeList takes this a step further by always ensuring it returns itself from one of its own calls. Understanding how these return values are used in this manner is pivotal to understanding the NodeList style plug-in.

NodeList as an array

Because a dojo.NodeList is *just* an array, you can access any of its nonchainable properties just as you would a normal array. You're also provided with all the standard built-in array functions (slice(), pop(), shift(), and so on).

The most common property you'll see when working with an array is length:

```
var list = dojo.query(".foo");
if(list.length){
  list.style("color", "blue");
}else{
  console.warn("no nodes found?! adding one:");
  list.push(dojo.create("div"));
}
list.onclick(function(e){ /* some onclick handler */ });
```

JavaScript has a concept of "truthyness," meaning many values other than a literal false will cause a conditional check to evaluate to false. Zero (0) is one such "truthy" value. If an array has a length equal to 0, it has no elements, so you can check the length in this shorthand way.

The previous example is admittedly a bit convoluted, though it avoids calling the style() function in the case where there are no nodes in the NodeList. Even for empty NodeLists there is a tiny piece of overhead from calling chained functions. The act of calling a function alone costs *something*; NodeList is just smart enough to take no action while still returning itself, preventing throwing exceptions for accessing undefined values. For instance, a common way of accessing a single item from a NodeList is to access the array's value at a given index:

```
var list = dojo.query(".nodes");
var first = list[0];
first.innerHTML = "<p>New content for the first item</p>";
```

This may seem like an entirely safe operation, though in practice it could come back to bite you. If there are no nodes in the document with class="nodes", then query() will find nothing. If query() doesn't find anything, list.length is

0, meaning there is no node at index 0 in the array (remember, arrays are zero-based indexes). The variable first would then be *undefined* (a "falsey" value). This undefined value doesn't have an innerHTML property, and an exception would be thrown. In the best case, a very cryptic error message would be thrown: "first is undefined." With luck, the browser will point you to the line where this occurred, though in lesser browsers you will be provided a message like "object expected" with no hint as to where, why, or how. This is why it is safer to either program defensively (by checking list.length first) or use the built-in methods for NodeList, as you'll see in the next section.

Iterating with a NodeList

To program more defensively, you could rewrite the previous example using NodeList's built-in iterator forEach() to go over each node in turn. If the list has no length, the forEach() call will be a no-op (or null operation) and allow for code to further execute:

```
dojo.query(".nodes").forEach(function(n){
  n.innerHTML = "<p>New content!</p>";
});
```

If accessing the first item only is the desired behavior, you have a function for that too called at(). By adding a call in the chain before forEach(), you can reduce this NodeList to a single-item NodeList:

```
dojo.query(".nodes").at(0).forEach(function(n){
  n.innerHTML = "<p>New only for the node at index 0</p>";
});
```

Again, because at() returns the reduced NodeList, you are able to chain the forEach() call. The forEach() will run only once unless the list's length is 0, in which case it is still a null operation and your code will safely execute past this potential error.

Sometimes, however, violently failing is the desired behavior. If you've written some code dependent on a query() call returning at least one node (or only one node) and you've used only NodeList built-in functions like at() and forEach(), your code will "fail silently." You needed something to happen, and it didn't, with no explanation as to why or even where, which could be more tedious to debug than something that throws an exception because you tried to access an undefined variable.

Bear with me here. I know this may seem tedious at this point, but understanding these fundamentals will go a long way in helping you write really robust and interesting plug-ins of your own.

What else does NodeList provide?

You've seen only a few of the available functions built into dojo.NodeList: at(), forEach(), and style(). Although they make for nice simple examples, the full power of NodeList is almost entirely self-contained. There are dozens of built-in helper functions such as forEach() and style() inside dojo.NodeList, and knowing how to best utilize them will serve you well when writing your own plug-ins.

The available NodeList functions are described in full in the API documentation, though we'll peek at most of them in this section briefly.

By far the most common built-in NodeList function is the previously described forEach(). At the heart of most plug-in functionality, this method iterates over the NodeList just as dojo.forEach() would iterate over any array. The difference of course is that the array being iterated over is the NodeList instance. A passed callback function is passed the same arguments as dojo.forEach() would be: item, index, and a reference to the original array. item in this case is an actual DomNode reference, just like the object returned from a call like dojo.byId(). Here, I'll quickly iterate over all the anchor nodes found from the query() call and log them to the debugging console:

```
dojo.query("a").forEach(function(item, index, reference){
  console.log("node is", item, "at index in array", index, reference);
  if(item == reference[index]){
    // this is always true
  }
});
```

Using forEach() in this way has its advantages. When you look at the next most common method, connect(), you'll see one such advantage. Consider the following snippet:

```
// just like dojo.connect(node, "onclick") though registers a click
// for each anchor found dojo.query("a").connect("onclick", function(event){
  window.location.href = "/search.php?url=" + event.target.href;
});
```

This seems an entirely useful and safe example though in some situations yields incorrect behavior. If the anchor tag has complex markup within, the event.target could be a node other than the anchor. The onclick event bubbles, so any child element that triggers this event will become the .target. Such complex markup could look something like this:

```
<a href="foo.html">Hi <span>Dojo User</span>, Click Me Anywhere!</a>
```

If the text "Dojo User" is the origin of the mouse click, event.target will be a span and thus have no .href attribute.

Single-node equivalent functions

Most NodeList functions have single-node equivalents: dojo.style() and NodeList.style(), dojo.connect() and NodeList.connect(), and so on. By using forEach(), you can connect directly to the node and reference that node from within the registered onclick function:

```
dojo.query("a").forEach(function(n){
  dojo.connect(n, "onclick", function(){
    window.location.href = "/search.php?url=" + n.href;
  });
});
```

In the case of NodeList.connect() vs. dojo.connect(), by using the forEach() method, you can disconnect the event when you choose. NodeList.connect(), although it will clean up connections as necessary between pages, does not have a NodeList way to disconnect the handler at a later time.

```
dojo.query("a").forEach(function(n){
 var handle = dojo.connect(n, "onclick", function(){
   dojo.disconnect(handle);
  });
});
```

In this example, you locate all the anchor elements in the page and call a forEach() loop to iterate over them. In the iterator function, you make a call to dojo.connect to bind a click handler to the node, storing the connection information in a variable named handle. This example doesn't "do" anything except connect the click handler and disconnect it upon first calling.

DOM-style functions

Next up are a host of DOM-style functions. These functions are also available in both Dojo and NodeList forms: addClass(), removeClass(), toggleClass(), and the ever-popular style(). The following snippet, though redundant, will add, remove, and then re-add the class name added to each found anchor in the document. toggleClass() will add a class if not present or remove the class otherwise.

```
dojo.query("a")
  .addClass("added")
  .removeClass("added")
  .toggleClass("added")
  .style("opacity", 0.5);
```

The style() method accepts a (prop, value) pair or an object hash of properties and values:

```
dojo.query("div").style("opacity", 0.5")
  .style({ color:"red", backgroundColor:"blue" });
```

In addition to the standard NodeList.connect() utility (also available for single-serve use as dojo.connect()), Dojo provides a number of common DOM event connections as named methods. This allows you to concisely register common event handlers in a very terse form. The events used are stored as an array on the NodeList object:

```
// give this a try in Firebug: dojo.forEach(dojo.NodeList.events,
  function(eventName){
  console.log("Available: ", eventName);
});
```

All the standard DOM Level 2 events are available: blur, focus, change, click, error, keydown, keypress, keyup, load, mousedown, mouseenter, mouseleave, mousemove, mouseout, mouseover, mouseup, and submit. These events are registered directly by calling the "on" version of those name. For example:

```
// our list of nodes:
var list = dojo.query("a");
// a common event handler for this example:
var handler = function(e){
  console.log("Event is: ", e.type, "Target:", e.target); e.preventDefault();
};

// both chains are identical
list.onclick(handler).onmouseenter(handler);
list.connect("onclick", handler).connect("onmouseenter", handler);
```

Events are a key component to rich JavaScript web pages.

That's enough on built-in NodeList functions for the moment. There are enough tricks and neat techniques available in NodeList to constitute its own chapter, and you haven't even begun adding your own custom methods yet. The key to remember here is most standard Dojo DOM functions exist on the NodeList as well and can be harnessed both directly on the list or on a per-node basis within a forEach() loop. You'll also see more built-in NodeList functions as you get into writing your own plug-ins as examples.

I'll provide just a tiny bit more background before you get into actually writing the plug-ins. You're almost there.

A brief history of this

In JavaScript, this has a very special meaning. It refers to the context in which a function has been executed. Every function scope has its own this, though JavaScript allows you to easily manipulate the meaning of this at any time. Understanding how to harness this will enlighten your JavaScript too.

By default this is the object from which a function was executed. Everything in JavaScript is an object in one way or another and is able to refer to this in some meaningful way. To visualize, think of it more of a "parent-object" relationship. If an object has members and functions, executing the function from the object will set the context (sometimes also referred to as **scope**) to the parent object. Here is a simple example:

```
// define the object. a Singleton:
var myObj = {
  count: 0,
  adder: function(value){
    this.count += value;
  }
}

// add 5 to myObj.count
myObj.adder(5);
console.log(myObj.count);
```

Calling adder() from the myObj object sets the context of this within the adder() function to be myObj. In the previous code, you're accessing this.count, referring to the count member of the myObj object. Although this may not seem like an overly enlightening concept, it is an essential aspect of JavaScript and the cornerstone of its flexibility.

Suppose you had a second object with a separate count variable. You can reuse the original object's adder() function to manipulate the second object simply by changing the meaning of this when you call it. To do this, JavaScript has two handy built-in functions: call() and apply():

```
var otherObject = { count:0 }
myObj.adder.call(otherObject, 1);
console.log(otherObject.count); // 1
```

This time, when adder() is called, you've set the context (this) to mean otherObject, so the this within the adder() function actually references otherObject.count. The code has not changed, only the way you call it. call() accepts any number of parameters, the first being the scope in which to execute the function and the rest become positional arguments to whatever is being executed (in this case, you're passing a single extra argument to adder(), which is translated into the value parameter).

apply() is almost the same but accepts only two arguments: the first again being the scope to set the context to and the second being an array that is translated into the positional arguments:

```
var myFunction = function(a, b, c){
  console.log("got", a, b, c);
}
myFunction(2, 3, 4); // got 2 3 4
myFunction.call(this, 2, 3, 4); // got 2 3 4
myFunction.apply(this, [2, 3, 4]); // got 2 3 4
```

The three calls to myFunction() are identical in every way. Using apply() or call() effectively depends entirely on you and what is needed at any given time. Sometimes it is easier to generate an array to pass to apply(), although other times using call() makes more sense. You can, of course, simply call the function directly, though you lose the ability to manipulate the scope.

Using dojo.hitch()

Dojo has a handy built-in function for manipulating scope: dojo.hitch(). hitch() is, in my opinion, the most magical of functions available within Dojo. It creates a new function that will only ever execute in a given scope, currying along arguments passed to the new function. Going back to the adder() function, you can see immediately how useful it can be:

```
var hitchedFunction = dojo.hitch(otherObject, myObj.adder);
hitchedFunction(2);
console.log(otherObject.count);
```

In this code, you save the function returned from hitch() into a new variable. You call the new function directly, though the scope has been predetermined to be otherObject. Ultimately, hitch() is simply a shorthand wrapper around call(scope, ...) and makes for some very terse, though powerful, code.

Preserving this

Not only is hitch()/apply()/call() useful for manipulating the scope, it also comes into play when you want to preserve the scope. Preserving scope across anonymous functions is probably the single most difficult concept for beginners to JavaScript to comprehend. Once mastered, however, having complete control over your code comes naturally. You can accomplish nearly anything armed with a good understanding of scope.

The most common place where "lost scope" will bite you is in asynchronous callbacks: anonymous functions passed to other functions where the intent is to retain the original scope. Consider the following example:

```
var myObj = {
  url:"/foo.html"
  cache:"", // an empty string
  getData: function(){
    dojo.xhrGet({
      url: this.url,
      load: function(data){
        // unfortunately, "this" is out of scope
        this.cache = data;
      }
    });
  }
};
myObj.getData(); // window.cache will be the result, not myObj.cache
```

This happens because the load: callback has its own scope. The typical way to handle this would be to store a reference to this in the getData() function and reference that within the anonymous callback. Something like this:

```
...
getData: function(){
  var self = this; // store the reference
  dojo.xhrGet({
    url: this.url,
    load: function(data){
      self.cache = data; // use the reference
    }
  });
},
...
```

Another (much cleaner) alternative would be to use dojo.hitch() to scope the load: callback to the original context. this means the same thing anywhere in a function until a new function scope is reached, so you can pass this to hitch() and preserve its meaning in place, still allowing an anonymous function inline and manipulating the scope simultaneously:

```
...
getData: function(){
  dojo.xhrGet{{
    url: this.url,
    load: dojo.hitch(this, function(data){
      this.cache = data;
    })
  });
},
```

...

Finally, hitch() allows a very clean shorthand syntax for creating a hitched function simply from the context and a string name of a method in that scope. The previous example can be made more DRYish by breaking the load: callback into a separate function directly on your object, allowing you to use it manually or as a callback:

```
var myObj = {
  url:"foo.html",
  cache:"",
  getData: function(){
    dojo.xhrGet({
      url: this.url,
      // calls this.handleData in scope of "this"
      load: dojo.hitch(this, "handleData")
    });
  },
  handleData: function(data){
    this.cache = data;
  }
};
```

Now the handleData() function is responsible for setting the cache (and potentially any intermediate processing that may need to take place) in a single location, and the getData() function is responsible for nothing more than fetching the URL and passing along that data to the handleData() callback. Functional programming for the win.

The secret of chaining

Chaining function calls on one another may seem like some sort of magic, but once you understand the nuances of scope/context/this, it becomes painfully obvious how simple a technique it is.

So, the secret is (quickly, make sure no one is behind you stealing this nugget of knowledge) return this;. Any function that returns its context from the call can be chained indefinitely. I touched on this concept briefly in the previous pages. To illustrate how easy this is, create another plain object:

```
var myObj = {
  count:0,
  add: function(value){
    this.count += value;
    return this;
  }
};
```

```
// chain three add() calls
myObj.add(2).add(3).add(5);
console.log(myObj.count); // 10
```

By returning the context (or parent object, in different words), you are able to chain other commands directly on that return value. The return value doesn't even have to be this; it can be whatever object you choose, provided you understand that you are able to call only functions on the return object in place. Take, for instance, String instances. In JavaScript, Strings are immutable, and most operations return a new instance of the String. Because each String operation returns a new String, you can still chain string functions indefinitely, just quietly throwing away the previous return value each time. Only when the end of the chain comes does the return value matter:

```
var myStr = "The quick brown Fox";
var finalStr = myStr.replace("Fox", "Cow").toUpperCase().replace("QUICK",
"slow");
console.log(finalStr); // THE slow BROWN COW
```

Chaining appears in many places in Dojo, most notably on dojo.NodeList. This is why you are able to call such magic chains as you do with dojo.query(). Most every NodeList method returns this (though some return values or even newly created NodeLists). If a NodeList method returns a new NodeList, chaining can continue. However, the chained functions after the new list has been returned apply to a different list than was originally specified. An example of a NodeList function that returns a new NodeList is query(). NodeList.query() will execute a CSS3 selector query rooted in the original list. For instance:

```
var ul = dojo.query("#someid ul");
// find all <ul>'s under id="someid"
var listitems = ul.query("li");
// find all <li>'s within the found <ul>'s
```

This of course could be chained. Perhaps you wanted to set the opacity of the unordered list and then immediately locate the children to register an onclick:

```
dojo.query("#someid ul")
  .style("opacity", 0.75) // applies to the original NodeList
  .query("li") // search NodeList for <li>'s
    .onclick(function(e){
      // applied to the found list-items
    })
  ;
```

And that's it. You now know everything there is to know about chaining. There is only one final concept remaining before you get into writing your NodeList plug-ins. All these concepts come to a head with this final installment: the prototype.

What is a prototype?

JavaScript doesn't have classes *or* classical object inheritance. Whether this is a blessing or a curse is not the goal of this appendix. I will spare you the lengthy discussion (you will thank me in the end). Understanding how to use an object's prototype, however, is not only required for plug-in writing but is the one last bit that ties everything mentioned thus far together.

Every object in JavaScript is an instance of *something*. That *something* has a .prototype that defines the functions (or members) shared by all instances of the object. When an object of some type is created, it inherits these items from the .prototype. An example of a prototype function would be Array.prototype.push():

```
var x = []; // create the empty Array object. this will be typeof "Array"
x.push("a");
x.push("b");
console.log(x); // ["a", "b"]
```

All arrays have the push() method. This function has been around for quite some time. A function that has not existed on the array prototype (nor does it exist in all versions of JavaScript in all browsers) is forEach(). Dojo has a dojo.forEach() function to which you pass an array, but the array itself doesn't contain iteration functionality. Some browsers have gone ahead with "spec" (which refers to the ECMAScript specification, which defines JavaScript as a language) and have provided Array.prototype.forEach(), though it cannot be used consistently across browsers. As an example of how to augment an object so that all objects inherit the augmentation, here I'm implementing forEach() in places where it is not available:

```
if(!Array.prototype.forEach){
  // it doesn't exist. Let's add it.
  Array.prototype.forEach = function(callback, thisObj){
    thisObj = thisObj || this;
    for(var i = 0; i < this.length; i++){
      // call some callback for each item in this array.
      // pass the item, the index of the item, and a reference to the array
      // to each call of the callback. callback.call(thisObj, this[i], i,
      // this);
```

This implementation of forEach() is based on the Mozilla Developer Center forEach() and is available in browsers implementing JavaScript 1.6 and newer. It also mimics Dojo's own forEach(). If you were to implement this prototype extension using Dojo, you would simply do the following:

```
if(!Array.prototype.forEach){
  Array.prototype.forEach = function(callback, thisObj){
    return dojo.forEach(this, callback, thisObj);
  }
}
```

Extending *native* prototypes like this is typically not a recommended practice in Dojo, which is the reason the array utility functions like dojo.forEach() and dojo.filter() exist in the first place. They attempt to follow the recommended spec and provide functions in the Dojo namespace to avoid pollution of the native objects. But, as mentioned, everything has a prototype, including your own classes and functions. Although JavaScript does not possess a way to create classes with multiple inheritance, Dojo provides a utility to handle it for you: dojo.declare().

```
dojo.declare("my.Thing", null, {
  url:"foo.html",
  cache:"",
  constructor: function(args){
    // mix any passed kwArgs into this instance
    dojo.mixin(this, args);
  }
});

var x = new my.Thing({ url:"bar.html" });
```

The object my.Thing has a .prototype. Decorated on that prototype are two defined default values: url and cache. Each *new* my.Thing obtains these defaults. Changing the *instance* value (x.url, or x.cache) does not affect other instances of my.Thing. Changing the my.Thing.prototype will apply the changes to all *new* instances created. You can see this in action with a few lines of code:

```
// sanity check:
var x = new my.Thing();
console.log(x.title); // undefined. No .title on my.Thing.prototype

// give all instances a .title member:
my.Thing.prototype.title = "Default Title";

// create a new thing after augmenting my.Thing
var y = new my.Thing();
console.log(y.title, x.title); // "Default Title", undefined

// the mixin call in the constructor will override the default:
var z = new my.Thing({ title:"Overridden Title" });
console.log(z.title); // "Overridden title"

x.arbitraryTitle = "You can put any member on an instance";
```

Now here's how you can utilize the .prototype and this together to augment the my.Thing class more:

```
my.Thing.prototype.showTitle = function(){
  console.log(this.title);
};

var x = new my.Thing({ title:"Foo!" });
x.showTitle(); // "Foo!"
```

Again, when you refer to this within an instance function, you refer to the parent object. In this case, you are referring to x, the variable referencing the instance of my.Thing you just created.

So, this all may feel very abstract. For that I apologize. You're here now. Ready to start writing plug-ins. Did you miss it? You've already written a few. Let's get back to my earlier comment about the word *plug-in* being exceptionally generic. Not only did you create your own class-like object, you created a "plug-in" to show the title. *That's* the secret. Define your plug-ins on dojo.NodeList.prototype, and remember to return this.

Starting simple

Armed with all the intimate details pertaining to JavaScript's flexibility, you are ready to start writing your own NodeList extensions (also known as **plug-ins**). The most basic of plug-ins you can write would be a null operation. Let's call it doNothing():

```
dojo.NodeList.prototype.doNothing = function(){
  return this;
}
```

dojo.query("a").doNothing().doNothing().doNothing();

This plug-in literally does *nothing*. It is a function, defined on the prototype that returns this to allow chaining. A do-nothing plug-in is less than useful, but I hope all the reading you've done to this point makes the concept crystal clear. All you need to do now is add actual code to your plug-in—making it useful.

Let's start simple. You can reuse an existing NodeList method and create a super-simple plug-in to do something not provided out of the box by Dojo:

```
dojo.extend(dojo.NodeList, {
  makeRed: function(){
    return this.style("color", "red");
  }
```

```
    });
```

```
    // to use it: dojo.query("div.foo").makeRed();
    // or continue chaining.
```

I referenced a new Dojo method here and snuck in a bit of shorthand within the plug-in. dojo.extend() is a utility function that mixes a passed object of items onto a passed object's .prototype. Instead of continually typing dojo.NodeList.prototype for each plug-in you want to write, you can simply use extend() on that prototype with a list of the functions you want to add:

```
    dojo.extend(dojo.NodeList, { /* plug-in hash */ });
    // is identical to:
    dojo.mixin(dojo.NodeList.prototype, { /* plug-in hash */ });
```

You could write the makeRed plug-in out in a longer form, though it provides only a marginal performance boost by avoiding calling the extend() function:

```
    dojo.NodeList.prototype.makeRed = function(){
      return this.style("color", "red");
    }
```

The shorthand introduced into the plug-in is something you will see often. I'm calling this.style() within the function. In this scenario, this refers to whichever NodeList instance you are currently in. For the same reason you can continue chaining after calling style(), you can return the return value of style() in your own plug-in code. You can expand the example to be more verbose to help visualize what is taking place here:

```
    dojo.extend(dojo.NodeList, {
      makeRed: function(){
        var x = this.style("color", "red"); // style returns a NodeList
        if(x == this){
          console.log("See, they reference the same object");
        }
        return this;
      }
    });
```

So, you get to skip the intermediate steps and simply return this.style(...), knowing the returned value will eventually become your expected this in the end. Probably the most common of plug-in patterns mimics this behavior: the plug-in will do something for each node in the list.

```
    dojo.extend(dojo.NodeList, {
      makeCaps: function(){
        return this.forEach(function(node){
          node.innerHTML = node.innerHTML.toUpperCase();
        });
      }
```

```
});
```

Because there is no built-in Dojo function for uppercasing a node's content, you have to write a bit of extra code, and because this plug-in must act upon all nodes in the list, you put this code within a forEach() call (again using the built-in NodeList.forEach() referenced by using this). Again, it could be more verbose, but no one really wants *that*.

You can chain multiple times within a plug-in and return the result of that chain directly as well. Another function missing from the Dojo core functionality is a shorthand way to apply hovering behavior to a node. You can add that bit of syntactic sugar with just a single line of plug-in. You can call it hover:

```
dojo.extend(dojo.NodeList, {
  hover: function(overFn, /* Optional */exitFn){
    return this.onmouseenter(overFn).onmouseleave(exitFn || overFn);
  }
});

// to use: dojo.query("ul > li").hover(function(event){
// when the <li> is entered or exited, this function will fire
});
```

The plug-in is simple and reusable. As shown here, it is just a shorthand for two existing NodeList methods, passing along a function to execute for the mouseenter and mouseleave events. There is a smidge of magic taking place with the onmouseleave call, but only to make the exitFn optional. If an argument is not passed in the second position to hover(), it will evaluate to a "falsey" value. The logical OR operation (||) simply registers the overFn in its place, enabling a user to register a single function to handle both hover states.

You can even build off your own plug-ins; you first provide the reusable hover() function and then create a new function that uses those events to add or remove a class. This is also a good opportunity to see how to use dojo.extend() to mix multiple properties:

```
dojo.extend(dojo.NodeList, {
  hover: function(over, out){
    return this.onmouseenter(over).onmouseleave(out || over);
  },
  hoverClass: function(className){
    var re = /over|enter/;
    return this.hover(function(event){
      var isOver = re.test(event.type);
      dojo.toggleClass(event.target, className, isOver);
    });
  }
```

```
});
```

You test the `event.type` against a simple regular expression to determine whether the callback was fired for the `mouseover` event or `mouseout` event. When you know this, you call `dojo.toggleClass()`, passing the original intended class name and the Boolean `isOver` to force either adding or removing.

You've also just seen the first example of another exciting feature of JavaScript: a closure.

What is a closure?

A **closure** is the most magical of all JavaScriptisms. A closure is created any time a new scope uses a reference from an enclosing scope. Although a seemingly simple concept, a lot of the power and flexibility afforded in JavaScript comes from this idiom.

Closures are a lot easier to visualize than to explain. First, imagine the following code:

```
for(var i = 0; i < 5; i++){
  dojo.connect("nodeId" + i, "onclick", function(e){
    alert(i);
  });
}
```

Logically, you'd expect the alert to correspond to the value of the variable i sequentially in each of the `onclick` event listeners. Unfortunately, the variable i is updated for each iteration of the loop, making every *reference* to that variable the same. Clicking any of the five nodes (for example, id="nodeId1" to "nodeId5") will alert the last value of the variable i, or four.

The solution to this is to create a closure. You'll pass the current value of the i variable to a function, thus creating a new reference to the value. This value is "closed" in the new function you've created, so you can use it inside and know it is "locked" to the original value passed:

```
for(var i = 0; i < 5; i++){
  (function(i){
    dojo.connect("nodeId" + i, "onclick", function(e){
      alert(i);
    });
  })(i);
}
```

Now it may seem complicated, but really it isn't. The funky function definition wrapped inside parentheses is called a **self-executing anonymous function**. You know already functions are defined with the function keyword, and by adding () to the name, you execute the function:

```
var foo = function(i){
  console.log(i);
}
foo(2);
```

So, with that knowledge, you can decipher this seemingly complex definition. Parentheses are used to group sections of JavaScript code. You wrap the anonymous function definition in parentheses and then add a second pair on the end to immediately execute the function:

```
(function(){ /* code */ });
// wasteful, just create an anonymous function
(function(){ /* code */ })();
// create and immediately execute an anonymous function
```

Earlier, you passed the number 2 to the function call, which passes that as a parameter to the internal function. It is by mere coincidence I used the same variable i twice initially, though because they are in different scopes, they are different variables. The original example could be expanded to be clearer by using different variable names:

```
for(var i = 0; i < 5; i++){
(function(inneri){
// inneri becomes a "closed" variable saved as the value of the "outer" i
// value at the time of calling dojo.connect(node, "onclick",
    function(e){ alert(inneri); });
})(i); // here is where we pass the current value of i
}
```

All you're doing is making a new scope with a new closed variable. By using the inner i variable within the click handler, you avoid using the parent scope's i variable directly and have created a closure.

A downside to the earlier self-executing anonymous function is that the JavaScript engine will create that same function five times (which could be hugely expensive, depending on the size of the function). A better solution would be to make a *named* function once outside the loop and simply call that function, remembering to pass the current value of i to each call:

```
var handler = function(myi){
// "myi" is local to THIS function only here dojo.connect("nodeid" +
    myi, "onclick", function(e){
    alert(myi);
});
```

```
    }

    for(var i = 0; i < 5; i++){
      handler(i);
    }
```

By *passing* the variable i to the handler execution, you avoid storing a reference to the changing value. It is like a snapshot of the value at the time, passing it to the function and storing it as a new variable name. You create a closure in that the click handler function references the variable myi from the parent scope.

The key here is to know variables defined within a particular function scope are local to that scope. You may reference them inside other inner functions (creating a closure). Doing so not only prevents leaking variables to the global scope but also has bonus side effects such as compressing better with ShrinkSafe or creating relatively "private" variables.

How does this apply to plug-ins?

This has everything to do with plug-ins. First, plug-in authors often create a large self-executing anonymous function scope, localizing all the internal variables:

```
    dojo.provide("my.plug-in") // my/plug-in.js; this is so we can
    dojo.require("my.plug-in")
    (function(){
      // our plug-in code goes inside this scope, created by the self executing
      // anonymous function. In here we can create local variables and export
      // our plug-in onto dojo.NodeList.prototype
      var plug-inName = "setColor";
      dojo.NodeList.prototype[plug-inName] = function(color){
        return this.style("color", color);
      }
    })();
```

Another convenient practice is to pass a parameter to the self-executing anonymous function, using it as a local variable in the new scope:

```
    dojo.provide("my.plug-in");
    (function(d, $){
      // we can use "d" as if it were "dojo", and "$" instead of "dojo.query"
      d.extend(d.NodeList, {
        setOpacity: function(alpha){
          // summary: Set the opacity to some value
          return this.style("opacity", alpha);
        }
      });
    })(dojo, dojo.query);
```

309

Here I've passed a reference to the Dojo library in the first position (which becomes the variable d internally) and a reference to the dojo.query() function in the second position (aliased internally as $). This allows you the convenience of having to type less and provides a small performance boost by referencing a local variable over a global one.

Perhaps most important, creating a closure is the first step in writing plug-ins that do more than simply apply a style setting or register convenient event listeners. Most plug-ins will act upon each of the nodes of a NodeList. The internal this.forEach() function is used in these cases, and by passing a callback function, you create a new scope to work within. This way, each iteration of your plug-in will have its own local variables but can still use variables from parent scopes should the need arise.

```
dojo.provide("my.plug-in");
(function(d){
  // a regular expression we can use anywhere in this scope
  var re = /enter|over/;

  // create the plug-ins:
  d.extend(d.NodeList, {
    hover: function(over, out){
      return this.onmouseenter(over).onmouseleave(out || over);
    },
    multiClass: function(cName){
      return this.forEach(function(n){
        d.style(n, "color", red);
        d.connect(n, "onclick", function(e){
          // referencing variables from all scopes in this file
          d.toggleClass(n, cName, d.hasClass(n, cName));
          e.preventDefault();
        });
      }).hover(function(e){
        d.toggleClass(this, cName + "hover", re.test(e.type));
      })
    }
  });
})(dojo);
```

Notice within the onclick handler that you're using variables from every scope you created. The n comes from the forEach() callback and is a reference to the target node. You do this because of the nature of the click event: it bubbles, so any node clicked inside the target node will be e.target when the event object is passed. The intent here was to add or remove the class from the explicit node you selected with dojo.query(), so you do it directly rather than rely on the event target. The className variable is shared from the original NodeList call. You pass this in from the user code utilizing this plug-in:

```
dojo.query("a.specialLink").multiClass("selected");
```

Now, clicking the node will toggle the class selected from each anchor node found with the class specialLink attached, as well as toggle the class selectedhover when the node is entered and exited. (You just created your own support for the :hover CSS selector and can now style the anchors to react to the various classes applied much easier than is possible in pure CSS, especially considering older browsers support.)

Finally, the e variable is part of the innermost local scope, which is the callback attached to the onclick event and hover events. You can use this variable to stop the default click event from occurring and later to determine whether the event was an enter or leave trigger.

As you create more complex plug-ins, the benefits of scope and closures will become more apparent (though you've seen a few solid use cases already).

Functions as plug-ins?

Most dojo.NodeList/dojo.query() functions have identical parts in the dojo namespace. The functions in the dojo namespace all typically accept a string ID or domNode reference in the first position and a number of positional arguments following. For example, here's dojo.style():

```
dojo.style("someId", "opacity", 0.2);
// identical to:
dojo.query("#someId").style("opacity", 0.2);
```

In the dojo.query() case, the node reference in the first position is assumed. The nodes are iterated over using forEach(), which ultimately calls the dojo version and passes the reference in each iteration. A simple example would be to find a function that does *not* follow this pattern and implement it: dojo.setSelectable(). For whatever reason, dojo.setSelectable() isn't available in dojo.NodeList operations. You can remedy this with relative ease:

```
(function(d){
  // map the dojo.setSelectable function into NodeList
  d.extend(d.NodeList, {
    setSelectable: function(selectable){
      return this.forEach(function(n){
        d.setSelectable(n, selectable);
      });
    }
  });
})(dojo);
```

This is such a common practice that Dojo even provides a developer helper for doing just this. The previous plug-in can really be reduced to a single line:

```
(function(d, nl){
  nl.prototype.setSelectable = nl._adaptAsForEach(d.setSelectable);
})(dojo, dojo.NodeList);
```

It may seem like voodoo, but the concept is simple: only .prototype items are copied onto all instances. dojo.NodeList is just an object like any other, so the adaptAs functions are just stubbed there, dangling on the namespace to use as needed. They are not copied over or useful in the .prototype context but rather are simply utility functions with a home.

So, you create a local nl variable as a reference to dojo.NodeList with the wrapping function. Then, you set the value of nl.prototype.setSelectable to whatever the return value of calling nl._adaptAsForEach happens to be. adaptAsForEach() is designed specifically for converting a single-node function into an iterator-based function and returns a function masquerading as the original (assuming the first parameter to be each node in the nodelist). In other words, you're creating a plug-in using an existing function in Dojo and "plugging" it into dojo.NodeList to make more functionality for multinode operations. Now you have dojo.query("span").setSelectable() after the one line of code.

There are a number of reasons for doing this. Most important, a *lot* of functionality is useful outside the syntactic sugar NodeList provides. The single-node variant can be considered the fast path, because it doesn't have to go through the work of finding the node using query(), instantiating a NodeList, or even iterating a single time in a loop. The performance benefits are astounding.

The pattern also reduces a lot of code needed to match both situations. Consider the following modified excerpt from dojo/_base/NodeList.js, which is the core of dojo.NodeList functionality:

```
(function(d){
  var each = d.NodeList._adaptAsForEach;
  d.forEach(["addClass", "removeClass", "toggleClass"], function(fn){
    d.NodeList.prototype[fn] = each(d[fn]);
  });

})(dojo);
```

All this is doing is taking an array of function names that already live in the dojo namespace and running adaptAsForEach() on them, saving the reference to a prototype member.

You can write your own functions that mimic this behavior quite easily as well. The only requirement is that the single-node function accepts a node in the first position and some number of arguments following that.

Let's go back to the hover plug-in for a moment. It accepted two arguments: an over callback and an optional out callback. If out is not specified, the over callback will be reused for both. You don't use a node reference in the NodeList-only version because the node is assumed. But in the single-node variant, you need the reference. To make it more "Dojo-y," you pass the node through dojo.byId() to ensure the function can accept either a string ID or a domNode reference:

```
(function(d){

  // a single node variation
  d.hover = function(node, over, out){
    node = d.byId(node);
    d.connect(node, "mouseenter", over);
    d.connect(node, "mouseleave", out || over);
  }

  // reuse above with dojo.query
  d.NodeList.prototype.hover = d.NodeList._adaptAsForEach(d.hover);

})(dojo);
```

Now you can call either of the examples, depending on the use case:

```
(function(){

  var re = /enter|over/;
  var handler = function(e){
    // event handler for hover states
    dojo.toggleClass(e.target, "hovered", re.test(e.type));
  }

  // both are the same: one acts on id="someId" the other on class="someNodes"
  dojo.hover("someId", handler);
  dojo.query(".someNodes").hover(handler);
})();
```

This pattern isn't limited to only the dojo namespace either. In fact, Dojo typically recommends *not* extending the dojo namespace with your own functionality (dojo.NodeList being one of the exceptions to that rule). A common use case would be to make your own mini utility library in your own namespace (thus far referred to as my) and adapt those functions into NodeList. Here you'll create a superCoolFunction that does literally nothing. You then adapt that function into dojo.NodeList as superCool(). The one function will handle the execution needs of both single-node operation and bulk operation.

```
dojo.provide("my.plug-in")
(function(d){

  my.superCoolFunction = function(node, args){
    node = d.byId(node);
    // do something to node.
  }

  // the alternate way to modify NodeList.prototype:
  d.extend(d.NodeList, {
    // it doesn't have to be the same name even
    superCool: d.NodeList._adaptAsForEach(my.superCoolFunction)
  });


})(dojo);

my.superCoolFunction("nodeId");
// or
dojo.query(".someNodes").superCool();
```

Again, both have identical results, though one is optimized for a single-node case and the other has been adapted. The adapter function takes care of the return this; for you, so you can use the adapted plug-in with the standard chaining technique with dojo.query().

More adapter functions

Other (slightly less common) adapter functions are available on the dojo.NodeList object: _adaptAsMap(), _adaptAsFilter(), and _adaptWithCondition(), all of which are worthy of explanation.

Both _adaptAsMap() and _adaptAsFilter() behave exactly like _adaptAsForEach() with one small though significant difference: they behave like dojo.map() and dojo.filter(), respectively. map() returns a new list of values or nodes, and filter() reduces the list to a smaller list based on a return value.

The easiest explanation of _adaptAsMap() would be to show how to convert a list of nodes to their immediate parent nodes. You first must make a single-node function that returns the node you want:

```
my.parent = function(node){
  node = dojo.byId(node);
  return node.parentNode;
```

```
}
```

Then you simply adapt it:

```
dojo.NodeList.prototype.parent = dojo.NodeList._adaptAsMap(my.parent);
// to use:
dojo.query(".bar").parent().style({ padding:"20px" });
```

First you find all nodes with class="bar" and then chain the parent() function on, returning a new NodeList comprised of the node's parent nodes. Because that return value is too a NodeList, you continue chaining and set the style setting for passing to 20px.

Filtering is hugely useful, too. It allows you to filter elements out of a list simply by running some conditional check. If the function returns true, the element is to be included. false indicates the element should be excluded. A very simple example would be to return the odd or even members of a NodeList:

```
dojo.NodeList.prototype.even = dojo.NodeList._adaptAsFilter(function(n, i){
  return i % 2 == 0
});
// to use:
dojo.query("table tr").even().addClass("even-row");
```

_adaptWithCondition() will simply toggle between _adaptAsMap() and _adaptAsForEach() depending on a conditional test function. Many functions in Dojo act as a getter and setter function, either returning a value (getter) or setting a value (setter). One such function is the reliable dojo.style() method. You can see this in action here:

```
dojo.style("someId", "opacity", 0.3); // setter
var opacity = dojo.style("someId", "opacity"); // getter
```

This function is defined on dojo.NodeList using _adaptWithCondition(). If only two arguments are passed and the second is not an object hash of arguments, the NodeList function returns something *other* than this, stopping chaining. Otherwise, the style() function acts as a setter and returns this to allow further chaining.

```
var styles = dojo.query("a").style("marginLeft");
// an array of marginLeft properties
// or setter
dojo.query("a").style("marginLeft", "9px");
```

You can use this with your own code. Simply determine whether the function is to act as a getter or a setter, and return a value appropriately. When using _adaptWithCondition(), you must supply a conditional function as a helper. This is passed to the adapter function as a second argument, and the return of this function is used to differentiate whether map() or forEach() will be used. The arguments passed to the original call from the plug-in are passed to this conditional function to help in determining the intent.

The theoretical plug-in here will either set or get the full class="" value for some node. Let's call it doClass and use _adaptWithCondition() to determine which route to take:

```
(function(d, nl){

    // just make the function as you would:
    my.doClass = function(node, className){
      node = d.byId(node);
      if(className){
        // we are a setter. return nothing.
        node.className = className;
      }else{
        // we are a getter. return something.
        return node.className;
      }
    };

    nl.prototype.doClass = nl._adaptWithCondition(my.doClass, function(args){
      // conditional test function. if true is returned, use map()
      // if false, just use forEach. if we were passed no args, we'll be acting
      // as a getter. If we were passed args, we'll be a setter
        (and use forEach)
      return args.length > 1;  // Boolean

    });

})(dojo, dojo.NodeList);

// NodeList style:
dojo.query(".foo").doClass(); // returns an array of classNames
dojo.query(".bar").doClass("baz"); // overwrites class="baz" with class="baz"

// single-node style:
my.doClass("nodeId", "newClass"); // setter
var current = my.doClass("nodeId"); // getter. current == "newClass" here
```

When you pass only one argument to the adapted function, the conditional checking function returns false. This causes the function to behave as a getter and returns an array of class names.

That's about as advanced as it can get in theory. If you kept pace, pat yourself on the back—you are on course to becoming a true functional JavaScript ninja. If you feel like you missed a step along the way, don't fret. Review the material until you become comfortable with the concepts. If you have questions, the folks in #dojo (irc.freenode.net) are usually around (myself included) and provide top-notch JavaScript discussion companions.

Index

XMLHTTP object, 52
XMLHttpRequest (XHR) object, 52,
172

Y
Yahoo! user interface, 50

Z
Zend PHP framework, 260
zero-based indexes, 293
zero-index arrays, 26